JANE AUSTEN
AND
THE WAR OF IDEAS

Jane Austen
and
the War of Ideas

Marilyn Butler

Clarendon Press · Oxford
1975

Oxford University Press, Ely House, London W.1

GLASGOW   NEW YORK   TORONTO   MELBOURNE   WELLINGTON
CAPE TOWN   IBADAN   NAIROBI   DAR ES SALAAM   LUSAKA   ADDIS ABABA
DELHI   BOMBAY   CALCUTTA   MADRAS   KARACHI   LAHORE   DACCA
KUALA LUMPUR   SINGAPORE   HONG HONG   TOKYO

ISBN 0 19 812068 0

*Printed in Great Britain by
Butler & Tanner Ltd, Frome and London*

ACKNOWLEDGEMENTS

THIS book was substantially written during my tenure of the Gamble Research Fellowship at St. Hilda's College, Oxford. I am deeply grateful to the Principal and Fellows of St. Hilda's, as well as to my new colleagues at St. Hugh's, for much stimulus and kindness.

Among other friends I owe special debts to Christina Colvin, Elizabeth Mavor, Victoria Love, and Stephen Gill, for their criticisms; to Jane Crisp and Gary Kelly, who shared their expertise; and to my pupils, enthusiastic or challenging. Above all I should thank my husband and three sons, who make the times when I am not working the best part of life, but otherwise have been the book's allies.

M. S. B.

St. Hugh's College, Oxford.

July 1974

CONTENTS

INTRODUCTION

JANE Austen is by common consent an author remarkably
sure of her values. She skewers a moral solecism as confidently as a verbal infelicity. At the end of her novels the
standing of the heroine's soul in the light of the next world
seems as decisively settled as her future financial security in
this. The familiar Austen moral abstractions avoid seeming
abstract, so closely are they bound up with an orderly pattern
of behaviour, a set of assumptions imposed by the material
circumstances of leisured middle-class life. The nouns which
convey her positives—'powers', 'grace', 'elegance', 'understanding'—are general, but the effect is never cloudy. The
syntax Jane Austen gives to those characters she favours is
decided and clear, revealing that, for her, personal merit is
bound up with perspicuity—the power to discern general
truths. What those truths are is never spelt out, and yet the
very last impression left by an Austen novel is one of doubt.

It is by virtue of her certainties that Jane Austen is called
Augustan. Certainly satirical writers before her time had
criticized manners or behaviour they deplored by confident
reference to an understood standard, such as that of Christian
doctrine, or of certain classical literary forms. But these are
criticisms of the actual by reference to an ideal; whereas Jane
Austen finds her ideal within a world she deliberately makes
resemble the actual. By implication she is far less critical of
contemporary society in its essence than Ben Jonson, Dryden,
Swift, Pope, or Fielding had been. For at least four of her
heroines, moral progress consists in discerning, and submitting
to, the claims of the society around them. This is certainly not
the moral position of the authors of *Volpone*, *Gulliver's Travels*,
or *The Dunciad*. In fact it is not a typical neo-classical
position at all.

If Jane Austen's moral goals seem nearer at hand, more
realizable, than Pope's, how are they to be defined? The
essence of her certainty is that the reforms she perceives to
be necessary are within the attitudes of individuals; she calls

for no general changes in the world of the established lesser landed gentry. Most modern commentators on Jane Austen assume that her reasons for adopting her matter and manner are aesthetic rather than moral: she writes about '3 or 4 families in a Country Village' because she knows she can do it well, not because she wishes to validate a way of life. Yet it is always dangerous to make unhistorical assumptions, and in the period itself it would have been customary to think in very different terms about what such preferences showed. Critics of the novel, from Samuel Johnson to Clara Reeve and Henry Mackenzie, all ponder thoughtfully the moral impression the novelist makes upon the reader, and (in print at least) give cursory attention to the means he employs to do it. Jane Austen's twentieth-century reader will probably exclaim that this is precisely where she differs from the rest. If so, he must explain why her naturalism operates only within carefully defined limits. Her style, confident and generalizing, and her openly apparent arrangement of character and plot, all suggest an ideal order, which at the same time they present in terms of an actual order. It is not demanded of a Charles Musgrove that he should aspire to be a good man in any very lofty or spiritual sense. '. . . A more equal match . . . might have given more consequence to his character, and more usefulness, rationality and elegance to his habits and pursuits.'[1] It would have been enough if he had realized his capacity to be a gentleman.

This is not to suggest that Jane Austen is merely a snob, as a crass vein of criticism of her novels has held. Her distinctions between true gentlemanliness and the shell of it are keen, perhaps because—like Elizabeth Bennet—she has experienced social rebuffs at first hand.[2] She is certainly no sycophant of wealth or rank, and she does not deal intimately with—or apparently much like—the great aristocracy. The class she deals with has local and not national importance: in eighteenth-century terms, she is a Tory rather than a Whig. She believes that the gentleman—as her words 'consequence' and 'usefulness' imply—derives his personal dignity from the

---

[1] *Persuasion*, ed. R. W. Chapman, Oxford, revised ed. 1965, p. 43.
[2] Cf. D. J. Greene, 'Jane Austen and the Peerage', *PMLA* lxviii (1953), 1017–31.

contribution he makes at the head of an organic, hierarchical, small community. It is for such a community, ideally perceived, that her novels speak.

The novel of Jane Austen's day was not just didactic. It was also seen as relevant to contemporary issues, and, since these issues were unusually deep and clearcut, inevitably partisan. Indeed, at the period when Jane Austen began to write, literature as a whole was partisan, in England as well as on the Continent: so were the other arts, as Kenneth Clark observes in drawing a general parallel with painting. 'Doctrine was found in works which seem to us very harmless. We may think that *The Marriage of Figaro* was written solely to give us pleasure, but in 1785 it was considered a political bombshell, for from 1780 to 1790 every play and every ballet was interpreted in a political sense.'[1] To qualify this a little, at the very least a representation of man in a setting which resembled the natural world would be seen as making certain statements about man's nature and about his social role, all of which were capable of translation into the political sphere. There may well have been artists who thought relatively little about politics. But some artistic forms implicitly seemed to convey certain general principles or prepossessions about man, and if, in this sensitive period, an artist did not care much what they were, his critics and readers were liable to care for him. As it happens, Jane Austen's novels belong decisively to one class of partisan novels, the conservative. Intellectually she is orthodox: more orthodox than a contemporary with whom she has otherwise much in common, Maria Edgeworth. Her important innovations are technical and stylistic modifications within a clearly defined and accepted genre.

In order to determine Jane Austen's values it is necessary to survey partisanship in other novels of the period, a neglected and fascinating area of intellectual history. Modern literary criticism, so often narrowly aesthetic, has patronized eighteenth-century 'didacticism', and in the process obscured the pressure of ideas that helped to give contemporary fiction its form. No doubt a great novel, a *Tristram Shandy* or an *Emma*, can also be understood on our terms: each has a vitality that transcends its genre. But no book is improved by being

[1] *The Romantic Rebellion: Romantic versus Classic Art*, London, 1973, p. 26.

taken out of its context. Every book, even a masterpiece, yields a little more if its assumptions, its language, are understood. And whatever may be true of *Emma*, it is open to question whether *Sense and Sensibility* and *Mansfield Park* can in fact ever be fully independent of their historical context. The hope with which this study sets out is that by placing Jane Austen within her genre, we help to define her meaning; and, in the process, to isolate what is unique in her work, its ultimate originality.

PART I

THE NOVEL AND THE WAR OF IDEAS

All well-written books, that discuss the actions of men, are in reality so many histories of the progress of mind.
Thomas Holcroft, Preface to *Hugh Trevor*, 1794.

[In 1797] the cry spread like a general infection, and I have been told that not even a petty novel for boarding-school misses now ventures to aspire to favour unless it contains some expression of dislike or abhorrence to the new philosophy.
William Godwin, quoted by H. N. Brailsford, *Shelley, Godwin and their Circle*, 1913, p. 156.

CHAPTER 1

SENTIMENTALISM: THE RADICAL INHERITANCE

THE received view of the English novel in the latter part of the eighteenth century is hardly encouraging. 'Between the work of the four great novelists of the mid-eighteenth century and that of Jane Austen and Scott there are no names which posterity has consented to call great.'[1] If the general reader or undergraduate of today were required to name a novelist writing two hundred years ago, he would be hard put to it to find one he had read: Fanny Burney; Henry Mackenzie, perhaps; from a little later, Ann Radcliffe. Yet even in a decade which Miss Tompkins identifies as particularly arid, the 1770s, minor writers, intellectuals, and dilettantes were tentatively staking out new ground in a highly significant area. The middle of the eighteenth century was a period of growing insight into the subjective mind, so that when, for example, its novelists became engrossed in the triangular relationship between hero, author, and reader, they were reflecting an intellectual innovation of great importance. With few really good novels to its credit, the movement known as sentimentalism is nevertheless fascinating for the contribution it makes towards the representation of the inner life, and its active engagement of the reader's imaginative sympathy.

Both man's moral nature, and his mental processes, were the subject of much general intellectual inquiry, and some controversy, in the middle of the century; of bitter partisan strife in the French Revolutionary period. By the mid-1790s reaction against all that Revolution stood for encompassed most of the important features of sentimental narrative writing. Writers of the 1790s looked back on their predecessors of the earlier generation, and saw subversion in work that in

---

[1] J. M. S. Tompkins, *The Popular Novel in England, 1770–1800*, London, 1932, p. v.

its day was at most mildly reformist. Even progressives in 1790 had their doubts about some of the disturbing implications of mid-century psychology. But by far the most numerous and influential of the attacks on sentiment came from the swelling ranks of political and religious orthodoxy. With some justice, and much exaggeration, the sentimentalists came to be read as moral relativists who threatened to undermine established religion and society. The anti-sentimental writing of Jane Austen has been taken as primarily burlesque of a *style*; but essentially it was the absorption of the earlier movement in the conscious and unconscious mind which offended, because implicitly it put the individual before the group. Sentimentalism has received a bad press in our times because the rigorous philosophical impetus behind it is misunderstood; in the 1790s it was understood only too well. At the same time it was simplified, as a form or idea will be caricatured in a second, changed generation. For the purposes of this study, which is concerned with Jane Austen and her contemporaries, the sentimentalists are significant less for what they first intended than for what they shortly afterwards conveyed. Almost every novelist of Jane Austen's day is in some degree or other in the most literal sense a reactionary. To understand the nature of the reaction, it is necessary to turn the perspective of a nervous era upon its sentimental inheritance.

Among the most controversial positions of the sentimentalist—in the eyes of the next generation—was his proposition that man's instincts were good. This tenet has often been attributed to the influence of Shaftesbury and of his Scottish disciple Francis Hutcheson; but it is probably more helpful, as R. S. Crane suggests, to look back to an earlier period and a broader, more popular influence, that of the latitudinarian divines of the Restoration.[1]

Eighteenth-century optimism about the nature of man had its earlier equivalent in the sermons and writings of Tillotson, Barrow, South, Parker, Burnet, Clarke and Bentley. Most

---

[1] 'Suggestions towards a Genealogy of A Man of Feeling', *ELH* i (1935), 205–30. For a discussion of the special importance of Thomas Burnet, and his possible influence via Shaftesbury on eighteenth-century theories of human nature, see Ernest Tuveson, 'The Origins of the Moral Sense', *HLQ* xi (1947–8), 241–59.

clearly in these early stages, its reading of man's nature challenged the basic conceptions of some very diverse types of Christian. The latitudinarians began in strong reaction to that harsh Puritan pessimism, according to which post-lapsarian man was too sinful to be redeemed by his own unaided efforts. But the Puritans were not the only Christians to take a gloomy view of man's depravity, as Swift's writings amply illustrate.

Broad Church belief in man's goodness and rationality confronted the pessimism which remained a live tradition on both wings of Christian thought. As the eighteenth century advanced, discussion about man's nature became increasingly secular in tone. Confidence in the innate soundness of the natural instincts was so general that at least in Britain it largely lost its power to offend. The new philosophy of the human mind that flourished in mid-century Scotland was ostensibly without theological prior assumptions. It claimed to be a science, based on empirical evidence of how the human animal behaved. Hume and Hartley on the workings of the mind, Smith and Ferguson on the workings of society, all wrote in the dispassionate spirit with which Newton had uncovered the laws of an organic universe. Their tone implied that they were offering not controversy but fact. And yet, across the Channel in authoritarian France, the *philosophes* used these very 'facts' as political dynamite.

Even in England, there was a long-standing connection between the 'natural' view of man and political liberalism. In the reign of William III the latitudinarian divines supported Whig policies and sided with the liberal philosophy of Locke, while opposing the case for a strong monarchy advanced by Thomas Hobbes. Hobbes had taken the pessimistic view of human nature and drawn political conclusions from it. If man was naturally self-seeking and depraved, it followed that an enlightened despotism might be the wisest form of government. Without strong external curbs, men's passions would lead them to seek to master or destroy one another. 'Hereby it is manifest, that during the time men live without a common Power to keep them all in awe, they are in that condition which is called Warre; and such a warre, as is of every man, against every man.'[1] Latitudinarians such as Isaac Barrow

1 Thomas Hobbes, *Leviathan*, ch. 13.

waged a ceaseless war against Hobbes' 'monstrous paradox', and urged instead, as Matthew Tindal afterwards put it, that man 'is a social creature, who naturally loves his own species, and is full of pity, tenderness, and benevolence'.[1] Throughout the next century a kindly view of man's nature tends to go hand in hand with a belief in the safety and indeed wisdom of political liberty. Among the Scots, Hume alone expresses faith in man's impulses together with scepticism about the wisdom of giving him scope to practise them.[2] Ferguson and Gibbon both believe that the health of a nation depends upon the personal liberty and voluntary participation of its citizens.[3] Adam Smith takes entrenched power as his favourite target, and berates the self-defeating tactics throughout history of landed aristocracies and merchant guilds, together with their typical tool, an oligarchic central government. Despite Hume, the consensus links faith in the individual with impatience of constraints imposed upon him from without.

In broad terms the novel is associated from the beginning with the more individualistic, optimistic, and politically liberal strands in eighteenth-century thinking. It is true that Fielding seems unusual in openly preaching a latitudinarian theology, and that at first glance Defoe and Richardson put forward an opposing faith, the old Puritan concept of man's sinfulness and his need for grace. But more important than this difference is the fact that over a broad area the form of the novel itself pleads for the individual, for his innate well-meaningness and for his value. Ronald Paulson has observed that the ethics of the novel are more relativist than those of satire. The novelist concentrates on the man or woman, the satirist on the deed. The novelist is in effect engaged in explaining and understanding a chronological sequence of actions in terms of the man who performs them; the satirist judges the single objective fact.[4] The intrinsically progressive

---

[1] From 'Christianity and the Creation': quoted by Crane, op. cit., p. 226.

[2] Hume's sceptical treatment in his *History* of the libertarian arguments of seventeenth-century parliamentarians aroused anger and dismay among his Whig readers. Cf. Duncan Forbes, introduction to Hume's *History of England*, Pelican Books, 1970, pp. 18 ff.; and below, pp. 34–6.

[3] See below, p. 35.

[4] R. Paulson, *Satire and the Novel in Eighteenth Century England*, New Haven, 1967, pp. 3–11.

element in the novel, which distinguishes it from earlier forms, lies in the unique dominance over the action of the personality of the hero or heroine, for this in itself implies a subjective attitude to reality. But if a tendency towards relativism is present in the novel from the beginning, it becomes conscious and explicit in the 1760s and 1770s.

The broad characteristics of the sentimental movement—its conscious intellectuality, its belief in man, its dislike of dogma, and its political liberalism—are well illustrated in the work of Henry Mackenzie (1745–1831). This versatile and representative man of letters ('our Scottish Addison', as Walter Scott called him) grew up in an Edinburgh dominated by the two greatest figures of the Scottish Enlightenment, Hume and Smith.[1] He inherited the concerns of that gifted group, especially its interest in psychology and its observation that in practice the mind is governed by irrational associations rather than by the conscious will. He also inherited its liberalism. It is possible to miss this vein in Mackenzie, for he has none of the campaigning zeal of his fellow-Scotsman Smollett, as manifested in the brilliant assault on naval inefficiency in *Roderick Random*. Yet, despite its more muted expression, Mackenzie's sympathy with the victimized individual and his dislike of the system has the same general connotation as Smollett's—or, at least, has every ingredient that is seen as tendentious a generation later.[2] After Harley, the Man of Feeling, is deceived by the ex-footman pretending to gentility, he reflects that 'the fault may more properly be imputed to that rank where the futility is real, than where it is feigned'.[3] Later Harley hears a lecture from the misanthropist, denouncing British rapacity in India. Throughout, Mackenzie shows the woes of victims of the rich and powerful, from Miss Atkins, seduced by the squire's son, to the old soldier Edwards, who is successively the pawn of a heartless landlord, a partial magistrate, a press-gang, brutal naval discipline, and a generally unfeeling society.

[1] Both figure in Mackenzie's entertaining and far from egotistical *Anecdotes and Egotisms*, ed. H. W. Thompson, London, 1927.

[2] See below, pp. 88 ff.

[3] *The Man of Feeling*, ed. Brian Vickers, Oxford English Novels, 1967, p. 29.

Yet, although the element of social criticism so typical of the 1760s and 1770s is present in Mackenzie, his real radicalism lies elsewhere. His psychology has deeper implications than his politics for the traditional ethical system. He goes far further than writers of any earlier generation in finding artistic expression for the authentic psychology of Hume. His presentation of human consciousness is fleeting, impressionistic, emotional rather than rational. He does not attempt to realize the social scene by objective means; truth for Mackenzie is essentially subjective. Both the formalized social structure—the State—and the formalized ethical structure—the Church—are diminished not by being attacked, but by being ignored. The entire action is located in Harley's feelings, the external world appears to exist only in so far as it makes an impression on him, and value exists not in any predetermined code of ethics, but in Harley's intuitive sympathy for his fellow-man.

Mackenzie is neither the first of his movement, nor the most brilliant. He lacks Sterne's humour, his originality, most if not all of his outstanding literary talent. Nor does he have the peculiar personal radiance which Goldsmith communicates in *The Vicar of Wakefield*. He is, however, more useful for our present purpose because he is more representative than either Sterne or Goldsmith. The eccentricity and exuberant play of fancy in *Tristram Shandy* partly obscures the book's intellectual point, although this can certainly be seen as characteristically sentimental: the vindication of Toby's simple and benevolent human instincts by comparison with the systematizing of Walter, the inhumanity of the Catholic Dr. Slop, even the calculation of the Widow Wadman. Like Sterne, Goldsmith casts his book in a characteristically sentimental mode, one in which a highly sentient, sympathetic family is assailed by a hard fate, and harder world. But Goldsmith blends his sentimental theme with some orthodox moralizing, and his other purpose, of schooling the Primrose family in Stoic or Christian resignation, is untypical of the movement. Mackenzie is plainer, more direct and consistent than either of them.

He is so partly because he is the most fully steeped of the three in the contemporary body of thinking for which sentimentalism is one kind of expression. When he first describes *The Man of Feeling* in a letter to his cousin, he does so in terms which, although casually and modestly worded, bring out the intellectual ambitiousness of the book. True to the empirical Scottish spirit, it contains 'observations . . . on men and matters'; its fragmentariness is not a sign of carelessness, but a calculated attempt to speak directly of the sensational aspects of the mind without imposing factitious rationalizations:

. . . I have seldom been in use to write any prose, except what consisted of observations (such as I could make) on men and matters. The way of introducing these by narrative, I had fallen into in some detached essays, from the notion of its interesting both the memory and the affections deeper than mere argument or moral reasoning. In this way I was somehow led to think of introducing a man of sensibility into different scenes where his feelings might be seen in their effects, and his sentiments occasionally delivered without the stiffness of regular deduction.[1]

The Man of the World, 1773, with its contrast between the simple, unworldly Annesly family, and Sir Thomas Sindall, who preys on them, has more social criticism than close psychological observation: it follows a pattern familiar in novels which imitate the manner and sentiments of Rousseau.[2] But the aim of *The Mirror*, the journal of which Mackenzie was the guiding spirit, is to observe human nature, in order, presumptively, to liberalize a society which tends to confine or distort it. *The Mirror* declares that it means 'to trace the progress of character through the mazes in which it is involved by education or habit' and 'to investigate those passions and affections of the mind which have the chief influence on the happiness of individuals, or of society'.[3] Mackenzie's tales in

---

[1] H. Mackenzie to Miss Elizabeth Rose, 8 July 1769: H. W. Thompson, *A Scottish Man of Feeling*, London, 1931, p. 108.

[2] Other novels which arrange their characters in order to contrast vicious rich and virtuous poor are Henry Brooke's *Fool of Quality* (1767), Thomas Day's *Sandford and Merton* (1783–9), and Mrs. Inchbald's *Nature and Art* (1796). (See below, p. 31 and p. 89.) But cf. D. G. Spencer, 'Henry Mackenzie, a Practical Sentimentalist', *Papers in Language and Literature*, iii (1967), 314–26, for a different view of Mackenzie's attitude to his virtuous protagonists.

[3] *The Mirror*, no. 1 (23 Jan. 1779).

The Mirror often illustrate at its best his talent for simple pathos, and they are among the most direct of all his assertions of natural man's innate goodness. 'Father Nicholas' is eloquent on the 'Power of Corrupt Society and False Shame over the Natural Feelings of Virtue'. In 'Louisa Veroni' the hero seduces a poor Italian girl, and afterwards learns that she is more deserving than respectably married English ladies of his own class. 'La Roche' portrays religion not as 'a system' but as 'a feeling'. All three were much admired, and often reprinted in miscellanies. During the last three decades of the century they were probably as familiar as any expressions of sentimental faith in man and mistrust of society.

The Man of Feeling, Mackenzie's first work of fiction, arrived on the scene relatively late, in 1771. The 1760s, in politics the decade of Wilkes, in literature of Sterne and Goldsmith, had already familiarized the reading public with a radical change in narrative techniques. The most obvious characteristic of sentimental narrative writing is that it shifts the emphasis from the action—what a character does—to his response to the action. 'Plot' indeed as such ceases to be continuous, or clearly defined, since events in real life are seldom seen as the direct fruits of our endeavours. The scene is what matters, and the focus of each scene is the character's state of mind in response to external stimuli. The scene therefore becomes a vivid, isolated entity. The total movement of the book, what traditionally would have been the plot, becomes obscure, complex, perversely malign, in imitation of the real-life manner in which the environment impinges upon the individual. Even in *The Vicar of Wakefield*, for example, a novel in which far more of a traditionally novelettish kind happens than in *Tristram Shandy*, events occur in a random sequence, to reflect a destiny which is never within the characters' control. The replacement of the plot based on the protagonist's conscious actions—the plot equally of *Robinson Crusoe, Clarissa*, and *Tom Jones*—with an impressionistic sequence of scenes reflects the mid-century flight from rationalistic abstraction, its interest instead in mental activity as it can actually be observed. At its best the old type of plot is both consecutive, and deeply significant for the ethical life of the hero. For example, Robinson Crusoe's decision to defy his father and go wandering, Clarissa's decisions to leave home and afterwards not to marry Lovelace, are events so decisive as to order everything that follows, and to cast the entire novel into the form of a moral drama, in which the protagonist's conscience has the decisive role. But this kind of action really belongs to an older universe, sure of its moral absolutes, in which the fallen individual has to make a positive action in order to be saved. Mackenzie's generation sees human activity not in terms of black-and-white ethical choices, but neutrally, naturalistically, as a behavioural fact. The changed attitude to plot is not perverse, but the reflection of a sophisticated new perception of psychological reality.

The novel is not the only form affected. Plays written during the eighteenth century show the same shift away from a continuous action, the same concern, instead, with the hero's subjective experience. Sentimental tragedies and comedies have much in common with each other: typically, innocent protagonists are caught in a series of affecting situations. In performance, especially, the drama was manifestly subject to the same intellectual pressures which influenced the development of the novel. Shakespeare, so often all things to all men, was acted in a manner that brought out the dominance of the hero. It was the period which saw the rise of 'star' actors—Garrick, Kemble, and later Kean—who exploited their different personal qualities for the same purpose of focusing the audience's sympathy upon the hero rather than allowing it to be distributed among a number of characters. Plays with a 'strong' hero, simultaneously attractive and repellent, such as *Richard III* and *Macbeth*, became increasingly popular as the century wore on. The drama of the villain–hero's situation and the acuteness of his sufferings outweighed the 'objective' moral consideration that he had done wrong. Garrick for example freely adapted Shakespeare's text, and gave individual scenes a wholly personal reading, in order to make each of these plays seem as subjective as his art could contrive.[1]

1 See the chapter 'Garrick's Shakespeare and Subjective Dramatic Character', Joseph W. Donohue Jr., *Dramatic Character in the English Romantic Age*, Princeton, 1971, pp. 216–42.

But structurally the drama was less responsive to sentimentalism than the novel was. In production the stress could
shift from plot to scenic effect, and all sorts of devices could
be used to focus attention and sympathy on the hero. Nevertheless, strong formal conventions persisted, to give a perhaps
unwanted significance to the working-out of the action. In
consequence, there is nothing in eighteenth-century drama to
approach Sterne's wayward narrative procedure, nor even
Mackenzie's simple pretence that he has only incomplete
fragments of manuscript.[1] Moreover, although he may stress
the role of the hero, the dramatist is obliged by the nature of
his medium to pay adequate attention to lesser characters.
He is handling a form which emanates, like epic and satire,
from a much older period, and he finds it considerably more
difficult to adjust from an external to an inward presentation
of reality. It is no wonder that closet drama, enabling greater
and greater predominance of the central character, and greater
inwardness of interest, begins to gain in prestige on drama
really meant for the stage; nor that critics of the Romantic
period, like Lamb and Coleridge, often stress that Shakespeare's plays are better read than in performance.[2]

The dominance of the hero in the mid-century novel is more
complete. A little earlier, both Richardson and Fielding presented minor characters in sharp focus, giving them an
objective existence independent of the hero or heroine's consciousness. In the sentimental novel minor characters tend to
make an impression by way of the hero, or by virtue of their
emotional link with him. The lesser characters in *The Man of
Feeling*, like the mad girl, the prostitute, and Edwards, make
a vivid impression upon Harley by arousing his pity. Sometimes, however, the force of feeling is on the other side. Stock
minor characters of sentimentalism are those possessed by a
strong, pure stream of love: the elderly servant who gives up
everything to follow his master; the innocent, helpless child;
the faithful dog who dies, sometimes through the cruelty of
an enemy, sometimes of a broken heart. The relationship

---

[1] See below, p. 27.
[2] For a full description of the comparable evolution of drama in the period,
see Donohue, op. cit., and Arthur Sherbo, *English Sentimental Drama*,
Michigan, 1957.

between figures like these and the hero is fleeting, partial, and often one-sided. The inevitable result is that minor figures, to some extent in Sterne and Goldsmith, to a greater extent in Mackenzie, lose their substance, their otherness. This, at any rate, is true of those who are benign. Enemies take on a different kind of colouring: they merge into a background which in general suggests an intransigent or malign outside world. Like the lesser characters, the physical background is perceived subjectively, as if through the hero's own eyes. Perhaps it appears to change in sympathy with his moods, and is cheerful, lowering, or romantic precisely in tune with his state of mind. Alternatively it takes sides against him as the embodiment of his harsh destiny, like the gloomy and terrifying landscapes of Mrs. Radcliffe. In either case, its objective existence is suspect. The firm outlines of Defoe's social universe, Richardson's or Fielding's or Smollett's, are shaded away into a Humeian scepticism.

With the fading of secondary characters within the world of the novel, a new relationship comes for the first time to the fore. The reader's attitude to the central character becomes an active element, and even, in extreme examples, more important than relationships within the fictional world. The tendency already noted from the form's beginning, to induce the reader to identify with the hero, takes on a new dimension and consciousness in the sentimental period. Heroes and heroines are employed who readily attract identification. They are often very young and inexperienced, and hence easy victims of the corrupt or designing; or more positively, more radiantly innocent—like Harley, Uncle Toby, the Vicar of Wakefield, or Brooke's Fool of Quality. The reader's sense of involvement with these older innocents is encouraged by the characters' own ready fund of sympathy: at the faintest hint all will shed a tear for the suffering of others. They are thus model human beings, as first the latitudinarians, afterwards the empiricists sketched the proper Man. They are acutely sentient, expressive, and, above all, responsive through sympathy to the woes of their fellows.

Some recent critics have taken the view that a form which shows an undue interest in the reader, outside the world of its own creation, has entered a period of decadence. Miss

Tompkins, for example, argues thus about the comedy of Beaumont and Fletcher and about the novels and plays which develop the same techniques in the sentimental period.[1] But the conscious development of the author–reader relationship, its attempt to involve the reader actively in a series of discoveries and discriminations parallel to those of the character, is surely a real technical achievement by the minor writers of the mid-eighteenth century. The responses of the reader are perceived to be potentially rich and various, and authors develop techniques to elicit them which are often exceedingly subtle. The fragmented narrative makes it possible to play with mood, moving swiftly between terror and pity, or laughter and tears. Reading these works demands the same kind of energy as living through the events they describe: it is a positive, ever-varying emotional response, of the type that Dickens and Thackeray can still evoke a century later. The reader is made aware that what is expected of him is an experiential self-surrender quite different in kind from the older pattern of reader's attitudes. Writers of both drama and novel are explicit that whereas the received notion requires judgement, the new and more proper response is sympathy. Favourite characters are warm-blooded and sympathetic; pressure, sometimes subtle and often extreme, is put upon the reader to enter into the spirit of the action, with the same impulsive generosity.

Among the most successful stage characters of the later eighteenth century is a group whom in real life the audience might have been very ready to condemn. Macklin, for example, launched the lovable stage Irishman with Sir Callaghan O'Brallaghan (*Love à la Mode*, 1759). O'Brallaghan was soon followed by a host of other Irishmen, Scotsmen, and West Indians, all representatives of unpopular minorities. Each of these is made fallible, but endearingly, generously so; the audience is virtually obliged to take them to their hearts. Two of the most significant characters in the entire period are certainly Tom Jones, in Fielding's novel, and Charles Surface, in Sheridan's play *The School for Scandal*. In each case the reader is encouraged to begin by identifying as wise a well-

---

[1] *The Popular Novel in England, 1770–1800*, pp. 92–112. Cf. Brian Vickers, in his introduction to *The Man of Feeling*, p. xi.

meaning, in old-fashioned terms highly virtuous character, who for the best of apparent reasons passes an unfavourable judgement upon the hero: Squire Allworthy in *Tom Jones* and Sir Oliver Surface, Charles's uncle, in *The School for Scandal*. In the terms of the older orthodoxies with which each 'judge' sets out, the young men continue to fail the test they are set.[1] Each goes on acting according to a fallible, generous nature, recklessly, imprudently, in Tom's case immorally. Yet the purpose of both books is to put the reader into an entirely different frame of mind from the orthodoxy implied by having the hero tested by a wise older man: if anyone is judged it is the judge himself. We do not find Tom or Charles innocent of the first charge against them, but the notion of judging them by these criteria becomes irrelevant as their fundamental good nature is proved. Much has been said in criticism of the passivity of sentimental heroes, who seem to act as they do involuntarily, out of mindless instinct. Censor-characters like Allworthy and Sir Oliver undergo a process of intellectual discovery of a notably active kind, and, what is more, the reader experiences the same revelation along with them. He is forced to perceive the limits of cerebral judgement and to embrace in its stead spontaneous sympathy. The moment when judgement is voluntarily suspended is the equivalent of the even more characteristic moment when tears are shed. It is another sign that the reader takes an active role in relationship to the imagined world, and, by giving his sympathy, realizes his own nature. The conscious use within so many plots of wise–foolish moralists, whose standards change from rational to emotional, dispassionate to sympathetic, shows how clearly sentimentalists recognize what is at stake. They are giving dramatic expression to a new concept of man—humane, subjective, naturalistic.

If modern critics have not paid much attention to the proselytizing element in sentimental fiction, contemporaries

---

[1] The motif of a hero judged by a censorious father-figure, often lurking in disguise, is a favourite in the drama of the period, though it is as old as Terence's *Adelphoe*. It is a classic comic plot, signalizing reconciliation between the generations; but in this period the stress is put on the abdication of authority and inherited precept, in the face of youthful instinct.

take it entirely seriously. Samuel Johnson questions power-fully whether it is proper for the novelist to be concerned primarily—as Fielding in *Tom Jones* declares he is—with a naturalistic account of man, drawn from experience and not from books.[1] It seems to Johnson that all writers have a duty not merely to entertain but to instruct; and he questions whether, 'if the world be promiscuously described', the novel might not be actively subversive. The chief danger (and here he is surely thinking not of Fielding's critical commentary in *Tom Jones*, but of the presentation of Tom himself) is the novel-ist's deliberate effort to attract sympathy for the hero and to induce the reader to suspend the habit of ethical judgement:

> If the power of example is so great, as to take possession of the memory by a kind of violence, and produce effects almost without the intervention of the will, care ought to be taken that, when the choice is unrestrained, the best examples only should be ex-hibited. . . .
>
> Many writers, for the sake of following nature, so mingle good and bad qualities in their principal personages, that they are both equally conspicuous; and as we accompany them through their adventures with delight, and are led by degrees to interest our-selves in their favour, we lost the abhorrence of their faults, because they do not hinder our pleasure, or, perhaps, regard them with some kindness for being united with so much merit. . . .
>
> In narratives, where historical veracity has no place, I cannot discover why there should not be exhibited the most perfect idea of virtue; of virtue not angelical, nor above probability, for what we cannot credit we shall never imitate, but the highest and purest that humanity can reach, which, exercised in such trials as the various revolutions of things shall bring upon it, may, by conquering some calamities, and enduring others, teach us what we may hope, and what we can perform. Vice, for vice is necessary to be shown, should always disgust; nor should the graces of gaiety, or the dignity of courage, be so united with it, as to reconcile it to the mind.[2]

Johnson's essay anticipates the sentimental era proper. Yet the issue continues to be debated in the terms in which he sees it: exemplary heroes (like Richardson's) who illustrate

---

[1] *Tom Jones*, ix. 1.
[2] *The Rambler*, iv (31 Mar. 1750): reprinted by Ioan Williams, *Novel and Romance, 1700–1800*, London, 1970, p. 142.

virtue, versus 'natural' heroes (like Fielding's) who arouse
fellow-feeling; and the majority of serious essayists side with
Johnson through the following decades. Curiously enough the
ablest development of Johnson's argument is by the arch-
exponent of 'feeling', Mackenzie himself. It is true that
Mackenzie's important essay in *The Lounger* criticizing sentimental fiction appears after his own creative work in the
genre; it seems in fact to be a striking symptom of the reaction
against sentimentalism that begins in the 1780s.[1] Nevertheless it is ironic that Mackenzie picks up Johnson's central
criticisms, which can certainly be applied to his own fiction of
the previous fifteen years. Sentimental literature is dangerous
because it involves unreflecting identification with a hero who
is presented 'naturally', and by absolute standards often errs.
Mackenzie now concedes that the positive values of the sentimentalist offend against orthodox morality, since they place
love, friendship, and compassion higher than parental duty,
justice, and prudence. He makes two further points which
become favourite themes with moralists by the end of the
century. The highly subjective, internalized mode of writing
tends 'to separate ideals from action and conscience from feeling'; readers are deliberately induced to 'surrender to impressions which never have any effect upon their conduct'.
Another danger of subjectivism is that it fills the mind 'with
false and inflated ideas of happiness', which are unlike life in
the real world and indeed inimical to it; and this he characterizes as 'a sickly sort of refinement'.[2]

There is a temptation for the modern reader to take Johnson's preference for exemplary central characters over mixed
ones as an instance of the great critic nodding. And, of course,
we are aware that his interpretation of what is 'moral' differs
radically from that of Fielding: the latter certainly thinks
himself a more stalwart champion of middle-of-the-road Christianity than his opponent Richardson. To Fielding, *Pamela*
appears to be written with the kind of indulgence towards

---

[1] See below, pp. 33 ff.

[2] *The Lounger*, xx (18 June 1785): reprinted by Ioan Williams, op. cit.,
p. 331. The tendency of essayists such as Mackenzie to adopt conservative
Johnsonian critical positions is discussed by R. D. Mayo, *The English Novel in
the Magazines, 1740–1815*, Evanston, 1962, pp. 140 ff. For his discussion of
Johnson's novel-criticism, see ibid., pp. 96–100.

the central character which Samuel Johnson finds in *Tom Jones*. The paradox is an interesting one, which shows how very sensitive Christian critics in the eighteenth century are to the un-Christian quality of moral complacency: because, it seems, they equate the reader's willingness to indulge the central character with his willingness to indulge himself. In relation to Fielding, and on this issue, Johnson sees himself just as Fielding sees himself in relation to the early Richardson—a champion of Christianity in the Augustinian tradition, a sceptic about human nature and an upholder of the old absolutes. The issue for both turns on a single question: with what degree of moral stringency is the hero presented?

After Johnson, *Tom Jones* becomes a key case in the dispute about the novel's underlying tendency to moral relativism; just as *The School for Scandal* in borrowing from it becomes a key case for the drama. Not for nothing is Sheridan's indulgence towards Charles Surface cited by critics at the end of the century as, in effect, the wilful abnegation of objective ethical criteria.[1] The critics make the further point, that in drawing the converse case, Joseph Surface, Sheridan is guilty of an invidious blow against morality. Joseph, like Fielding's Blifil, is a hypocrite, a man who seems virtuous to all the world, but is not. He is an even blacker (and less credible) case than Blifil, an out-and-out villain capable of indulging in all sorts of vice, including lechery. Conservative critics point out with some reason that here Sheridan really plays fast and loose with morality. The reader takes the action as yet another demonstration that intuitive responsiveness is better than more formal and correct goodness. There is casuistry here, becase we are never really shown orthodox goodness: instead Sheridan equates outward prudence and proper behaviour with the deliberate hypocritical calculation of self-interest. The suspicion with which those who hold to the old absolutes come to regard sentimental literature can be seen, in this extreme case, to be not unreasonably founded. The liberal or sentimental tendency is indeed to work against the

---

[1] The morality of *The School for Scandal* is attacked by Mackenzie, *Anecdotes and Egotisms*, p. 205, as well as by two of the anti-jacobins discussed below, pp. 112–14. Cf. Robert Bisset, *Douglas, or the Highlander*, 1800, London, iii. 111 ff., and Charles Lucas, *The Infernal Quixote*, London, 1801, i. 252.

exercise of the ethical sense, and actively to enlist the reader, by half-conscious and almost subliminal means, in the party of unlimited toleration.

A single novel, one which was popular and influential in the last quarter of the eighteenth century, will illustrate how radical sentiment could be. Though pallid beside two translations—Rousseau's *Nouvelle Héloïse* and Goethe's *Sorrows of Young Werther*—Mackenzie's *Julia de Roubigné* (1777) was among the most admired love-stories to appear in England in the second half of the century. This in itself increases its significance, because the opposition to sentimental literature which built up in the 1790s—when the apprentice Jane Austen formed her literary attitudes—centred its case on sentimental attitudes to love. All Jane Austen's stories concern a young girl's choice of a partner in marriage, and all make the choice the occasion for a number of critical and far-reaching ethical decisions. Mackenzie's handling of the same situations in *Julia de Roubigné* is therefore a more useful contrast to Jane Austen than his better-known *Man of Feeling*, or than the work of Sterne or Goldsmith.

It was the Scottish judge and philosopher Lord Kames who challenged Mackenzie to write a novel in which all the characters were virtuous.[1] Mackenzie went to the plot of *La Nouvelle Héloïse* (perhaps encouraged by the final footnote, in which Rousseau comments with some pride on the lofty natures of all his characters).[2] Like the original Julie, Mackenzie's Julia is a girl of Richardsonian elevation of soul. Her father has been wealthy, and it was as a rich girl that Julia fell in love with her poor cousin, Savillon. He, though loving her, was too scrupulous to declare his feelings. Savillon has left for the West Indies to make his fortune, and since his departure M. de Roubigné has lost almost everything. The action opens at this point, with M. de Roubigné and his family living in picturesque poverty in a cottage. They have a neighbour,

---

[1] H. W. Thompson, *A Scottish Man of Feeling*, p. 148.

[2] *Julie, Ou la Nouvelle Héloïse*, was translated into English in 1761. Julie is in love with a young man socially beneath her, and is married against her will to an older man; afterwards St. Preux, who still loves her, comes to visit her as a married woman. But for a significant difference between the two Julias, see below, p. 44.

Louis de Montauban, a rich nobleman of Spanish background who falls in love with Julia. She, unable through delicacy to reveal her undeclared love for Savillon, cannot fully account for her reluctance to marry Montauban.[1] Then Montauban saves M. de Roubigné from prison by paying a debt, and Julia, who has high-flown ideas of honour, feels obliged to accept him out of gratitude—though she agonizes over whether she ought to marry someone whom she cannot love as well as Savillon. Despite her doubts and forebodings, the first volume ends with their marriage.

The second volume centres on Savillon. He has made a fortune in the West Indies while always, it now appears, loving Julia. There is no longer any reason why he should not ask her to be his wife. He hurries home to France, only to find her married to Montauban. In his despair he begs for a last interview, and Julia, though again with foreboding, agrees. By this time her husband has discovered hints of her feeling for Savillon, and (being a man of conventional ideas) he assumes that she is unfaithful. His suspicions seem confirmed by the meeting, and he administers poison to Julia. (The extremity of his jealous reaction is given psychological plausibility, like Othello's, by the alien, chivalric code of personal honour he derives from his Spanish upbringing.) Before dying, Julia tells him the exact truth about her relationship with Savillon, and in an agony of remorse for his mistake, Montauban goes mad and kills himself.

The essence of the story is that it vindicates passion. Julia is bound to Montauban by the honourable motives of filial obedience and gratitude. But she loves Savillon with all the force of instinct; and Mackenzie obviously considers her scruples correct when she argues that marriage ought to be the sanctification of our deeper emotions, and not of rationalizations based on even the worthiest motive. Her case is put by her friend and confidante, Maria de Roncilles:

I have ever thought as you do, 'that it is not enough for a woman not to swerve from the duty of a wife; that to love another more

[1] The literary echoes in the plot are strong. The de Roubignés' sinking in two stages into poverty seems borrowed from *The Vicar of Wakefield*. Julia's dealings with her mild mother and angry father when Montauban wants to marry her are obviously based on *Clarissa*.

than a husband, is an adultery of the heart; and not to love a husband with undivided affection, is a virtual breach of the vow that unites us.'[1]

Julia's feeling for Savillon is a total emotional identification. 'Must I forget the scenes of our early days, the opinions we formed, the authors we read, the music we played together? There was a time when I was wont to retire from the profanity of vulgar souls, to indulge the remembrance!'[2] For Montauban she feels gratitude, and respect, but there is a kind of sternness about him which demands justice rather than spontaneous affection, and this she deplores. 'There is an [sic] yielding weakness, which to me is more amiable than the inflexible right; it is an act of my reason to approve of the last; but my heart gives its suffrage to the first, without pausing to inquire for a cause.'[3] Readers of Jane Austen will note how totally different is this reliance on intuition from the later writer's prudent rationality. Julia's fond memories of her conversations with Savillon on literature and music anticipate Willoughby's courtship of Marianne Dashwood; and Mme de Roubigné's last letter of prudential advice might have been written by Elinor: 'The rapture of extravagant love will evaporate and waste; the conduct of the wife must substitute in its room other regards, as delicate, and more lasting.'[4]

The difference is that in Mackenzie's novel Mme de Roubigné proves quite wrong, and so does poor Montauban, whose sanguine expectation that gratitude and esteem is a sufficient basis for marriage rings from the first like hollow self-deception:

If they [romantics] say, that affection is a mere involuntary impulse, neither waiting the decisions of reason, nor the dissuasives of prudence, do they not in reality degrade us to machines, which are blindly actuated by some uncontrollable power? If they allow a woman reasonable motives for her attachment, what can be stronger than those sentiments which excite her esteem, and those proofs of them which produce her gratitude?'[5]

Montauban, connected as he is with an old aristocracy and a traditional, objective code of ethics and propriety, is a fair

---

[1] *Julia de Roubigné*, 4th ed., London, 1787, i. 90–1.   [2] Ibid., i. 95.
[3] Ibid., i. 33.   [4] Ibid., i. 183.   [5] Ibid., i. 160–1.

spokesman for the conventional point of view, and he puts what indeed proves to be a deeply felt ethical objection to intuitional psychology. Julia and Savillon are the helpless creatures of their passions; they *cannot* dispose their feelings voluntarily, according to their conscious will. The problem is that, according to Mackenzie's observations of human nature, our mental processes are indeed like that. Montauban, possessed with unreasoning passion, and eventually mad, himself ends by proving the force of involuntary emotion.

The purpose of the story is not indeed to recommend a changed attitude to marriage or an adjustment of the marriage laws—a campaign of Mary Wollstonecraft's in the 1790s—but to observe the sexual behaviour of a triangle of lovers placed in an acute dilemma. The spirit of the book is not ethical or not in any simple sense; unlike other eighteenth-century novelists, before and after, Mackenzie is not nearly as much interested in what people ought to do as in what they actually do. His novel is outstanding for the nice quality of its observations. Commenting on her father's friendship for Montauban, Julia remarks, 'Perhaps it is from something amiss in our nature, but I have often observed the most strict of our attachments to proceed from an alliance of dislike.'[1] The whole tendency of the technical devices is to throw the emphasis away from the action as such and on to the principal characters' perception of them. It is, for example, a novel told in letters, in imitation of *Clarissa*. But virtually all the letters are from principals; the function in the earlier novel of a confidante like Anna Howe or Belfield was to provide an external view, an independent perspective which is the very opposite of what Mackenzie is after. Where he does use a minor correspondent it is in order eventually to heighten, not detract from, the sustained subjectivity of his over-all effect. Twice in a crisis it is not Julia, but her maid Lisette, who writes to Mme de Roncilles. The first occasion is the death of Mme de Roubigné, when Julia is supposed too afflicted to write—a device which usefully gives us Lisette's description of Julia's refined symptoms of distress. The second occasion is Julia's marriage, which Lisette in her simplicity assumes to be a happy occasion. The reader knows the heroine better—

[1] *Julia de Roubigné*, i. 33.

knows, for example, that when Lisette describes Julia's pallor she should be attributing it not to joy but to grief. Once more, the effect of the introduction of a minor character is not to diversify the reader's information about events, but to produce a heightened awareness of the principal's consciousness.

As in *The Man of Feeling*, Mackenzie uses the device of the incomplete bundle of papers discovered after the event by an impartial editor.[1] Poignancy is added by the neglect with which an indifferent world now treats this record of deep sorrow and suffering; the papers have been handed over for use in a grocer's shop. In conjunction with the immediate and necessarily discontinuous letter-form, the technique plays a less central part in the total effect than in the earlier novel. But Mackenzie remains very anxious to establish the seriousness of his performance—as a collection of accurate observations of human behaviour rather than mere fiction—and the circumstantial detail surrounding his 'editorship' is an attempt at simulating actuality. He claims, for example, that he has not tampered with the manuscript he found—there has been no attempt to impose a cerebral pattern upon the living record of sensation:

I love myself (and am apt, therefore, from a common sort of weakness, to imagine that other people love) to read nature in her smallest character, and am often more apprised of the state of the mind from very trifling, than from very important circumstances.[2]

Julia de Roubigné is a novel of considerable merit, sensitive, intelligent, and—apart from the theatrical climax—carefully controlled. It is also strikingly radical. Its 'revolutionary' qualities do not depend upon the digression in the second volume, about the liberal reforms Savillon introduces on his sugar plantation, which is the novel's other ill-judged sequence. Far more significant in the long run are the attitudes revealed towards human behaviour, and especially the relations between the instincts and the judgement. The three

---

[1] Charles Johnston's *Chrysal, or the Adventures of a Guinea*, 1767, may be the immediate source of the idea. A modified form of the same device occurs in Mackenzie's *Man of the World*, 1773. The duplication of narrators which results is further evidence of the technical inventiveness of the period, and of its obsessive interest in a subjective focus.

[2] *Julia de Roubigné*, pp. x–xi.

central characters are indeed all made morally admirable; where they fall into error it is because they rely on conventions, or on their own rationalizations, rather than upon the truth of instinct. This is an exalted view of intuitive human nature, and there is no example in the novel of a character who follows impulse acting selfishly or even cruelly. Mackenzie's trio of characters succeed in destroying one another: but only because, with the best intentions, they allow sophisticated, 'unnatural' ideas like gratitude or duty or honour to prevail over the truth of their sensations.

The radical nature of the representation is underlined by the fact that the truly 'pure' passion in the novel is extramarital. It seems likely that *Julia de Roubigné*'s central triangle, with the hero loving a married woman, also owes something to Goethe's *Sorrows of Werther*, first translated into English in 1771. If so, Mackenzie was lucky to escape the odium heaped by English conservatives on Goethe, for *Werther* became, and long remained, the notorious symbol of the sentimentalists' sexual immorality. It must be that Julia's carefully stressed innocence, and the extreme pathos of her fate, prevailed in critics' minds over the potentially dangerous example offered by her situation. For, in spite of Julia's respectability, this is a novel which goes as far or further than *Werther* in justifying not merely general instinct, but sexual passion, as a guide to conduct. It is the quality of feeling that sanctifies the marriage; not, as the anti-jacobins were to have it, the other way around. And of all the propositions advanced by liberal novelists during the century, this soon came to seem personally the most liberating, and socially the most dangerous.

CHAPTER 2

THE JACOBIN NOVEL I:
REVOLUTION AND REASON

THE debate about whether man's nature is virtuous or vicious, and the related arguments which compare primitive with advanced society, underlie much of the human science, the philosophy, the history, and the polemic of the last two decades of the eighteenth century. Inevitably these are key issues for the novelist too. R. G. Collingwood observes that between the sixteenth and the nineteenth century man's central intellectual effort was 'with laying the foundations of natural science, and philosophy took as its main theme the relation of the human mind as subject to the natural world of things around it in space as object'.[1] The novel is the major new literary genre of this period: and by its special treatment of the hero, which is quite unlike that of older forms such as epic or drama, it isolates 'the human mind as subject' from the 'world of things around it in space as object'. In the sympathy or otherwise with which he regards his hero's sensations, the late-eighteenth-century novelist is likely to reveal his partisanship in the terms of the contemporary debate on man. When he sketches in the society of contemporary England or France with any attempt at verisimilitude, he probably commits himself to a general view about advanced society.

The twentieth-century reader, habituated to the post-Freudian psychological novel, naturally does not think of 'inward interest' as tendentious. But then the novel as he knows it no longer generically raises live controversy—apart, perhaps, from science fiction, which has to evaluate whole societies, and so retains a unique licence to be didactic. The great majority of late-eighteenth-century popular novelists were modest hacks who did not set out to propagate a world view. But there was too much moral-essay writing, and too

---

[1] *The Philosophy of History*, Oxford, 1946, pp. 4–5.

much portentous criticism, for them to hide their heads successfully in the sand. They knew that their heroes and heroines were supposed to offer a moral pattern. The outcome of
the action, since it would be just, would betray a sense of
values. No bid for irresponsibility, no plea that their stories
merely set out to entertain, could absolve them from the
burden of their implicit meaning.

It is not difficult to see why the sentimentalist, with his
focus on the hero or heroine, comes to be identified as individualistic, libertarian, unorthodox, anti-social. Writers in a
subjective genre which is really related to the sentimental—
the Gothic horror-story—lay themselves open to like suspicion, unless they take careful steps to proclaim their
orthodoxy. Clara Reeve and Ann Radcliffe dwell upon the
sensations of their central characters, and Mrs. Radcliffe
especially learns to present her narrative subjectively, every
scene tense because it is permeated by the irrational terror
experienced by the heroine. Mrs. Radcliffe's symbolic 'meaning' is the progressive one: her innocent heroine, pure, passive,
acutely sensitive, is acted upon by the evil, all-powerful
tyrants who govern the world about her. *The Romance of the
Forest*, 1792, *The Mysteries of Udolpho*, 1794, and *The Italian*,
1797, might well have championed the individual oppressed
by a corrupt society, to judge alone by their central situations
and their emotive style. But Mrs. Radcliffe, although bent on
exploiting her period's discovery of abnormal nervous conditions, remains resolutely orthodox in her religion and morals,
and conservative in her politics. Her evil society usually
belongs to a past century, and to a country of Southern
Europe; her typical tyrants are aristocrats of the Spanish type,
narrow cold abbesses, or monks associated with the Inquisition.[1] (Topically, though not very consistently, since the
tale is set in the seventeenth century, the villainous Marquis
of Montalt in *The Romance of the Forest* is an adherent of the
new philosophy.) By contrast Mrs. Radcliffe's heroines are
pious and unassertive, and her virtuous minor characters tend
to be faithful servants. While cunningly giving her readers the
imaginative experience they crave, she manages at the same

[1] Cf. J. M. S. Tompkins, *The Popular Novel in England, 1770–1800*, pp. 249 ff.

time to pay sufficient tribute to the established order of a liberal but Christian England.

Even the care taken by Mrs. Radcliffe underlines how dangerous the novel was felt to be: as Johnson and his critical followers supposed, it was a form made to convey moral relativism. It was not therefore surprising that in the early 1790s, in the immediate aftermath of the French Revolution, a group of English radicals made use of it to circulate their ideas. The first to publish an explicitly revolutionary novel was Thomas Holcroft (1745–1809), former stable-boy, shoemaker, and actor, practising playwright and translator, and now author of *Anna St. Ives* (1792) and *The Adventures of Hugh Trevor* (1794–7). His friend William Godwin (1756–1836) brought out *Caleb Williams* in 1794; and in the same year Elizabeth Inchbald (1753–1821), already a successful novelist by virtue of the domestic *A Simple Story* (1791), was working on *A Satire on the Times*, which was to have included a harsh portrait of George III. When 'A Satire' eventually appeared in 1796, it was renamed *Nature and Art*, and had lost its subversive political portraits.[1] But with its motifs of the honest savage versus the corrupt artistocrat, and the simple country girl seduced by the vicious young squire, *Nature and Art* remained a progressive statement in the tradition of Rousseau or of Rousseau's English disciple Thomas Day.[2] Associated with the same group of London radicals were the feminists Mary Wollstonecraft (1759–97) and Mary Hays (1760–1843). A few practising novelists like Charlotte Smith and Mary Robinson were not such conscientious polemicists, but intermittently they would reveal liberal sympathies, so that by the end of the decade they incurred some of the odium attached to the 'jacobinical' clique.[3] Meanwhile, away in the provinces, the papermaker Robert Bage (1728–1801) continued his irreverent series of satirical novels,

---

[1] The 'Lord of the Bedchamber', Lord Bendham, remains in the finished novel, but he is scarcely recognizable as George III: the fears of her publisher, and the prudential advice of friends, persuaded Mrs. Inchbald to tone down the political content. C. Kegan Paul, *William Godwin, his friends and contemporaries*, 1876, i. 140–1, and G. D. Kelly, 'The English Jacobin Novel and its Background, 1780–1805', unpublished thesis for the University of Oxford, 1972, pp. 170 ff.

[2] See above, p. 13n.   [3] See below, p. 112.

which, since they began in the 1780s, were not strictly of the Revolution at all.

Two of the best of the 'jacobin' novels—Godwin's *Caleb Williams* and Bage's *Hermsprong* (1796)—will be analysed independently in Chapter 3, and what is essentially radical in them, their steady championing of Individual Man against a corrupt society, will emerge in that discussion. Meanwhile the question at issue is how far the jacobins as a group seized their opportunity; what, if anything, they were contributing to the novel at the time when the youthful Jane Austen was beginning to write. The answer is at first sight puzzling. Three decades earlier the sentimental novelists made technical innovations which reflected a new awareness of the subjective life of the individual. The so-called jacobins, for all their doctrinal individualism, do not follow the sentimentalists' lead. Gone is Sterne's associationism, or Mackenzie's artful fragmentariness. The revolutionaries do not even make sustained use of that commonest of all sentimental techniques, the harnessing of the reader's uncritical sympathies. Scene after scene in *Anna St. Ives* or *Nature and Art* parrots stock situations designed to call forth the reader's ready tears. Yet at times Holcroft and Mrs. Inchbald explicitly criticize sentimental emotionalism; and, significantly, neither of them *when writing as a progressive* shows any of that interest in the psychological processes which is the hallmark of the sentimental liberal.[1] As for the related genre, the Gothic, Godwin alone has an inkling of its potential for the writer who wants an image for the oppressed human spirit. He gives a Gothic colouring to *Caleb Williams*, and his *St. Leon* (1799) is a sustained essay in the genre. And yet if the heart of the Gothic novel is its sensitivity to nervous, or irrational, experience, even Godwin is partly out of sympathy with his medium. For all their energy, their idealism, and, at least in Godwin's case, their imaginative power, in the novel the revolutionaries voluntarily limit themselves, with the result that their subversion—like their artistic achievement—goes

---

[1] *Anna St. Ives* contains idealized, generalized character-studies, not closely observed from life (see below, pp. 47–8); Mrs. Inchbald, whose *Simple Story* is an impressive psychological novel, treats the characters as types in her more consciously radical *Nature and Art*.

only so far. The modern reader who wants to understand what a conservative like Jane Austen reacts against had better read the sentimentalists.

The course of intellectual history seldom runs smooth. The conservative Mrs. Radcliffe uses subjective techniques, though she hedges them about with safeguards; the radicals who are her nearest contemporaries shy away from them. In general the most marked trend in the English popular novel of the 1790s (in spite of its being the decade of the Terror and of *Lyrical Ballads*) is its resolute rationality, its suspicion of the uncontrollable workings of the unconscious mind. No feature is more common in novels of any ideological complexion during the revolutionary era than an unremitting hostility to that central plank of Mackenzie and other leading sentimentalists, the intuitional psychology of Hartley and Hume. Conservative critics of the novel, and conservative novelists too, see that the true threat to orthodoxy lies in the moral relativism implicit in the sentimental movement. It is therefore cunning of them, though inaccurate, to ascribe to the 'jacobins' of the 1790s subjectivity, emotionalism, indulgence towards human weakness, and belief in sexual freedom, all of which the jacobins explicitly renounce. For the time being the English progressive novelist speaks resolutely to the Reason. Sentimentalism has many critics in the period, but no one who is juster, more penetrating, or, for a while, more whole-hearted, than William Godwin.

The reaction against sentiment no doubt owed something to that most arbitrary and unanalysable of factors, the pendulum of fashion. Sentimentalism's heyday had been in the 1760s and 1770s, since when a torrent of novels, plays, and poems had devalued its serious intellectual content by turning its familiar characters, situations, and attitudes into clichés. Certain features of the manner, especially perhaps its exclusivity, its air of conscious refinement and superiority, proved both irritating and wonderfully parodiable. Absurdity hovered, and still hovers today, around Anna Seward, the Swan of Lichfield, and her self-admiring coterie. It is even harder to take seriously the della Cruscan movement, established in Florence in the mid-1780s: the episode in which its

leader, Robert Merry, exchanged extravagant professions of
love in the columns of *The World* with 'Laura Matilda'—only
to discover when at last they met that she was fat, middle-
aged Mrs. Hannah Cowley—itself reads extraordinarily like
burlesque.[1] Satirical attacks on sentimental affectation seem
to have had much more prestige in the last two decades of the
century among the cultural élite than any new sentimental
poetry. *The Rolliad*, 1784, Gifford's *Baviad*, 1791, and *Maeviad*,
1795, Mathias' *Pursuits of Literature*, 1794, and the poems of
The Anti-jacobin, 1797–8, all tended to go into far more
editions than any of the works or styles they satirized. But
why did the art of sinking become so popular? In order to
account for the resurgence of satire in the 1780s and 1790s, it
is necessary to look outside literature to general intellectual
history.

For the revolutionaries the disturbing features of sentimentalism lie not in style but in content, in the psychology of
Hume, and in the sociology of Montesquieu or of Hume's
fellow-Scot Adam Smith. Hume himself is too dispassionate
a seeker after truth to be either a partisan of the liberal
position, or an easy optimist. If man is the creature of his sensations, current and remembered, and of his involuntary
powers of association, he cannot be at the same time the
dignified and rational captain of his own mental universe.
Hume recognizes as much; both he and his contemporary
Scottish psychologists and physiologists produce a picture of
the mind dominated by the external environment and by the
individual nervous system, and this is a state of affairs as
obnoxious to the humanist as it is to most Christians.

The anxieties induced by Hume in a careful reader do not
stop there, for implicitly the picture of society he gives in his
History is a disturbing one. As a historian Hume has struck
most modern critics as a little disappointing, for with typical
scepticism he rejects earlier theories of historical causation—
such as the conscious activities of great men—without putting
anything coherent in their stead. Yet this in itself is expres-

---

[1] The episode is described in full by Kenneth Hopkins, *Portraits in Satire*,
1958, pp. 174–83. In Maria Edgeworth's story *Angelina*, 1801, a high-flown
literary correspondence is followed by a similar dénouement. (See below,
pp. 134–6.) Although the Merry story became widely known when Gifford
satirized it in *The Baviad*, the resemblance is presumably coincidental.

sive: for one of the most widely read historians of the century, historical change seems to be a chaotic, formless flux, which dwarfs the human actors caught up in it. Other historians of the period are readier to account for events without being more reassuring. Montesquieu's *Esprit des lois* popularizes a conception of organic societies developing in response to impersonal geographic forces. Adam Ferguson, comparing pastoral with advanced societies, shows forcibly how far the individual's role is in practice determined by the social world into which he was born. Gibbon, who acknowledges a debt to Scottish historiography and sociology,[1] produces the late-eighteenth century's most powerful imaginative picture of a world of individuals caught in the web of social change. He is intrigued by the diversity of the human beings on his stage. For the sake of variety and richness he will pause to consider, for example, Mahomed, St. Bernard, the Courtenay family, and of course the individual emperors. Occasionally he arrives at a man who in the very nature of things has unusual importance: the four virtuous and effective Antonines, for example, who, succeeding one another in the second century A.D., might—if such a thing had been humanly possible—have arrested the Roman decline. The point is that for Gibbon personal intervention on this scale and at this time was not possible. The massive size of the Roman empire and the Augustan centralization of its offices under the emperor had destroyed the possibility of effective human action. Even the coming of Christianity, which Gibbon sees as another factor to encourage personal passivity and quiescence, was not necessary to bring about the empire's moral decline.

Gibbon does not argue that in all circumstances the individual is helpless. He considers that simpler communities, such as those of the barbarians, or the Roman Republic, allow a man considerable freedom and dignity. In the middle of the eighteenth century, and from his Swiss vantage-point, he can point to a political solution which still allows liberty to the individual citizen, that of the very small, or pastoral, state. Nevertheless, the imaginative picture Gibbon has drawn of the actual historical civilization under review is a compelling

---

[1] *Decline and Fall of the Roman Empire*, ed. J. B. Bury, 7 vols., London, 1909, i. 143.

one, the more so because it has features in common with Hume's *History,* and with much—and very various—imaginative literature of the period. There is a futility about what men do; but what they are may be subtle, even marvellous. While Gibbon's villains are the superstitious Christians, or tyrants like Augustus and Severus, who helped to extend the sway of institutions, his heroes are men like Boethius, who retained their intellectual independence. And Gibbon himself, observer, philosopher, intellectual, is always present, pacing about in the wings, to reinforce the influence of the wise men on his stage, and to provide at least an alternative focus of interest to the otherwise soulless, impersonal pressure of events. In a less formulated sense, it is the same in Hume's *History of Great Britain.* There are no effective great men, but the best among the pygmies are those like Blake and Monck who have no personal ambition, and merely represent a wise consensus. The most typical hero of the era of sensibility is not the master of events, nor even the actor, but the sensitive observer—Gibbon and Hume's *personae* in their histories, Gray's in his *Elegy,* Sterne's as Yorick or Mackenzie's as Harley. All are men who record a rapid and endlessly varied sense of impressions, and all are helpless to influence the onward movement of destiny.

It is clear, in short, that the most prestigious portraits of man in society in the 1760s and 1770s tend to be optimistic about human nature only in a special and very limited sense. Even though they hold the intuitive side of man's nature to be naturally benevolent, the stress they place on the irrational makes man the tool of processes over which he has no control. Precisely because they observe this aspect of human nature with accuracy, the better sentimental novelists allow a potentially disturbing picture to emerge, even though it is no part of their purpose to lay stress on it. Sterne's Uncle Toby is not only benevolent, but ineffectual, perhaps impotent. Mackenzie's Julia is, as her husband observes, a creature who cannot command but is commanded by her own deepest feelings.[1] The disturbing feature of sentimentalism is that it has much to say about sensation, little about action; indeed, the more the complexities of the inner life are understood, the

[1] See above, pp. 25–6.

less confident can an observer be that the individual's nature might ever be satisfactorily realized in action. The same spirit of cool scientific appraisal is directed at man's broader social conditions as at his inner life, with similar results. The consequence of a growing understanding of economics and of political institutions is to make it seem as hard for the individual man to control his environment as it is for him to control himself. It is hardly surprising, therefore, that at the very end of the sentimental period a great writer adapts the characteristic tools of the progressive in order to make a pessimistic and conservative case.

In the *Reflexions on the Revolution in France* (1790), Edmund Burke advances two main propositions, both of them adapted from familiar positions of the Anglo-Scottish science of man. First he proposes that an advanced ('civil') society, such as contemporary France or England, is an organic whole, the equivalent in political life of inter-related systems of plant-life (since Linnaeus a fashionable study), or of the cosmos, which Newton had shown as answerable to its own law. Second, Burke implies a view of the nature of man which is in line with the psychology of the irrational. His human beings intuitively feel love or sympathy for family, for neighbours, and, by a natural associative process, for the head of the wider family, in the person of the head of state. Only the perverted think in terms of their selfish individual 'rights' or advantages. It is only by obeying his deepest instincts, which are social, and by mistrusting his reason, which may delude him with false notions of where his advantage lies as an individual, that man can achieve happiness and fulfil his nature. Burke has in fact seen the political logic of Hume's more pessimistic side, his picture of man as the involuntary servant of his affective experiences and instincts. That inclination in Hume's *History* towards political quietism becomes the major theme of the *Reflexions*, and it is cunningly worked out with the full range of sentimental effects.

Like all sentimental writers, Burke is aware above all of the reader. He knows how to enlist his active participation by evoking a series of rapidly changing reactions. The *Reflexions* is a typical sentimental performance because it goes far beyond either rational political discussion or even detached treatment of matter seen as irrational: it tries to evoke the living experience—alternately of belonging to the community and of threatened alienation from it—in the half-consciousness of the reader. Through a subtle web of association Burke evokes the living organism of English society as it has existed in its continuity over centuries; and he shows how inseparable the life of the community is from the life of the individual. Exploiting the mind's natural process of building up impressions by association, rather than proceeding by logic, he moves apparently at random from the English Revolution Society and Dr. Richard Price to a legalistic discussion of the seventeenth century, to events in France, and back again to the Revolution's English supporters. It is only gradually that the desired effect builds up: the clustering on one side, that of the existing English constitution, of a vast range of images, from the homely and endearing, to the venerable, and even, by virtue of Miltonic associations, to the cosmic. Of those who resort to anarchy, for example, he comments:

If that which is only submission to necessity should be made the object of choice, the law is broken, nature is disobeyed, and the rebellious are outlawed, cast forth, and exiled, from this world of reason, and order, and peace, and virtue, and fruitful penitence, into the antagonist world of madness, discord, vice, confusion and unavailing sorrow.[1]

A densely peopled community, made up of lords and peasants, the English living and dead of many centuries, dwarfs the revolutionaries as he presents them, for they are seen as mere individuals, a faction, outcasts; or, worse, as dehumanized 'metaphysicians', 'theorists', 'philosophical fanatics' who rely on cold mathematical calculation and scraps of paper. The spontaneous human instinct is to exist unassertively in a community made dear by association. Thus the man who guides himself and others by cerebral means is linked—by images that are thin, pared-down, non-sentient—to a less-than-human order:

We know that *we* have made no discoveries; and we think that no discoveries are to be made, in morality; nor many in the great principles of government, nor in the ideas of liberty, which were

[1] Edmund Burke, *Works*, London, 1826, v. 185.

understood before we were born, altogether as well as they will be after the grave has heaped its mould upon our presumption, and the silent tomb shall have imposed its law on our pert loquacity. In England we have not yet been completely embowelled of our natural entrails . . . We have not been drawn and trussed, like stuffed birds in a museum, with chaff and rags and paltry blurred shreds of paper about the rights of man.[1]

Of the sixty or so authors of books and pamphlets who tried to refute Burke's position and to defend the Revolution, the majority responded indignantly to what they regarded as the sophistry of his appeal to the irrational.[2] E. Erämetsä records how the word 'sensibility' became a pejorative term before the turn of the century, and the process could for example be illustrated in Mary Wollstonecraft's strictures on Burke:

Sensibility is the *mania* of the day, and compassion the virtue which is to cover a multitude of vices, whilst justice is left to mourn in sullen silence, and balance truth in vain . . . Quitting the flowers of rhetoric, let us, Sir, reason together . . .[3]

No doubt one effect of Burke's tactics was to drive his opponents towards a sometimes exaggerated posture of rationality, which is handled with poise by the lawyer James Mackintosh, but assorts ill with the natural style of a humane, impassioned individualist like Mary Wollstonecraft herself. In general, though, it is probably a mistake to lay at Burke's door the difficulties of his opponents. The tide of sentimentalism had turned; and already, in the late 1780s, progressives like for example Bage and Holcroft had censured, independently, the tendency to quietism which is latent in the sentimentalist's stress on the irrational. It remained for the greatest of the revolutionaries, William Godwin, to survey half a century of attitudes to man in society, in order to put his finger on the point where the radical of the 1790s had to part company with his predecessors.

Godwin's *Political Justice*, 1793, is a book which goes back

[1] Ibid., v. 166–7.
[2] See James T. Boulton, *The Language of Politics in the Age of Wilkes and Burke*, London, 1963.
[3] *A Vindication of the Rights of Man*, 1790, pp. 5–6. Cf. E. Erämetsä, A *Study of the Word 'Sentimental' and of Other Linguistic Characteristics of Eighteenth Century Sentimentalism in England*, Helsinki, 1951.

in English tradition to the Commonwealth and to Puritan political dissent, in French tradition to the Enlightenment as represented for example by d'Holbach and Helvétius. But for all the breadth, and at times the intricacy of its arguments, there are two broad points which it is primarily concerned to establish. The first, as the opening passage makes clear, is the refutation of that conception of Montesquieu, long dear to English and Anglo–Scottish liberals, and latterly the starting-point of Edmund Burke: the notion of civil society as organic, 'natural', and, in the life of the individual man, essentially wholesome.[1] Godwin sees the organized social mechanism as a clog on the freedom of the individual; government as a repressive combination favouring the rich against the poor; kings and aristocracy as vested interests, and their institutions, such as the law, as not merely often unjust but necessarily unnatural, because they impose a fixed code upon a world which is continuously in flux. But perhaps more central from our point of view, because more crucial to his development as a novelist, is Godwin's conception of human nature. He totally rejects that view recently exploited by Burke, but really implicit in Hartley, Hume, and most of their followers, that man's inner life is primarily instinctive, and his attitudes and actions involuntary. He does not deny the almost limitless influence of existing society, with its entrenched opinions and attitudes, and he deals with such prior conditioning in a chapter grimly entitled 'The Characters of Men Originate in their Social Circumstances'. Nevertheless, he distinguishes carefully between voluntary and involuntary actions, while admitting that in the current state of things the latter may be much the more common, and that 'this consideration must greatly overcloud the prospect of the moral reformer'.[2] But

in the meantime it is obvious to remark, that the perfection of the human character consists in approaching as nearly as possible to the perfectly voluntary state. We ought to be upon all occasions prepared to render a reason of our actions. We should remove

[1] Godwin claimed that the starting-point of *Political Justice* was 'a feeling of the imperfections and errors of Montesquieu'. C. Kegan Paul, *William Godwin, his friends and contemporaries*, i. 67.

[2] *Political Justice*, 3rd ed., ed. F. E. L. Priestley, Toronto, 1946, i. 55.

ourselves to the furthest distance from the state of mere inanimate machines, acted upon by causes of which they have no understanding. We should be cautious of thinking it a sufficient reason for an action, that we are accustomed to perform it, and that we once thought it right . . . In our speculative opinions and our practical principles we should never consider the book of enquiry as shut.[1]

Instead of the sentimentalist's benevolent intuition or fellow-feeling, he believes in the conscious, willed understanding as the essentially human thing, the guarantee of man's dignity and his sole hope for improvement. He minimizes those aspects of man's nature which limit the freedom of his mind, such as the pleasures of the senses, tastes, and 'involuntary affections', which include emotional attachments to family and friends. In a less corrupt society these would, he thinks, wither away, or assume their properly subordinate place. Godwin is often censured for the coldness of his theorizing; he uses some injudicious examples to illustrate his case, such as the notorious passage in which he remarks that in a fire a perfectly just man would save the life of Fénelon before that of Fénelon's chamber-maid, even though the latter were the rescuer's wife or mother.[2] So much play was made of this that in the third edition Fénélon's valet was consigned to the flames instead of his chamber-maid, but as far as the popular impression went the damage was done. Yet it is fair to recall that this celebrated instance of Godwin's 'inhumanity' occurs in the context of a strong assertion of human value. Godwin is rejecting the idea that we are totally the slaves either of our passions or of social conditioning, though he has admitted the power of both. He is maintaining that we reach our full humanity only when we are capable of perceiving our power to choose, and of exercising it. *Political Justice* has a place in what is for the student of literature a recognizable tradition, that of Milton in *Comus*, *Areopagitica*, and *Paradise Lost* and Richardson in *Clarissa*, a tradition in which individuals master their destiny through a conscious act of choice. Godwin has therefore defied the dominant tendency both of eighteenth

---

[1] Ibid., i. 68. Both these examples come from the important chapter v, 'The Voluntary Actions of Men Originate in their Opinions'.

[2] Ibid., ii. 2; in the 3rd edition, i. 126–9. For the changes to the 3rd edition of 1798, and the change in attitude which occasioned them, see below pp. 66–7.

century sensationalist philosophy, and of historiography after Montesquieu, to render the human being will-less.

The English progressives of the 1790s thus gave sound intellectual reasons for rejecting the passivity of the sentimentalists; but perhaps less conscious factors influenced them too. For example, their English lower-middle-class origins, and in several cases their Nonconformity, may have done as much as their French sympathies to account for the austerity of some of their attitudes. Bage, the Midlands paper manufacturer, who was little if at all subject to metropolitan fashion, produced four novels in the 1780s which poked fun at the sentimental heroine and her characteristically passive, merely responsive behaviour.[1] At the same time his heroes were not the effete aristocrats favoured by the sentimental school, but sons of sturdy farmers or merchants, who made it a point of honour to work for a living. The class from which Bage came was active and rising; more often than not its members were Dissenters, and thus heirs both to a tradition of opposition to the *status quo*, and of doubt about human nature.[2] Bage's favourite plot involves a trial: a young man or woman must prove worthy to marry, not, as in the sentimental tradition, by sheer ardour, a willingness to die for love, but by cooler, more rational tests of probity, unselfishness, and practical worth. The emotion of love is no longer central. The traditional plot merely provides an occasion for an extended probation in which the moral qualities of the hero are explored.[3]

[1] *Mount Henneth*, 1782, *Barham Downs*, 1784, *The Fair Syrian*, 1787, and *James Wallace*, 1789. Each has a sentimental heroine and a more robust friend or sister whose energy and self-reliance is seen as morally preferable. The same pattern is repeated in *Hermsprong*: see below, pp. 82–3.

[2] Bage was described by his friend William Hutton as 'barely a Christian, though one of the best'. (*Monthly Magazine*, xii (1 Jan. 1802), 479.) Scott mistakenly associated him with the Quakers, perhaps because of sympathetic portraits like that of Isaac Arnold in *Barham Downs*. Bage himself seems close to his creation in spirit . . . 'I am Isaac Arnold, by birth a man, by religion a Quaker, taught to despise all titles that are not the marks of virtue; and of consequence—thine. I rank above thee.' *Barham Downs*, i. 330.

[3] The most extended trial of this kind occurs in Bage's *Man as He Is*, 1792, in which the impoverished Quaker heroine, Cornelia Colerain, steadily refuses to marry the wealthy baronet, Sir George Paradyne, until he can command himself and prove a useful member of society. See below, p. 77.

Often Bage has a quaint out-of-fashion provincial flavour all his own, but his attitude to the sentimental ideal of womanhood is shared by the other, London-based, revolutionary novelists. All agree that the stress on feeling rather than on reason, and on fine sensation rather than on activity, holds particular dangers for women, since, by encouraging passivity, it leads easily to submission. How many late-eighteenth-century novels, for example, include a meek heroinely admission of the claims of a parent, however tyrannous; or of the beauty of self-abnegation at the mere mention of 'duty' or 'gratitude'? The outward manifestations of a delicate sensibility in woman become a source of provocation to progressives, as Thomas Holcroft reveals in an irritable outburst when reviewing a novel called *Louisa Matthews*:

> She [the heroine] is a sensitive plant, which shrinks, if the untutored finger of common accident approach it. We must warn the fair authoress, that this propensity of mind can neither conduce to her own happiness, nor teach happiness to her readers.[1]

It is not only female characters who attract strictures of this kind. Writers of revolutionary tendencies censure any symptoms of dangerous sensibility in their heroes. Edmund Oliver, in Charles Lloyd's novel of that name, spends the action wrestling with the weakness,[2] as does the hero of Mary Robinson's *Walsingham, or the pupil of nature* (1797). However, it is the heroine of the progressive novel of the 1790s who is most regularly seen in terms of a conflict between conventional fine feeling, and reason; and who is always enjoined to command herself, on pain of self-destruction. Elizabeth Inchbald is the best artist among the feminists of the period to argue against the sway of feeling. A lack of self-command is the vice of Miss Milner, heroine of *A Simple Story* (1791); and in *Nature and Art* (1796), the simple, innocent Hannah Primrose, who allows herself to be seduced, is compared kindly but unfavourably with the prudent Rebecca Rymer. Thomas Holcroft declares that the aim of his *Anna St. Ives* (1792), is 'to teach fortitude to females': he depicts Anna as weak in the

---

[1] *Monthly Review*, 2nd ser., x (Apr. 1793), 459: quoted by G. D. Kelly, 'The English Jacobin Novel and Its Background', unpublished D.Phil. thesis for the University of Oxford, 1972, p. 195.

[2] See below, p. 109.

first half of the novel, when her judgement is suborned by passion, and invincible in the second half, when her reason prevails. The same point is central in Mary Hays's *Memoirs of Emma Courtnay* (1796). That novel, with its bizarre action of a woman persistently importuning a man to marry her, is sometimes referred to (especially by its host of contemporary critics)[1] as a bid for greater sexual freedom for women. In real life, the thirty-six-year-old author, a humourless, passionate, evidently neurotic woman, was writing copious declarations of love to a man who was indifferent to her, and more long letters of exposition and self-revelation to William Godwin, to whom she had recently introduced herself.[2] Both these correspondences are incorporated into the novel, so that the urgency of real feeling, and the pain of real humiliation, all too recognizably break through. All the same, her contemporaries' laughter was cruel, and it did an injustice both to Mary Hays's moral character and to her plain intention. The theme of *Emma Courtnay*—at least at the conscious level—is that women will never be free unless they learn to submit their passions to the control of reason.

English novelists have always tended to be more prudish than their contemporaries on the Continent. For all the reverence for the instincts in the sentimental era, the sexual act itself is apparently too gross to be contemplated directly,[3] and it is extremely rare for an English heroine to survive a voluntary lapse from chastity.[4] Rousseau's Julie, who becomes St. Preux's mistress before her marriage to Wolmar, and ends her life not merely forgiven but adored and reverenced, is an unthinkable heroine for a Briton: Mackenzie's Julia, though in so many ways comparable, is impeccably chaste. Thus it was not the example of English sentimentalists, but that of Rousseau, Goethe, or Kotzebue, that the revolutionaries renounced when they refused to exploit sexual passion as a powerful

---

[1] See below, p. 117.

[2] A. F. Wedd, *The Love-Letters of Mary Hays, 1779–80*, London, 1925, p. 7.

[3] In sentimental fiction consummation is so often promised and withdrawn— as in Richardson's *Pamela* or Henry Brooke's *Juliet Grenville*—or withheld altogether—as for Sterne's Uncle Toby and Mackenzie's Harley—that the effect is a blend of sexual excitement with a veiled or explicit suggestion of impotence.

[4] Cf. J. M. S. Tompkins, *The Popular Novel in England, 1770–1800*, pp. 141–171.

natural ally against a moribund society and its repressive conventions.[1] At the conscious level, they could not use the libido
because they believed in reason, and were mistrustful of the
irrational. Unconsciously they were surely under the sway—
as their sentimental predecessors had been—of the puritanism
in sexual matters that is associated with English middle-class
and lower-middle-class life, and with nineteenth-century
Nonconformity. It is no accident that Godwin, their leading
intellectual and spokesman, began life as a Unitarian minister.

Even if, like Godwin, they renounced Christianity, in taste
and morality the English 'jacobins' proved truer to their class
and to its religious inheritance than to the more ardent ethos
of their Continental namesakes. The strongest of all influences
on English intellectual life during the next generation was
to be not the French Revolution, but the rise to a far greater
share of economic, social, and political influence of this very
class from which so many of the jacobins came.[2] Over the next
generation middle-class criticism was to be turned effectively
upon the aristocracy; not, immediately, on aristocratic
domination of political institutions, but on aristocratic moral
licence in private life. In sexual matters the jacobins thought
and as a group behaved (whatever their opponents claimed)
like forerunners of the Evangelicals. Their advocacy of reason
and restraint often makes them read like their opponents, the
conservative moralists. Occasionally, just because they are
middle class, while their opponents' base is aristocratic, the
jacobins actually succeed in giving a stronger appearance of
strait-laced respectability. Verbally, for example, *The Anti-
Jacobin* is much coarser than any of them.[3]

Whatever the historical explanation for the puritanical
streak in the English jacobin novel, which compares so oddly
with progressive writing on the Continent, artistically it
proves a major handicap. Unfortunately the jacobins are
slow to perceive the awkwardness of trying to graft Right
Reason on to the stock of sentimental fiction. Holcroft, for
example, is a competent journeyman both as playwright and

---

[1] The poets Burns and Blake wrote much more freely. For conservative
pressures on the novel, see below, pp. 120–1.

[2] See below, pp. 162–5, pp. 242–3, and pp. 284–6.

[3] See below, p. 163n.

as novelist, but he is always derivative,[1] and so he bases his plots on the conventional love-story. In *Anna St. Ives* he puts his heroine in the time-honoured dilemma of having to choose between two suitors for her hand. All the signs in the first half of the novel are that we are to be faced with a struggle between two warring elements: an internal debate, perhaps, between Anna's intuitive passion and her reason, or an externalized conflict between Anna's instincts and her father's worldly prudence. Neither develops, because Holcroft does not want Anna's passion to carry the day. He cannot have the essential Anna identified—as Julia de Roubigné is identified—with the inner life of her emotions. In the middle of the novel Anna discovers that *both* feeling and Right Reason direct her towards Frank Henley. Mary Wollstonecraft's semi-autobiographical *The Wrongs of Woman* is another revolutionary novel which seems to start as a conventional love-story, and to harness the reader's sympathy for the lover in the old intuitive way, only to falter in the middle of the action. At first the victimized heroine's love for her fellow-prisoner, Henry, is presented as a 'natural' and thus innately virtuous emotion (as indeed Mary proved in real life that she thought of sexual love). The novel is unfinished, but Henry was to turn unfaithful, and the apparent tendency of the whole was to be that a woman had better not trust a man's love. Mrs. Inchbald, a more sensitive artist than the others, does better by frankly making her two love-stories, *A Simple Story* and *Nature and Art*, studies in frustration, abnegation, or ultimate betrayal and tragedy. There is no conflict between form and meaning in the work of this reserved, inhibited woman. But Godwin, easily the finest intellect among the revolutionary novelists, is more positive than she is in rethinking his plot in terms of the philosophy he has to convey. *Caleb Williams* is rare and perhaps unique in the period in entirely leaving out love as a central motif.

---

[1] His plays—of which the most popular was *The Road to Ruin*, 1792—were in a familiar genre of late-eighteenth-century sentimental comedy, with a polemical element grafted on. (*Love's Frailties*, 1794, was booed when one of the characters spoke the daring line, 'I was bred to one of the most useless, and often the most worthless of all professions, that of a gentleman.') Among his novels, the main debt of *Hugh Trevor*, 4 vols., 1794–7, is to Smollett; that of *Bryan Perdue*, 1805, to Sterne.

The practical difficulties offered by romantic plots are only symptomatic of what is really the central difficulty. The essential core of the progressive's position is his faith in man; the jacobins share that faith with the sentimentalists, and what they are trying to do is to assert it more positively by bringing forward the active, voluntary side of man's consciousness while playing down involuntary sensations such as physical love. The ultimate difficulty of such a starting-point for a novelist is that it has, confessedly, little or nothing to do with that observable world which is the subject-matter of the novelist. The best sentimental novels, like Sterne's and Mackenzie's, were based on an increasingly sophisticated contemporary awareness of human behaviour. Their insights into the how and why of characters' actions had genuine psychological validity, whether or not they added up to a complete picture. The reaction of the 1790s (and this proves to be as true of the conservatives as of the revolutionaries) is not based on observation. When in *Political Justice* he describes a mental life that is voluntary rather than involuntary, Godwin admits that he speaks of the desirable human state, rather than of a situation which he sees existing in the society around him. He has difficulty in *Political Justice* in explaining, in terms which are satisfactory psychologically, how the individual indoctrinated by a corrupt society can ever arrive at a truth independent of his own fallible nature; and, aware of the old Protestant error of antinomianism, the confusion of our personal will with God's, he is led, like Richard Price before him, to a kind of Platonism. Truth or Right Reason awaits outside us, ready to be found if only our efforts towards rationality and mental independence are strenuous enough. Godwin and Holcroft were both interested in the work of the Platonist Thomas Taylor, and they discussed it, among other occasions, at the very time when Godwin was reading Holcroft's *Anna St. Ives* in manuscript.[1] It may be as the result of that discussion—it is certainly the fruit of the Platonist influence—that the psychology Holcroft employs in the

---

1 'Holcroft sups, talk of Plato', entry in Godwin's unpublished *Journal*, 20 Dec. 1791; quoted by G. D. Kelly, 'The English Jacobin Novel and Its Background', p. 236 n. Cf. Kathleen Raine and G. M. Harper, *Thomas Taylor the Platonist*, London, 1969, p. 444; and, for elements of Platonism in *Political Justice*, F. E. L. Priestley, Godwin's *Political Justice*, iii. 8–9 and *passim*.

novel is so strangely abstract, so remote from what is observable in life. Of the three principal characters, two, Anna and Frank, are partly or wholly ideal presentations of rational characters leading an active life of mind, and thus not only controlling their own destinies but potentially commanding their environment. The third, Coke Clifton, is a stage villain who speaks largely in quotations, and, with stage seediness clinging to him, fails altogether to suggest that Cavalier genealogy which gives his original, Lovelace, a genuine social representativeness. Originally, Holcroft's trio were to have been locked in a fatal conflict emblematic of the pressures of an unredeemed society upon the individual. Apparently it was Godwin who argued that it would be more 'true' to Platonist theory to end on the optimistic note which gives the novel so didactic and unlifelike an air.

It would be wrong to suggest that Holcroft is never moving and never effective. He resembles Mary Wollstonecraft, in that his life—courageous, passionate, indefatigable—is the best testimony he gives to his cause. One of the first and most fearless canvassers of radical ideas, in both novels and drama, he became a martyr to his opinions. After being arrested with eleven others in 1794 on trumped-up charges of treason, he carried through life the monstrous sneer Gifford fixed on him, that he was an 'acquitted felon'. By 1799 it had become virtually impossible for him to make a living by writing for the stage, and he went abroad with his wife and daughters, but his characteristic hopefulness never failed him. Although often sick, he believed too passionately in the human mind and spirit to submit to the merely physical; against the evidence of his senses, he willed disbelief in the reality of pain. In Germany in 1800 an incident occurred which typified the way in which a malign fortune often put his theories to the test. While he was preparing to bathe his feet in a solution of 'acqua fortis' (nitric acid), he broke the bottle and splashed the undiluted acid on to his hands, face, and eyes, burning himself agonizingly and endangering his never strong sight. Despite episodes like this, and an equally dreadful one in November 1789, when his runaway son shot himself rather than face his father, Holcroft will be remembered for the altruism and optimism with which he perfectly reflected the early stages of revolution: 'Hey for the New Jerusalem! The millennium! And peace and eternal beatitude be with the soul of Thomas Paine.'[1]

Mary Wollstonecraft also expresses the optimism and assertiveness of the early 1790s. In her life she was a doughty combatant of the evils women were heir to: she supported herself as a schoolmistress, governess and writer, championed her sister Eliza against Eliza's husband, went to revolutionary France and lived openly outside wedlock with Gilbert Imlay. After coming home in 1795, deserted, and with an illegitimate baby daughter, she twice attempted suicide: like her marital status, the suicides were an open secret. When she found herself pregnant again, this time by Godwin, she acknowledged propriety enough to want to get married, but retained her separate ménage: she had certainly not declined into tame domesticity when she died after the birth of the baby in 1798. Hers is an eloquent life, telling of battles fought against economic dependence and rigid, unequal sexual conventions. Yet in *The Wrongs of Woman*, the novel in which she tries to make use of this material, Mary Wollstonecraft creates a heroine who is what she ought not to have been, a passive vessel of suffering. With the partial exception of the wardress and ex-prostitute, Jemima, the novel is peopled with preconditioned characters who rarely break out of the rigid pattern society has taught them.

Holcroft, with his greater professionalism, makes rather better use in his fiction than Mary Wollstonecraft does in hers of scenes of real-life suffering. When he re-creates the hardships of his childhood, in his fragment of *Memoir*, he writes with a marvellous sense of external detail,[2] and much of the same material appears effectively in the opening section of *Hugh Trevor*. But Holcroft too finds it impossible

---

[1] Thomas Holcroft to William Godwin, n.d. [Spring 1791], on Holcroft's seeing *The Rights of Man* through the press. C. Kegan Paul, *William Godwin, his friends and contemporaries*, i. 69.

[2] *Memoir of Thomas Holcroft*, ed. W. Hazlitt, London, 1809. The two sequences of Holcroft's own writing, the long autobiographical fragment with which the book begins, and the journal describing his voyage into exile in 1799, both stand out strikingly from Hazlitt's more impersonal manner of narration.

to make sustained use of the best discoveries of recent fiction, which focused on close observation of the individual psyche. Apart from episodes borrowed from his own life, he is at his best when virtually plagiarizing. The second of his novels advocating the revolutionary cause, *Hugh Trevor*, models a passable social satire on one of Smollett's picaresque adventures, *Roderick Random* or *Peregrine Pickle*. In many respects the most effective moments in *Anna St. Ives* are those which most closely imitate Richardson. For by using Richardson's image of the imprisoned heroine defying her persecutor, Holcroft echoes old Puritan intensities, and gives Anna's resistance a resonance the English jacobins could not often manage on their own.

The protagonist undergoes the traditional imprisonment in most of the best jacobin novels: in Holcroft's *Hugh Trevor* as well as *Anna St. Ives*, in Godwin's *Caleb Williams* and *St. Leon*, in Mary Wollstonecraft's *Wrongs of Woman*. Often the prison-sequence is followed by a trial at which the prisoner speaks out against tyranny and in favour of the individual's right to liberty: eloquently and at length in Godwin and Mary Wollstonecraft, and, even better, with brevity in Mrs. Inchbald's *Nature and Art*.[1]

The symbols for the novel which sided with the oppressed individual were—like the lived experience—all there: but where was the form? Thorough-going sentimentalism, with its subjective narrative technique, was rejected, and in England at least the potential of the Gothic genre for the novelist of ideas was not yet tapped. It was only gradually that Godwin overcame his suspicion of the Gothic's connection with the abnormal and irrational, and not till the next generation, with *Frankenstein*, 1818, by Godwin's own daughter Mary Shelley, and *Melmoth the Wanderer*, 1820, by Maturin, that an ideo-

[1] In this novel the ruined woman, Hannah Primrose, is sentenced to death, unrecognized, by the man who years earlier seduced her. Hitherto silent, in spite of her wrongs, she cries out as sentence is about to be passed 'Ah! not from you!' This scene, imagined with the practising dramatist's flair for expressive action, is afterwards borrowed by Bulwer Lytton for his political novel *Paul Clifford* (1830). In Bulwer's version the judge is (unknown to himself) the father of the highwayman he is trying. Like Hannah, Paul was driven to his life of crime by the corruption of the very member of the Establishment afterwards appointed to judge him.

logical hatred of oppression and value for the person can be read into a sustained English Gothic tale.

Nothing better illustrates the jacobins' failure to find themselves a true form than their troubled relations with autobiography. Throughout the century there had been a close connection between on the one hand biography and autobiography, and on the other hand, the novel, which was very commonly a fictionalized memoir. As the eighteenth century progressed, so did interest in the technique of life-writing: notably, in the second half of the period the focus became increasingly domestic, and the materials used, anecdotes and familiar letters, were designed to build an impressionistic account of the complex, many-sided living man rather than the older, more formal, public, and rationalized 'Character'. Mason's *Life of Gray* and Boswell's *Life of Johnson* were seen as 'modern' performances in their day, and their day coincided with the sentimental period, but in biographical writing the process had by no means stopped at this point. The most influential *Life* of the closing years of the century was surely Rousseau's *Confessions*, the first part of which appeared in English translation in 1783, the second part in 1790. In this period of relative technical stasis in the novel itself, the *Confessions* ought to have had a special meaning for English fiction. As an impressionistic account of childhood and other early experience, an attempt to relive and to make the reader live the formative moments of a life, Rousseau's book is to earlier formal biography what *Tristram Shandy* is to fictional biography. Creative, sensational, fleeting, anti-moralistic, it applies a psychology similar to Hume's to the building of a portrait, and challenges the veracity of all other approaches to character, whether in real life or fiction.

The English progressives were fascinated by the *Confessions*. Mrs. Inchbald and Godwin made plans to translate it.[1] The more serious artists among the group all saw in biography the obvious form for an individualistic novel. The close relationship between Holcroft's Rousseauistic fragment on his early life and parts of *Hugh Trevor* has already been noted. Mrs.

[1] Godwin undertook a translation in December 1789; Mrs. Inchbald worked on hers in 1790. G. D. Kelly, 'The English Jacobin Novel and Its Background', p. 383, and J. Boaden, *Memoirs of Mrs. Inchbald*, London, 1833, i. 272.

Inchbald's *A Simple Story*, 1791, is essentially biographical in concept, as are all Godwin's novels to fall within what can roughly be called the revolutionary period—*Caleb Williams*, 1794, *St. Leon*, 1799, and *Fleetwood*, 1805.[1] But in many respects the two later novels of these three by Godwin, especially *Fleetwood*, reveal the Rousseauistic influence more strongly and clearly than does *Caleb Williams*. The immediate impact upon him of the *Confessions*, though powerful, must have been ambivalent. The reasons are easy to seek in *Political Justice*, which he shortly afterwards began to write. The *Confessions* evidently fascinated him by their air of truth as the record of the growth of a personality. They must have perturbed him because they made the process involuntary, the product of an infinitely complicated combination of chances.

It is interesting to find Mackenzie himself in later life also complaining in slightly different terms because this great record of experience lacks an ethical dimension. 'Autobiography, the confession of a person he himself instead of the priest,—generally gets absolution too easily. Rousseau without virtue, but having all the eloquence of virtue.'[2]

Another illustration of the insidious spread of moralism in opposition to the behavioural type of biography occurs in the work of Richard Lovell Edgeworth, the father of the novelist. Edgeworth was a liberal whose intellectual development owed something to Rousseau and French rationalism, but more to Scottish empiricism and to Hartley's psychology. In the late 1770s he began the most important work of his life, a study of the responses of young children to the knowledge they received, which was to provide a basis for a more scientific method of education. In 1789 Edgeworth learnt of the death of his friend Thomas Day, and by January 1790 he had half-finished an episodic biography of Day which used anecdotes and letters and built a rounded impression of the man by means that were plainly in keeping with associationist psychology. Before he could publish the material he learnt that his and Day's friend, the chemist James Keir, had written a more traditional *Memoir*, and he gave up his own proposed volume, after corresponding interestingly with Keir on the

---

[1] For Godwin's admiration of biography, see below, pp. 63–4.
[2] H. Mackenzie, *Anecdotes and Egotisms*, ed. H. W. Thompson, p. 184.

principles of biographical writing. Edgeworth's aim was to capture the experience, the impressionable moment; Keir's to write a formal 'éloge', 'a continued and connected discourse, with a beginning, middle and ending'.[1]

Edgeworth never abandoned his early belief in associationist psychology; the material he collected for his Life of Day reappears in his *Memoirs* of himself, published posthumously thirty years later, and it exhibits the impressionistic, fragmented approach to early experience that we should expect. But his belief as a scientist in keeping such records of actual experience, and in passing them on without superfluous generalization or interpretation, in fact became somewhat overlaid in later years by other considerations. Was it right to represent the growth of the mature personality as an evolutionary process, random, uncontrollable? Should man not rather be encouraged to master his environment—to form his own personality as a matter of active will, rather than in passive surrender to external forces?[2] Maria Edgeworth completed her father's autobiography after his death, with a conventionally organized volume to follow his impressionistic one. Her novels are commonly about education, and biographical in form; but they approach the topic in an entirely different spirit from Rousseau's example, or from her father's first venture. For her heroes and heroines, success or failure, happiness or tragedy, is determined initially by the parent's programme of education, afterwards by the child's taught attitude to life. If her controlled actions and contrived endings seem didactic to us now, it is because the novels of her day, of all shades of opinion, *are* didactic. External events are presented selectively, and indeed of the purely external there is less than at

---

[1] Keir to R. L. Edgeworth, Birmingham, 22 Feb. 1790 (unpublished letter in possession of Mrs. C. E. Colvin). Keir argues that two kinds of Life should be written of public men, the formal record, like his own, and the fuller, more intimate memoir, which gives 'a more striking likeness'. He cites recent French precedent. 'A very eloquent elogy [*sic*] was given of Mr. Turgot, the premier ministre of France, a man not unlike Mr. Day, & afterwards his memoirs respecting his life were published by an excellent writer and philosopher M. Condorcet.'

[2] For Edgeworth's growing dogmatism in later years about the possibility of a totally controlled educational environment, leading to a rationally planned personality, see M. Butler, *Maria Edgeworth: A Literary Biography*, Oxford, 1972, pp. 329–34.

other times in the history of the English novel. The multifarious reality of Sterne and Smollett has ceased to bombard the hero's mind; the complex social mechanism of Scott, Dickens, and Thackeray has not yet come to control his life. The era of the French Revolution and of the first generation of Romantic poets is the English novel's Age of Reason.

Meanwhile in Germany Rousseau's *Confessions* and Wordsworth's *Prelude* had their fictionalized equivalent in Goethe's *Wilhelm Meisters Lehrjahre* (1795–6), a *bildungsroman* in which a young man's growth to maturity is presented experientially and as a process of infinite complexity quite outside the hero's conscious control. In just the same period, the young person's arrival at maturity becomes a favourite topic of English novelists, but with a different end in view. Where the novel has a heroine rather than a hero, the range of possible experience is inevitably narrower. But in any case the emphasis has shifted sharply away from experience: it is an ethical emphasis, and the moral invariably turns upon the need to subject the irrational (or 'self-indulgent') side of the character to the rational (or 'prudent') side. The theme that maturing means conscious self-restraint is familiar to us from Jane Austen's novels. But (with or without reference to external religious sanctions) it is widespread in the work of her better contemporaries.

In England, from the French Revolution at least until the publication of *Waverley* in 1814, the novel of education, or of growing up, is rather similar whether it is written by a progressive or a conservative. Partisans of both sides are inflexibly severe towards self-indulgence; both denounce 'the passions'. In Elizabeth Inchbald's influential prototype, *A Simple Story*, Miss Milner shows waywardness and lack of control, and eventually ruins her life, because, as we are told in the closing lines, her father failed to provide her with 'PROPER EDUCATION'. Her story is contrasted in the second half of the novel with that of her firmly disciplined and ultimately happy daughter. Mary Hays's revolutionary novel about the need for self-control, *The Memoirs of Emma Courtnay*, appears in the same year, 1796, as Jane West's best-known conservative novel on the same theme, *A Gossip's Story*.[1] Among women

---

[1] See below, pp. 98–103.

novelists especially the format retains its appeal throughout the next fifteen years, becoming indeed if anything even more popular towards the end of the period. Maria Edgeworth is more absolute than ever before in equating early rational education with later self-command in *Vivian* (1812) and *Patronage* (1814). Mary Brunton urges the moral importance of the same qualities in two novels whose titles speak for themselves—*Self-control* (1812) and *Discipline* (1814). Fanny Burney adopts the theme of an education in self-control in *Camilla* (1796), and returns to it in *The Wanderer* (1814), where she contrasts the discipline, self-restraint, and capacity for independence of the heroine, who has known early wrongs and relative hardship, with the spoilt self-indulgence of the rich, ardent feminist, Eleanor. Jane Austen's *Mansfield Park* (1814), makes a similar comparison between the morally sound Fanny, schooled in hardship, and the indulged and uncontrolled young Bertrams.[1]

It was logical enough for the conservative moralist to preach suspicion of the passions, and of too close an interest in private experience for its own sake. It was less appropriate for the jacobin: his flight from the irrational represents more of an intellectual failure, just as his unwillingness to depict the inner life as a whole, naturalistically, is retrograde in terms of his form. The sentimental novelist won new ground, in terms of psychological realism; the jacobin is bent not so much on depicting an individual's growth to maturity, as on offering an ideal model for it. Because he is not at first primarily concerned with experience, even Godwin, the ablest of the jacobins, moves only slowly towards a manner which can be thought of as Romantic (as *Fleetwood* in 1805 can). In general Romanticism as an attitude and a style affects the English novel very little in the era of Wordsworth and Coleridge.

As a group, the jacobin novelists of the 1790s fail to find an artistic vehicle for what they most believe in, the conscious, sentient, unique individual. They end by creating central characters with less inward life than the sentimental heroes and heroines whose passivity gives them such offence. Ultimately those assertions of value which the novel is capable of making must be in terms of the experience of individual

[1] See below, pp. 219 ff.

characters. It is unreal to place miraculously rational, innocent beings in an irrational and wicked environment, as Holcroft, Elizabeth Inchbald, and Mary Wollstonecraft all do. People do not respond to great griefs and repeated injuries by formulating perfectibilian theories; at least the novel-reader does not think they do, and it is a case in which the reader, like the customer, cannot be wrong. The jacobins are certainly humanists, and their emphasis on reason is a crucial part of their faith in man. Unfortunately the inner life cannot be depicted as rational without a flight from observed psychology into abstraction, which for the purposes of fiction-writing sells the pass. It is a rare progressive novel which successfully makes its point by re-recreating the conscious mental life in fictional terms. It is an instance of how totally dependent meaning must be upon technique. In a cause of real merit, making claims for the individual that realistic fiction should have been peculiarly adapted to support, probably only William Godwin and Robert Bage succeed in writing a jacobin novel which quite deserves the name.

CHAPTER 3

THE JACOBIN NOVEL II:
CALEB WILLIAMS AND *HERMSPRONG*

As revolutionary novelists, Godwin and Bage are virtually as unlike as they can be. A highly theoretical student of liberty, Godwin creates a fictional world in which social reality is reflected symbolically through personal relationships, rather than re-created in detail. The businessman Bage prefers to deal in actuality: *Hermsprong* is a lively caricature of the world as it is. Godwin's mood is sombre, even tragic, Bage's sparkling and ultimately optimistic. Godwin's opinions influenced all the remaining jacobin novelists, and his pessimism, an understandable mood for an English radical of the period, extended itself in due course to his friends. Bage, the product of an older generation, was eventually to meet Godwin (in 1797), but in his work he never acknowledges his influence. Nevertheless, each was identified by nervous reviewers as a dangerously progressive figure, and the proof of their radical allegiance lies in the strong moral preference they show for what is private and individual. Each of them locates the action of his story within the consciousness of certain central characters, who learn (with the author's approval) to trust their own perceptions above the established codes of society. Both Godwin and Bage make the central assertion of the progressive when they assert the truth of the inner life over the mindless tyranny of the group.

1. GODWIN'S 'CALEB WILLIAMS'

In *Things As They Are: or the Adventures of Caleb Williams*, 1794, Godwin's subject is the mental life of men in society; and, though it is realized in imaginative, even stylized, terms, it is a portrait which (unlike the psychological essays of Holcroft and Mary Wollstonecraft) owes less to Godwin's wishes than to his sober assessment of reality. The psychology of most jacobin novelists is undermined by their desire, as

propagandists, to portray mental processes as essentially conscious and within the direction of the will. But Godwin, easily
the best mind among the revolutionaries, is also the least
prejudiced. *Caleb Williams*, which is the leading partisan novel
of the revolutionary period, is also that rare thing for the
times, an attempt at an objective portrait of the struggle
between the conscious and the unconscious, the individual's
need for self-assertion and the complex pressures of society.

Godwin's subject-matter in *Caleb Williams* has often been
considered to have far more to do with the irrational than it
really has, largely because the novel has the gloomy atmosphere and sensational plotting which is symptomatic of the
Gothic movement. In after years the author himself contributed many details which emphasized the romantic aspects
of his book. In his preface to *Fleetwood* for the Standard Novels
edition of 1832 he mentions, for example, how for *Caleb
Williams* he read many books about criminals, and about great
persecutions, which supplied helpful models for the most
exciting parts of his plot. His celebrated account in the same
preface of how he worked out the novel from the hunting of
Caleb *backwards* again emphasizes the mounting tension in
the action, and has prompted more than one modern critic to
notice a link with the technique of the even more thrilling
Edgar Allen Poe.[1] Godwin's description of his state of mind
at the time of writing emphasizes its abnormality, its heightened creative fervour, and so, again, stresses the strangeness
of the story he has to tell—as though it were an inexplicable
product of the subconscious, rather than an intelligible description of a reality which the reader might recognize in the
common world of every day. Finally, in dropping the first
part of his title in 1831, and so accepting the common name,
Caleb Williams, Godwin seems to direct the reader's attention
away from the outward scene to the inward, and to the bizarre
saga of suffering which is Caleb's personal story.[2]

Godwin's reason for writing of his novel long afterwards in

[1] René Wellek and Austin Warren, *Theory of Literature*, New York, 1949,
p. 335: cited by B. R. Pollin, *Education and Enlightenment in the Works of
William Godwin*, New York, 1962, p. 247, n. 5.

[2] This argument, and its accompanying evidence, is indebted to the case
made out by G. D. Kelly, 'The English Jacobin Novel and Its Background',
pp. 294 ff.

these terms is that over the years he became increasingly interested in the irrational, increasingly reconciled to Hume, and increasingly sceptical about the likelihood of real change in society through individual rationality. When the novel first came out his observations about it had a different tone. The original title suggested a work with a strong element of social description, or social satire: *Things As They Are.*[1] Furthermore, the statement of intention, suppressed in the first edition at the booksellers' request, showed that the novel was primarily designed to reflect the present political situation, in the hope of influencing it for the better:

The following narrative is intended to answer a purpose more general and important than immediately appears on the face of it. The question now afloat in the world respecting THINGS AS THEY ARE is the most interesting thing that can be presented to the human mind. While one party pleads for reformation and change, the other extols in warmest terms the existing constitution of society. It seemed as if something would be gained from the decision of this question, if that constitution were faithfully developed in its practical effects. What is now presented to the public is no refined and abstract speculation; it is a study and delineation of things passing in the moral world . . . It was proposed in the invention of the following work, to comprehend, as far as the progressive nature of a single story could allow, a general review of the modes of domestic and unrecorded despotism, by which man becomes the destroyer of man.[2]

It is true that even in the early stages Godwin worked cunningly to make his novel interesting. He already knew, perhaps from the theory or example of his opponent Burke, that a work must not merely state its truths, but must impress them direct on the imagination. He had noticed the impact made by the history of a criminal—such a man as Caleb is supposed by the world to be. The whole of those sections of the novel which deal with Caleb's imprisonment, his observations of his fellow-prisoners, his carefully detailed attempts to escape,

---

[1] It is fair to say that from the first the novel was usually familiarly known as *Caleb Williams*, and that this short form was used for the running titles.

[2] Suppressed preface to first edition, dated 12 May 1794; first published in the 2nd edition of 1796. Cf. Godwin's further explanation of his purpose, *British Critic*, vi (July 1797), 94.

and the prolonged hunt for him afterwards in Bristol, Wales, and London, all these episodes in *Caleb Williams* have the same appeal as in other novels of the genre. The fact that Caleb is not the great criminal of popular imaginings, but innocent, adds piquancy to his sufferings, and does nothing to detract from the excitement of the hunt for him.

Yet there are limits, and very obvious ones, to the use of 'Gothic' devices in *Caleb Williams*. The harassment which Caleb undergoes is neither the product nor the cause of an abnormally excited state of mind in its victim: the acute anxiety, suspense, and fear of the protagonist in the typical tale of terror is absent. Equally, Falkland is not presented as the figment of an overheated brain, nor with that aura of the supernatural that clings to a Montoni, Schedoni, or Monk: we shall see that only a few years later, exalted villains of this type are handled with quite another resonance. Again, few words are wasted on the physical setting, or landscape, two elements which afterwards become important for writers who focus on their central characters' irrational fears. Godwin's very considerable interest in Caleb's state of mind is in the rational side of his thought-processes, a fact which marks him off decisively from the Gothic writer. Nor is he free to create an imagined, nightmare world, since he must persuade the reader that it is the actual one: contemporary England, a society which tries to control the lives of its citizens by hierarchy and law, prejudice and prepossession. 'Things as They Are', and their bearing on the conscious mind of 'Caleb Williams', is the complete subject, and the strength of the novel lies in the coherence with which plot and characterization illustrate the original title.

To consider first the plot, which has too often been treated solely in terms of the nervous excitement it generates. The action gets properly under way only in the second volume, with the arousal of Caleb's curiosity about the secret harboured by Falkland; his realization that Falkland has committed a murder; and Falkland's consequent persecution of Caleb. The essence of this plot is that it effectively symbolizes the relationship of men in society. Caleb is an individual, an

almost nameless man sprung from obscure parents, but possessed with what for Godwin is the essential human quality,
a restless intellectual energy, or impulse towards truth. The
tragedy of his relationship with Falkland is that the latter is
committed to an evil and artificial pattern of behaviour imposed upon him by his social attitudes. Falkland's conceptions
of honour and virtue are wholly bound up in reputation: a man
hitherto seen as a pattern of goodness, he will nevertheless
commit crimes, even great crimes, to preserve his good fame
in the eyes of the world. At the level of personal ethics, the
plot poses the question, which of the two central figures,
Falkland or Caleb, is the good man? The answer the reader
finds to this question is exactly opposed to the universal
belief of the people in the world of the novel.

The issues the plot raises about society at large have to do
with the power exercised over individuals by the community
in general, and by rich or great men in particular; a power
which advanced societies have institutionalized as law. Godwin's case against the law, which was set out in *Political
Justice* in all its bold consistency,[1] is here developed with the
richness of documentation that is available to the novelist.
At the level of social satire, Godwin shows how far in practice
the administration of the law falls below the blind impartiality
it proclaims. Even in the England admired by Montesquieu
there are, he suggests, *de facto* Bastilles.[2] Between rich and
poor there is no equal justice. Legal processes do not touch
Falkland, who is a murderer, whereas they hound innocents
like Caleb, and the soldier Brightwel, who dies in prison
awaiting trial. The evidence of the rich man Falkland is auto-
matically preferred to Caleb's; his very reputation stops the
ears of judges and bystanders alike when Caleb is proclaiming
what the reader knows to be the truth. In the opening
volume, where Godwin concentrates on broad social criticism,
the brutal squire Tyrrel consistently uses the law to tyrannize
his social inferiors. Having attempted to force his kinswoman
Emily Melville into a marriage against her will, he has her
arrested for debt while she is in a fever, and thus brings about
her death. When the honest yeoman Hawkins resorts to law to

---

[1] See above, p. 40.
[2] *Caleb Williams*, ed. D. McCracken, Oxford English Novels, 1970, p. 181.

restrain Tyrrel from damaging his property, Tyrrel is delighted, for he knows that his tenant is now delivered into his
hands. 'It would, as Mr. Tyrrel argued, be the disgrace of a
civilised country, if a gentleman, when insolently attacked in
law by the scum of the earth, could not convert the cause into
a question of the longest purse, and stick in the skirts of his
adversary till he had reduced him to beggary.'[1]

But the philosophical nature of Godwin's opposition to law
is shown not by his attitude to its abuse, but by his attitude
to its virtues. Even granted impartiality, the law is an instrument of coercion which Godwin sees as pernicious to the
human spirit. His prison is a place of cruelty and degradation,
useless for the purpose of reform which is the only justifica-
tion Godwin can conceive for imposing punishment. He is
aware, moreover, of the possibility of reform without punishment, a possibility the law does not recognize. A celebrated
eighteenth-century criminal case haunted Godwin, and haunts
the novel: that of the schoolmaster Eugene Aram, who in 1745
murdered a man, and fourteen years later, after a blameless
life of scholarship, was detected, tried, and hanged. In the
1820s Godwin made notes for a life of Aram. He never wrote
it, but his disciple Bulwer Lytton did—although the latter's
conception was less Godwinian than he perhaps intended.[2]
Lytton's Eugene Aram is a romantic solitary, intermittently
tortured by remorse, but in general falsely persuaded that
his pure goal, knowledge, justified him in what he did.
Lytton thus changes the emphasis from the law to the
responses of the criminal; and his own ambivalent attitude to
Aram, his willingness to romanticize him, and his unwillingness (at least in subsequent editions) ever to believe him
guilty, all make his moral position suspect. In *Caleb Williams*
Godwin's attitude to Aram is more clear-cut and has to do
with the objective moral issue of the proper jurisdiction of
law over the individual. His Aram is an archetypal victim,
guilty in law, but a man for whom inflexible, impartial law

---

[1] *Caleb Williams*, p. 73.

[2] Kegan Paul's belief that Bulwer Lytton's novel was based on Godwin's
notes cannot be substantiated. The debt is more likely to arise from Bulwer's
longstanding interest in Godwin's writings. K. Hollingworth, *The Newgate
Novel*, New York, 1962, p. 243, n. 69. For Lytton's interest, during his radical
phase, in another novelist of the 1790s, see above, p. 50n.

is too stupid. As such he fits into a complex pattern of real-life analogy and becomes a significant parallel for Caleb.

The scope of the novel thus includes a broad sketch of how an existing society imposes itself on its individual members. Nevertheless, the form Godwin adopts is, deliberately, the most personal one possible, that of the confessional type of autobiography. The form supports Godwin's value-system: what is important to a man is his own mental life. Even history, which his contemporaries are increasingly prone to interpret as the evolution of whole societies, seems to Godwin more properly the study of the lives of individuals:

Laying aside the generalities of historical abstraction, we must mark the operation of human passions; must observe the empire of motives, whether groveling [*sic*] or elevated; and must note the influence that one human being exercises over another, and the ascendancy of the daring and the wise over the vulgar multitude.[1]

Among historians, the biographical Sallust is his favourite. Again, it follows that Godwin values novel-writing as, potentially, a careful record of a man's experiences; one, moreover, that has certain advantages over history, which is limited by the availability of evidence. In the preface to *Cloudesley*, 1830, he claims that 'fictitious history' . . . 'is more to be depended on, and comprises more of, the science of man, than whatever can be exhibited by the historian'.[2] In *Mandeville* he also depicts the novel as a semi-scientific record, claiming special seriousness for the *bildungsroman*, the novel of youth and education, which as an imaginative account of the growth of a personality may make a real contribution to man's perception of himself:

I have committed to paper what, during those years passed through my mind; I have nothing to do with vindicating or condemning that of which I am the historian. I may thus perhaps have performed a task of general utility; it is surely not unfitting,

---

1 'Of Romance and History', unpublished Essay written 'while the *Enquirer* was in the press' [i.e. shortly before 27 Feb. 1797]; quoted by G. D. Kelly, 'The English Jacobin Novel and Its Background', p. 322.

2 *Cloudesley*, London, 1830, p. xi.

that that which forms one considerable stage in the history of man, should for once be put into a legible and a permanent form.[1]

Caleb Williams is thus simultaneously a sketch of contemporary society conceived in general terms, and a close study of the inward life of a single individual. Godwin is true to his principles in placing the real action in Caleb's conscious mind. While the plot gets its forward impetus at a superficial level from the chase and its outcome, the really significant changes are the result of a growth in Caleb's understanding. At the beginning of the action Caleb is a callow country boy endowed with nothing but an aspiration towards knowledge. His desire to discover Falkland's secret hides no ulterior motive: he neither seeks personal power over his master, nor justice on behalf of the community. Caleb on the contrary is impelled by a virtuous impulse, his desire to base human relationships upon truth. When the secret is out, and Falkland knows it is out, he fears Caleb because the latter potentially has power over him. Falkland cannot help thinking in terms of competitive relationships; he conceives that either Caleb or himself must be the master, and the one who is not master must be the slave. Caleb however refuses to accept the necessity of such an assumption about human relationships. He wishes to be independent of Falkland, to go freely away without hurting him by telling his secret. He means to reject the whole traditional social concept, which is based on hierarchical relationships:

I thought with unspeakable loathing of those errors, in consequence of which every man is fated to be more or less the tyrant or the slave. I was astonished at the folly of my species, that they did not rise up as one man, and shake off chains so ignominious and misery so insupportable. So far as related to myself, I resolved, and this resolution has never been entirely forgotten by me, to hold myself disengaged from this odious scene, and never fill the part either of the oppressor or the sufferer.[2]

At his best Caleb lives up to this heroic resolve. His greatest moment is the one traditional to the Puritan novel. Confined

---

[1] *Mandeville*, London, 1817, i. 162; quoted by B. R. Pollin, *Education and Enlightenment in the Works of Wm. Godwin*, p. 217.
[2] *Caleb Williams*, p. 156.

in darkness in a prison-cell, Caleb discovers that he is free, for the essence of the self cannot be touched:

> I found out the secret of employing my mind . . . I tasked the stores of my memory and my powers of invention. . . .
> While I was thus employed I reflected with exultation upon the degree in which man is independent of the smiles and frowns of fortune. I was beyond her reach, for I could fall no lower. To an ordinary eye I might seem destitute and miserable, but in reality I wanted for nothing . . . Such is man in himself considered; so simple his nature; so few his wants. How different from the man of artificial society! . . .
> I was resolved at least fully to possess the days I had to live . . . Every sentiment of vanity, or rather of independence and justice within me, instigated me to say to my persecutor, 'You may cut off my existence, but you cannot disturb my serenity.'[1]

His exaltation now that he perceives he is master of himself enables him to defy the physical means taken to victimize him. He deploys his practical skills and ingenuity to escape from prison, and even when brought back and held in greater security he makes his getaway again. Once outside, he falls among thieves, but easily sees the fallacy with which they justify their way of life. The right weapon with which to fight society's tyranny cannot be another combination, for it is by submitting to the group—whether majority or faction—that a man gives up his proper reliance on his own reason. By using the analogy of the gang of thieves, Godwin dismisses the arguments in favour of violent revolution, and puts his faith instead in the individual's moral independence.

Caleb is not perfect, and he cannot always 'shake off the chains' that make man in society play the roles of tyrant or slave. He commits a moral error of Falkland's type when he is easily persuaded to return to face the judgement of Forester, on the grounds that it is 'of the utmost consequence to his future honour and character'.[2] Thus Caleb submits to the tyranny of a trial and allows himself to be victimized, solely for the sake of his public reputation. Afterwards, in London, he is goaded by Gines's persecution to try to denounce Falkland before a magistrate. He relates this action with a full sense of its enormity. 'I lost all regard to his intellectual

---

[1] Ibid., pp. 185–7.   [2] Ibid., p. 159.

greatness, and all pity for the agonies of his soul. I also would abjure forbearance. I would show myself bitter and inflexible as he had done.'[1]

Caleb is heroic when he stands out against the system, flawed when he stoops to collaborating with it. At first Godwin seems to be saying that such a hero cannot be made unhappy by the contempt of others, so long as his own conscience declares him innocent. Interestingly, however, there is a modification of this doctrine in the third volume, where Godwin explores as it were empirically the probable psychological consequences of enforced self-sufficiency. In succession Caleb is rejected by Laura, an idealized figure who has become a substitute mother, and by his fellow servant and adoptive father, Collins. It is his desperation when he looks ahead to a life without social affections that precipitates the novel's crisis, his last, successful denunciation of Falkland.

The appearance of this theme of the power of love at this point in Godwin's development is fascinating. Godwin's arguments in *Political Justice* against all forms of coercion of the reason had included the irrational prejudice we feel in favour of those we love best. He seems to have come within a few years to recognize that in 1792 and 1793—the years of *Anna St. Ives* and *Political Justice*—he and Holcroft had reacted excessively against Hume's observations of the irrational, and had overdone their stress on reason. Godwin's revisions to *Political Justice* in 1798 were an acknowledgement that in his eagerness to advocate mental and moral independence, he had formerly underestimated the part played by the senses, the habits, and the affections.[2]

He arrived at his new opinion partly as a result of conversation with friends, partly through published criticism, and partly through reading and rereading Hume's *Treatise*.[3] Critics of a more romantic or sentimental bent (in senses other than the technical) have liked to emphasize the part played by his brief, happy marriage with Mary Wollstonecraft, in converting the cold rationalist philosopher to a due

[1] *Caleb Williams*, p. 274.
[2] See F. E. L. Priestley, ed., Godwin's *Enquiry Concerning Political Justice*, iii. 12–13. Priestley comments that in the 3rd edition of 1798, Godwin's doctrine on the relations between reason and passion approaches Hume's.
[3] G. D. Kelly, 'The English Jacobin Novel and Its Background', pp. 365–6.

sense of the value of domestic life. But, although the character of Marguerite in Godwin's next novel, *St. Leon*, 1799, certainly suggests the real-life Mary Wollstonecraft, the first signs of Godwin's conversion to a subtler psychology encompassing the emotions pre-dates his marriage by several years. In *Caleb Williams* Godwin has had the intellectual independence to avoid the traditional love-story, but his concluding volume shows important concessions to some of the principal themes of sentiment. Caleb refrains from arguing with Laura or Collins: he puts their peace before his previously dominant passion, the love of truth. This second public denunciation of Falkland occurs not because (as on the previous occasion) he has to try to communicate the truth, but because he cannot bear the thought of a life lived without human ties. At least in the final version, Godwin takes another crucially important step towards sympathy: for Caleb ends by pitying his enemy, an act of feeling for his fellow-man which carries in it a germ of hope for the future, a possible way out of the continuous cycle of tyranny and submission.

Originally Godwin intended his novel to have ended differently. His diary shows that he finished the first version of *Caleb Williams* on 30 April 1794, but that he had a fresh idea for the ending, which he rewrote between 4 and 8 May 1794. In the original version Caleb fails to convince the magistrate that Falkland is guilty of murder; the conclusion of the novel consists of two fragments of manuscript written by Caleb in prison, the second of them in a drugged stupor, totally defeated, and obviously near to death. In his remarks accompanying his recent publication of the original ending,[1] D. Gilbert Dumas suggests that it is more tragic, consistent, and better than Godwin's second thoughts; but there are two views about this, and much to be said in support of David McCracken's argument that Godwin's second version 'is better Godwin and better prose fiction'.[2] The proposition, shared by Blake, that 'Truth can never be told so as to be understood, and not be believed', may be utopian rather than 'Things As They Are'; it may in itself even suggest a rather inappropriate

[1] D. Gilbert Dumas, 'Things as they Were: the Original Ending of *Caleb Williams*', *Studies in Engl. Lit.*, vi (July 1966), 575–97.
[2] *Caleb Williams*, p. xx.

happy ending; but the principle of truth is anything but the dominant aspect of the received version. The point is that the second ending is quite as tragic as the first, but for different and profounder reasons. Caleb breaks Falkland, with intense regret sees him carried off to die, and knows that at last he has done what all along he has sworn not to do— played the role of the tyrant. The first version is the more tragic at the level of external action, but it hands over responsibility for the dénouement to an external agent—the law— and so suffers from the rational but excessively neat and flat determinism of so many novels of the period. The new ending is a brilliant idea, a shift on to the inner plane which compromises neither the novel's political position, nor the starkness of its intellectual honesty. Caleb denounces Falkland, and at last he succeeds in making others believe him; but— and the sequel, having been prepared for, is perfectly convincing—by doing so he loses much of his own moral greatness, just as surely as he destroys Falkland. The vision of both protagonists enmeshed together in the same web of guilt and persecution is far finer than the earlier, more obvious dénouement.

Above all, the revised ending locates the action in Caleb's consciousness, which is as it should be. Caleb, with his epic struggle towards knowledge—not merely of Falkland's secret, but of himself and his world—is a hero of impressive stature. In his resistance to society's treatment of him, his indefatigable will to achieve his mental freedom, his 'life of mind', is symbolized the whole claim for human nature made in these times of revolution by the radical.

But in order to understand the true hero, Caleb, it is necessary for the reader to understand the anti-hero, Falkland. Falkland is deliberately given the attributes of the tragic hero, those of a great man bound for self-destruction. Every effort is made to interest the reader in his fate, and he is drawn not merely possessed of all the talents and graces, but also of the loftiest intentions. This very conception of greatness which he and we share is, however, his undoing: he is fatally attached to the outward worldly notion of superiority, rather than to the verdict of his conscience. In youth he has been much in love with the concept of chivalry, an outworn and in modern conditions pernicious notion of personal 'honour' which equates brute strength or skill in handling weapons with personal value.[1] The great man he most admires is Alexander, and it is striking how, in speaking of the cost of Alexander's victories, he forgets his benevolence: the lesser modern social virtue is driven out by contemplation of the extraordinary personal achievement. 'The death of a hundred thousand men is at first sight very shocking; but what in reality are a hundred thousand such men more than a hundred thousand sheep?'[2] His benevolence as a landlord leads him to censure Tyrrel's brutality towards Hawkins, and to appeal with great humanity and eloquence for gentle treatment of the lower classes. Yet in a short while Falkland himself is to complete the tyranny of Tyrrel, and to allow Hawkins and his son to hang, because his reputation demands it. He is tormented by guilt ever afterwards; his inward peace is totally destroyed. But he can do nothing about it, for in his final speech in the novel he demonstrates that he is unable to think in any but personal and competitive terms. 'My name will be consecrated to infamy.'[3] Falkland's very conception of personal merit—which the reader probably begins by sharing—is called in question by the events of the book.

If at times the treatment of lesser characters and social setting is somewhat thin and impoverished, this is compensated for by the richness of historical allusion in the treatment of the central figures, especially Falkland.[4] As a character he has been equated with Godwin's great real-life adversary, Edmund Burke, and the suggestion is a plausible one. Many of Falkland's characteristics are indeed matched in the character-sketch of Burke given in *Political Justice*. Burke, like Falkland, has wonderful personal talents, but because he

[1] Godwin was clearly fascinated by the manner in which gentlemanliness continued to be associated with military prowess, long after historical circumstances had made the knight an anachronism. His next novel, *St. Leon*, in which the knightly hero is among the defeated at the Battle of Pavia, is a study of clashing value-systems which contains historical insights worthy of Scott.

[2] *Caleb Williams*, p. 111.   [3] Ibid p. 324.

[4] The historical allusions in *Caleb Williams* have been fully examined by G. D. Kelly, to whom this discussion is indebted. Cf. 'The English Jacobin Novel and Its Background', pp. 321 ff.

chooses a wrong standard of values, 'chivalry', his gifts are perverted from the cause of truth to the service of tyranny.

> Our hearts bleed to see such gallantry, talents and virtue employed in perpetuating the calamities of mankind . . . He has unfortunately left us a memorable example of the power of a corrupt system of government, to undermine and divert from their purposes, the noblest faculties that have yet been exhibited to the observation of the world.[1]

It may even be, as Mr. P. N. Furbank has suggested, that Caleb's action in opening the box is equivalent to Godwin's in writing *Political Justice* (or, for that matter, *Caleb Williams* itself).[2] At the very least, there is an intermittent association between Burke and Falkland, two great and talented adherents of the existing system, on the one hand; Godwin and Caleb, two clear-sighted and would-be independent-minded opponents, on the other.

But this cannot be all. Falkland has a far wider range of reference than merely to Burke. In *Caleb Williams*, if not in *Political Justice*, Godwin attempts to emulate his opponent by glancing over human history, and particularly over the period that most fascinates him, English political history of the mid-seventeenth century. The name Falkland is after all associated with one of the best-known royalists of the Civil War—like the name of another aristocratic hero-villain of a Puritan novel, Richardson's Lovelace. Lucius Cary, Viscount Falkland, anticipated many of the traits of Godwin's Falkland. A man of great culture, with qualities which eighteenth-century historians found peculiarly admirable, he mourned the necessity which he felt impelled him into the Civil War, became slovenly in his dress, and, in his longing for peace, perhaps even courted the death which came to him at the first Battle of Newbury.[3] Falkland's association with the Royalist side in the Civil War is heightened by his

---

[1] *Political Justice*, ii. 545. The last sentence was added to the 3rd ed. of 1798 after Burke's death the previous year. If Falkland indeed echoes Burke, he is not the only Jacobin fictional character to do so. Mordent in Holcroft's play *The Deserted Daughter* has the same perverted talent, the same submission to accepted notions, the same hint at the 'fatal flaw' of classical tragedy, as Falkland and the Burke of Godwin's sketch in *Political Justice*.

[2] 'Godwin's Novels', *Essays in Criticism*, v (1955), pp. 251–6.

[3] Cf. Hume's description in the *History of Great Britain*, pp. 543–4.

marked physical resemblance to the Charles I of Van Dyck's portraits:

I found Mr. Falkland a man of small stature, with an extreme delicacy of form and appearance . . . His manner was kind, attentive and humane. His eye was full of animation, but there was a grace and sad solemnity in his air, which for want of experience I imagined was the inheritance of the great, and the instrument by which the distance between them and their inferiors was maintained.[1]

The grace, the air of refinement, and the sadness are also features of Charles's demeanour which impressed another Puritan, Marvell, in his *Horatian Ode Upon Cromwell's Return from Ireland*.

Like his echoes of tragedy, with its inimical suggestions of personal superiority and worldly greatness, Godwin's allusions to historical characters are entirely purposeful. He is in part writing a moral allegory of civil strife and, especially, oppression; so that to connect Falkland with the *anciens régimes* of both England and near-contemporary France is enormously to increase the significance of his persecution of Caleb. Falkland is the noble oppressor, with the virtues but also with the knowingness in oppression of real leaders in government at all periods. At different points in the novel he is associated with Alexander, and with the worst tyrants among the Roman emperors.[2] Tyrrel on the other hand is a mere brutish middleman, an instrument rather than an instigator of tyranny. His name links him primarily with Sir James Tyrrell, supposed murderer of the princes in the Tower.[3]

Caleb's antecedents are more humble and much more innocent. Instead of being associated with a succession of the more or less villainous great, Caleb springs from a race of small men, only just glimpsed in the pages of history. He is named after the spy whom Moses sent into the Promised Land—aptly, since curiosity is his chief quality, the search for truth his goal. Caleb stems from an anonymous but tough and

---

[1] *Caleb Williams*, p. 5.   [2] Ibid., pp. 110–12 and p. 314.

[3] Also with Walter Tyrrell or Tirel, reputedly slayer of William Rufus. Godwin may have known of other disreputable holders of the name, such as Anthony Tyrrell, the traitor and spy of Elizabeth's time. As English surnames go, Tyrrell is remarkably inauspicious.

independent-minded stock, that of the English yeomanry. The name 'Williams' (apart from the fact that it is Cromwell's original family name) is plebeian and Welsh: its associations are deliberately low. The tenant-farmer Hawkins plays a part parallel to Caleb's in the plot, and Hawkins has a clear sense of his own English inheritance, which to him means his historical and legal right not to be a slave. He cannot bear the idea of his son's being a servant—'The poorest neger, as a man may say, has some point that he will not part with.'[1] Hawkins is a figure with anonymous progenitors beyond the seventeenth century in the middle ages, or even in pre-Conquest times.[2] Rather more shadowily, Caleb perhaps suggests some of the simplicity and virtue of the plain citizen of the Roman Republic, in primitive days before the sophisticated and tyrannous emperors destroyed the fibre of that people. Elsewhere in his work Godwin consistently admired two periods, the Roman Republic and the English Commonwealth, as times when the egalitarian spirit had flourished. Allusions to the Puritans recur often in Caleb's history, especially echoes of their great literary monuments. The period of Caleb's imprisonment, which brings about his triumphant realization that his spirit cannot be enslaved, strongly recalls both the spirit and the phrasing of Milton's *Comus*—'You may cut off my existence, but you cannot disturb my serenity.'[3] The situation also echoes Bunyan's real-life imprisonment, and Clarissa's fictional one: the motif is, as we have seen, natural both to Puritan and to revolutionary literature, for it is the situation in which the stature of the individual ultimately proves itself. But in addition there are reminders of others, small men, victims, nearer Godwin's own time. At

---

[1] *Caleb Williams*, p. 71.

[2] For progressive propagandists, especially in the 1770s and 1780s, Anglo-Saxon times often provided a model for a free, simple society: the Conquest had brought strong kings, and a system of laws still in force. Cf. Duncan Forbes, 'Scientific Whiggism', *Cambridge Journal*, vii (1954), 661–3.

[3] Ibid., p, 187. See above, p. 65. The line is an echo of Milton's loftier 'Thou canst not touch the freedom of my mind.' *Comus* is a key work for Godwin, the chief literary source of his early novel *Imogen*, 1783. See Jack Marken's unpublished dissertation, 'The Early Works of William Godwin', Bloomington, 1953; and B. R. Pollin, *Education and Enlightenment in the Works of W. Godwin*, pp. 79–83. For the echoes of *Comus* in *Anna St. Ives*, see above, p. 41.

one stage, when Caleb is trying to support himself he becomes a watchmaker—a craft associated with Rousseau, since it was his father's. While in Wales he tries to make a contribution to philology. This was not merely the field of Godwin's contemporary, the radical Horne Tooke, whom he admired; it was also Eugene Aram's. Thus Caleb is linked consistently with the village Hampdens, who have been the victims for generations out of mind of the Alexanders, and whom Falkland willingly weighs light in the scale against the glory of a single great man. At a first or superficial reading, the novel seems to share the insubstantiality of other jacobin performances, and certainly to lack the solidity of Scott's rendering of history. Inspected with more care, it has considerable historical range and depth. With an allusive freedom possibly borrowed from Burke, it draws into a relatively simple contemporary story an exceptionally rich pattern of political reference, a pattern of class struggle, oppression, and attempted self-assertion unbroken from Alexander's times to Louis XVI's.

And yet, although Caleb and Falkland represent such different social traditions, they also resemble one another. 'In intelligence, in concern with personal reputation, and, by the end, even in crime and accompanying remorse, each character mirrors the other.'[1] When Falkland praises Alexander, he does so with an aristocratic bias unacceptable to Caleb, yet many of the ideal virtues he finds in Alexander—benevolence, liberality, and above all intellect—are the greatest of human qualities for Caleb (and his creator) too. 'It is mind, Williams, the generation of knowledge and virtue that we ought to love.'[2] Small wonder that 'there was a magnetical sympathy between me and my patron'.[3] Both men are outstanding individuals, who love virtue, but to a greater or lesser extent fall victim to the tyranny of 'things as they are'. Caleb, who is the book's more obvious victim, comes near to winning freedom through the life of his mind; Falkland, its ostensible oppressor, is wholly and tragically destroyed. Just as the central plot—the secret, and the persecution which follows its discovery—is a potent fable for the repressive social machine,

[1] David McCracken, *Caleb Williams*, p. xxi.
[2] Ibid., p. 111.　　　　[3] Ibid., p. 112.

so the structural equation between the two protagonists graphically conveys Godwin's central belief: that the individual is all-valuable, but in the present system tragically vulnerable too.

As a novel *Caleb Williams* is easy to find fault with. Elsewhere, in his letters and in the *Memoirs* of Mary Wollstonecraft, Godwin was often capable of a clear, terse style which admirably conveyed the Roman virtues he admired.[1] For some reason, the manner he thought appropriate to narrative was heavy, slack, and verbose. Moreover, in choosing the confessional stance, and the first person, he encounters a major technical problem, that of adequately realizing the other characters. Significantly, it is in the first volume, largely narrated by the lay figure Collins, that minor figures like Emily, Tyrrel, and Hawkins make a distinct appearance, and it is in this part of the book that Falkland is most convincing. Elsewhere, Godwin fails on the whole to put his characters into direct conflict, in fully dramatized scenes. Even at a crisis of the action, Falkland's unexpected accusation that Caleb is a thief, the dramatic value of the moment is half submerged by Caleb's ponderous reflections. This failure illustrates how totally Godwin rejected the technical discoveries of the sentimentalists, for whom the poignant, fully realized scene was the most meaningful of all units.[2]

As a whole, the faults are the obverse side of the novel's great strength. It is precisely because Caleb and his 'life of mind' are so central that the novel succeeds as a powerful representation of the individualist world-view. It is true that *Caleb Williams* is egotistical: so are *Pilgrim's Progress*, *Robinson Crusoe*, and *Pamela*. Consciously and unconsciously, its attitudes are often those of the earlier Puritan tradition; if they were not, its historical insights would probably not re-echo so eloquently, as a symbolic record of centuries of dissent and persecution. It is conceivable that the novel's reputation suffered less from its burden of reflection than from a speedy

[1] But cf. the passage quoted below, p. 118n.

[2] See above, p. 14. Some of the lesser jacobin novelists, like Holcroft and Mrs. Inchbald, were presumably saved by their dramatic training from like error, but it is very characteristic of Mary Wollstonecraft's fiction, and remains so of Godwin's.

hardening of public opinion against the ideals and traditions it proclaimed. In some quarters the battle-cries of the Commonwealth remained relevant throughout the eighteenth century, and they were powerfully revived in its last decade; but in the nineteenth century, with Nonconformity a respectable force within the legitimate political spectrum, the tradition could no longer speak so eloquently for the beleaguered individual. The author himself, nearly forty years on, apparently knew how much of his original meaning had been lost. It is possible that he bowed to necessity; more likely, that by then he shared the romantic solipsism of the early nineteenth century, and was content that his powerful early opposition to existing society as a whole should be obscured. It is ironic that Godwin, who once cared as much as Caleb or Falkland for his own fame, should have been among its most effective enemies. The vision he began with, of a powerful social mechanism, and a frail but genuine human will to resist it, was no idealist's chimera (like Holcroft's interpretation of perfectibility) but an imaginative realization of life in a modern society which two centuries have not falsified. For all its crudities, *Caleb Williams* remains easily the most impressive English novel of the 1790s.

2. BAGE'S 'HERMSPRONG'

Robert Bage,[1] the paper-maker from Elford, near Derby, is the revolutionary novelist who least resembles the others. He was older than most of them, and moved in a wholly different circle, though in the last few years of his life, after all his novels were written, he twice met Godwin. Bage's contacts in the Derby Philosophical Society included his friend William Hutton, Josiah Wedgwood, and Erasmus Darwin, the two latter also being members of the celebrated Lunar Society of Birmingham. This was a group, and a generation, which shared practical day-to-day interests, a taste for applied science, and a general intellectual approach shaped in the

[1] Bage's life (1728–1801) is summarized in William Hutton's *Memoir* in *The Monthly Magazine*, xii (1 Jan. 1802), 479, and in Scott's *Lives of the Novelists*. For his circle, see Eric Robinson, 'The Derby Philosophical Society', in A. E. Musson and E. Robinson, *Science and Technology in the Industrial Revolution*, Manchester, 1969, pp. 190–9, and Robert E. Schofield, *The Lunar Society of Birmingham*, 1963.

1760s and 1770s by the French *philosophes* and the Anglo–
Scottish empiricists. Bage's writings were evidently sufficiently typical for one member of the Lunar Society to detect
in them a kindred spirit. Richard Lovell Edgeworth, enjoying
Hermsprong in Ireland in 1797, believed that parts of it had
been written by one of his own most intimate friends, Erasmus
Darwin.[1]

Bage's circle of businessmen and entrepreneurs, inventors
and scientists, canal-builders, mechanics, chemists, educators,
is the key to an understanding of his intellectual position. It
was a world whose textbook was not Godwin's *Political
Justice*, still less Paine's *Rights of Man*, but Adam Smith's
Wealth of Nations. For three decades before the outbreak of
the French Revolution, Midlands industrialists had been
actively involved in a revolution of their own, and their
natural enemy was the only interest powerful enough to stop
it—the vested political interest in the capital, that of the
landed oligarchy, old corruption. The Lunar members tended
for example to be opposed to the American War: not merely
for the effect it might have on their immediate business
interests, but because Ministerial policy towards the colonists
was an interference from the centre with the liberty of the
middle-class subject. It was the principle which they detested.

Bage's first novels were written in the aftermath of the
American War, and in the end all six of them suggest the
period of that Revolution rather than the French.[2] Bage is
for individualism much as Adam Smith is for it, and it is for
this reason that the fictional format which most appeals to
him is that of Smith's compatriot and contemporary, Smollett. The fourth novel, *James Wallace*, indeed comes very near
to plagiarizing *Roderick Random:* a hero driven by necessity
to become a footman is too memorable a feature to be used
more than once. But the fifth, *Man As He Is*, 1792, shows
Bage deploying Smollett's loose-knit framework to real advantage, as his hero travels about England and the Continent
and purveys a representative, sharply satirical picture of

---

[1] Unpublished letter of R. L. Edgeworth to Maria Edgeworth, Belfast,
2 Mar. 1797: 'I am reading *Hermsprong* & am much pleased with the original
good sense which it contains—part of it is Dr. Darwins.' National Library
of Ireland, MS. 10166–7.

[2] For Bage's earlier novels, see above, p. 42.

contemporary men and manners. Bage excels at the pointed character-sketch, and in *Man As He Is* the aristocratic brother and sister, Lord Auschamp and Lady Mary Paradyne, are memorable comic creations, as solemn, self-important, and absurd as Jane Austen's Lady Catherine de Burgh. Unlike Holcroft, Bage is content to leave much as he found it the rambling picaresque format, with its haphazard sequence of events and its tolerance of coincidence. He appears innocent of the otherwise universal jacobin obsession with social determinism: his characters are only the pawns of their social environment inasmuch as they choose to be. Essentially free agents, in the aggregate they *are* society, as in the earlier, more naïve eighteenth-century comic manner.

If in social theory and psychology Bage is old-fashioned, he thereby avoids a great many technical difficulties. Moreover, it can at least be said of him that where he adopts stale conventions, he does not do so unthinkingly. The picaresque expresses well enough his individualistic egalitarian philosophy and his admiration for individual energy and effort. And where other conventions of eighteenth-century fiction-writing do not fall in with his themes, he has a neat way (which suggests far greater intellectual flexibility than Holcroft's) of standing them on their head.

The relationship in *Man As He Is* between Sir George Paradyne and Cornelia Colerain must for example have struck the contemporary reader as a most amusing democratic pastiche of Fanny Burney's snobbish central situation in *Cecilia*. And when Lady Mary Paradyne makes the same assumption as Fanny Burney's Mrs. Delvile, that the girl is socially unworthy to become her daughter-in-law, Sir George's rebuke is one that Mortimer Delville would have done well to utter (although it could never have come from Fanny Burney's deferential pen):

'The lady on whom you have made such liberal observation, rejects that honour. If she would accept it, I know not of your ladyship's acquaintance, in a comparison of merit, one who would not sink before her. If she would stoop to raise me to herself, I might still be happy; but she rejects me because—I am not worthy of her.'[1]

---

[1] *Man As He Is*, 1792, iv. 188. For a parallel with *Pride and Prejudice*, see below, pp. 200–1.

The plot of *Hermsprong*, 1796, plays havoc with cliché in similar terms. A totally unknown young man, strangely named and of supposed German origin, appears in a Cornish village, saves the life of Lord Grondale's daughter, and is supposed by that peer to be a fortune-hunter bent on marrying above him. Hermsprong does indeed love Caroline Campinet, but not her weaknesses;[1] she still thinks it right to play the part of a dutiful daughter, and it is Hermsprong who refuses to be married while she remains the slave of custom and prejudice.

In the plot of *Hermsprong*, the expectations roused by current literature are continually deployed, only to be overset. For example, the love-story begins in the standard romantic manner, with Hermsprong seizing the reins of the bolting horse as it drags Caroline's carriage towards the cliff. As a result of this episode, Caroline feels sentimentally bound to Hermsprong, although he drily points out that 'It was an impulse, and it was irresistible.'[2] At other points in the novel he behaves, or appears about to behave, according to the best manner of a hero. In a French garden he encounters Mr. Fillygrove, who is at the moment suffering from a hangover; but Mr. Fillygrove has eloped from Falmouth with Harriet Sumelin, Hermsprong is Mr. Sumelin's friend, and by a conventional sequence of events Mr. Fillygrove has soon challenged Hermsprong to a duel. The unorthodox outcome is in Bage's idiosyncratic vein. Hermsprong retaliates by picking up Fillygrove, and 'giving the young man a hearty shake' . . . 'Mr. Fillygrove was rather inclined to be sick.'[3] In a similar episode later in the novel Hermsprong encounters his rival for Caroline's hand, Sir Philip Chestrum, and, instead of duelling with him, he picks him up and deposits him on the far side of a fence.

The unexpected turns of event have the effect of throwing the protagonist's motives into relief. The reader is bound to ask himself what has made Hermsprong behave differently from other heroes, thus diverting the plot from its usual course. From here it is a short step to engaging the reader as

---

[1] *Hermsprong, or Man As He Is Not*, ed. V. Wilkins, London, 1951, ch. lxxvi, p. 233. Subsequent references are to this edition.

[2] Ibid., ch. lx, p. 33.   [3] Ibid., ch. xvi. p. 61.

a moral arbiter between the hero who refuses to act as heroes normally do, and the heroine who persists, despite the hero's disapproval, in acting merely like a heroine. The ironic disturbance of conventional expectations promotes an alert and critical attitude in the reader, an effect which is ably supported by further stylistic devices.

What we are to criticize in the principal action is very obvious. Lord Grondale is an archetypal Bage villain, a tyrant in each of his roles, as politician, landlord, and father. As usual, too, in Bage's portrayal of the upper classes, he is corrupt in his morals. He lives with 'a person of merit', Mrs. Stone, and has the impudence to justify himself by the precedent of those unorthodox father-figures, the Hebrew patriarchs.[1] In his garden he has a Temple of Venus, its walls adorned with suggestive pictures, and there he assaults his daughter's friend Maria Fluart:

> However capital these might be, they were such as ladies are not accustomed to admire in the presence of gentlemen. There was, however, a superb sofa, on which a lady might sit down with all possible propriety. Miss Fluart did sit down; but the prospect from thence rather increased than diminished a little matter of confusion which she felt on the view of the company she seemed to have got into.
>
> She was rising to leave the pavilion, when his lordship, in the most gallant manner possible, claimed a fine, due, he said, by the custom of the manor, from every lady who honoured that sofa by sitting upon it. His lordship meant simply a kiss, which I believe he would have taken respectfully enough, had Miss Fluart been passive; but, I know not why, the lady seemed to feel an alarm, for which probably she had no reason; and was intent only upon running away, whilst his lordship was intent only upon seizing his forfeit. A fine muslin apron was ill treated upon this occasion; a handkerchief was ruffled, and some beautiful hair had strayed from its confinement, and wantoned upon its owner's polished neck. She got away, however, from this palace of painting, and its dangerous sofa.
>
> 'Upon my word, my dear Miss Fluart,' said his lordship, getting down after her as fas as he was able, 'you are quite a prude today. I thought you superior to the nonsense of your sex,—the making such a rout about a kiss.'

1 Ibid., ch. xxv, p. 83.

'A kiss! Lord bless me,' said Miss Fluart, 'I thought, from the company your lordship had brought me into, and the mode of your attack, you had wanted to undress me.'[1]

Lord Grondale's chief aide—and jointly with him the satiric target of the main plot—is a servile pluralist, the Reverend Mr. Blick. This harsh portrait of a clergyman of the Established Church, in whom religion and every other moral principle are sacrificed to the worldly interest of his patron, is darker in tone than Bage's characteristic satire of earlier years, probably because the circumstances of the times made it so. Bage's friend William Hutton had been a sufferer, along with Joseph Priestley, of the Birmingham Riots in 1791, in which the mob had zealously burnt Dissenters' property in the name of King and Church. It is not merely the oligarchic tendencies of the upper classes and their syco-phants that Bage attacks; but, with a more special aptness in this novel, their crimes against religious toleration and free speech. Dr. Blick's actions recall real-life acts of repression which at the time of writing were fresh in the memory —the prosecution of men for their opinions in the Treason Trials of 1794, and the notorious Two Acts of 1795. Blick the so-called divine takes the most energetic part in the prosecution of Hermsprong, and, as perhaps his most generalized and representative act of sycophancy, preaches a sermon on the necessity of submission to the temporal power.

Equally, however, the themes of the novel are developed in the subplot, which concerns the family of Mr. Sumelin at Falmouth. The heroine's friend Miss Fluart is Mr. Sumelin's ward, a fact which often takes Caroline there; luckily for her since, by one of Bage's unashamed coincidences, Hermsprong is Mr. Sumelin's associate in business. The Sumelin *ménage* is the mirror-image of Lord Grondale's household: Mr. Sumelin, dry, intelligent, not at all severe, is the very reverse of a domestic tyrant, while his silly wife and their daughter Harriet are also the reverse of the rational Caroline Campinet. The lesson of the Falmouth family is that the freedom Mr. Sumelin allows is of little use unless women have minds, and are pre-

---

[1] *Hermsprong, or Man As He Is Not*, ch. xxxv, pp. 110–11.

pared to use them; for Mrs. Sumelin and Harriet voluntarily submit to the tyranny of fashion and appearances. Even if the action's periodic removal to Falmouth is not well accounted for in terms of plot, the thematic link goes a long way to justify it. Besides, few readers would be willing to forgo conversations which delightfully, and significantly, anticipate *Pride and Prejudice:*

. . . Mrs. Sumelin, in the course of rapid declamation, so far forgot things as to defend her dear Harriet from head to foot, imprudence and all.

'Then,' my guardian asked as soon as he could be heard, 'why do you eternally scold her for faults, if she has committed none?'

'You catch one up so, Mr. Sumelin; to be sure, I did not mean to say quite that; but for your part, you take no pains to instruct your children, nor ever did. I don't believe you have ever said one word to Harriet about this business.'

'What need? when I have a dear industrious wife, who takes the department of lecturing into her own hands, and performs it so ably.'

'You are enough to provoke a stone wall. I have not patience with you.'

"I don't expect it, my dear. Only have the goodness not to torment yourself. You were in the humour just now to think Harriet's fault a small one.—With all my heart. The law does not call it an offence at all. It gives young women leave to choose their own husbands after twenty-one; or before, provided they do not marry in England. Harriet, you see, did nothing illegal. She was going out of England, that she might not sin against the law. But the law also allows fathers to dispose of their acquired property as they please. To this inconvenience Harriet must submit. She loves Mr. Fillygrove, I do not. To him, therefore, I shall give nothing . . .[1]

It is largely in conversation at Falmouth, between Hermsprong, Caroline, and Maria Fluart, that the principal themes of the novel are developed. The most important of these is liberty, especially, in the terms of this novel, the liberty of women. Caroline has the first essential quality, which Mrs. Sumelin and Harriet lack—an educated understanding. But according to Hermsprong the problem for English women is that despite their relative liberty of action they employ too little liberty of mind. Without this, they become slaves to

[1] Ibid., ch. xv. p. 52.

fashion, convention, or their menfolk. To some extent the problem is one of education; but it is even more one of will.[1]

Caroline, too rational to be a slave to fashion or social ambition, nevertheless voluntarily submits to the tyranny of her father. Her combination of just perception and timid orthodoxy reveals itself when she is courted by Sir Philip Chestrum. He has inherited a fortune from his tradesman-father, and a long pedigree from his aristocratic mother, but Caroline rejects him on account of his want of education and intellect. To Lord Grondale, needless to say, he is an eligible suitor, and the peer enters into an unholy alliance with Lady Chestrum. In relation to the match, Caroline adopts the approved stance of the eighteenth-century heroine. She stands on her right to refuse the man she does not love; but she will not assert her right to the man, Hermsprong, whom she does love.[2] Bage criticizes his heroine's passivity by causing the lively Miss Fluart to put up an entertaining resistance on Caroline's behalf both to Sir Philip and to Lord Grondale. The former soon learns to fear the play of her irony—'Miss Fluart talked one thing always, and meant another.'[3] Lord Grondale, at first enchanted with her vivacity, eventually comes to hate her, as she thwarts his plans for Caroline's marriage and dismisses both it and his own suit with more than customary frankness:

Your Lordship requires Miss Campinet to return, in order to receive the addresses of Sir Philip Chestrum. I would recommend to your Lordship to receive those addresses yourself; for, if they are offered to Caroline in person, they must inspire her with invincible disgust . . . Indeed, my Lord, there should be a little affection, if it be no more than sufficient to prevent a nausea, which possibly might affect an elegant young woman upon the pawings of a bear or monkey. You know, my Lord, that is what I am waiting for: and when it comes, I am ready. But indeed, and indeed, I must wait till it does come; and so ought all sober minded young women, like.

Your Lordship's most obedient servant,
Maria Fluart.[4]

---

[1] *Hermsprong, or Man As He Is Not*, ch. xliii, pp. 135–7.
[2] Ibid., ch. lviii, pp. 183–6.
[3] Ibid., ch. lx, p. 191.
[4] Ibid., ch. xlix, p. 158.

What Maria Fluart does that her friend the conventional heroine does not do is to speak her mind with freedom. The reader comes to look for and to value a style in conversation which reveals liberty of mind. Hermsprong and Maria Fluart have the manner to perfection, so bracing that it hits their opponents like a bucketful of cold water. The Rev. Mr. Woodcock displays it in his finest hour, when he turns upon his superior, Dr. Blick.[1] Mr. Sumelin has it, together with other desirable intellectual qualities—decisiveness, as when he tells his wife to end her reproaches to Harriet, and discrimination, as when he corrects his wife's slipshod phrasing:

One morning, at breakfast, Mr. Sumelin had the misfortune to scald his fingers, simply for the common cause of such accidents, doing one thing, and thinking of another. Mrs. Sumelin, as is usual in these small domestic cases, began to scold.

'If I had broke the cup, madam,' Mr. Sumelin answered, 'it would have been a crime inexpiable but by a new set. This is, I suppose, a regular tax upon husbands; I submit to it; but I really cannot submit to the not being allowed to scald my own fingers.'

'It was so thoughtless, Mr. Sumelin,' said his lady.

'Was it not rather too much thought?' asked Miss Fluart.

'It's all one,' Mrs. Sumelin answered.

'To the tea-cup,' said the husband, 'or to things which want understanding.'[2]

The dialogue of admirable characters habitually suggests this kind of precision and here, if not in boldness, Caroline ranks among the angels. Her scene with Sir Philip Chestrum, in which she quietly discourages him, and in his complacency he fancies the opposite, has more than a touch of Jane Austen about it. Of course it anticipates the proposal scene of John Thorpe, just as it anticipates Sir Philip Baddely's courtship in Maria Edgeworth's *Belinda*: foolish young men who propose and are unexpectedly refused are a favourite stock-in-trade of comedy in the period, perhaps on account of the conceited Mr. Smith in Fanny Burney's *Evelina*. But even more interesting, and more fundamental to the art of Bage's successors, is the carefully controlled use in this scene of the heroine's intelligent tone. Nothing need be said by the author about Sir Philip Chestrum's inept proposal. The flavour of the heroine's

---

[1] Ibid., ch. xiii, p. 47.   [2] Ibid., ch. xlii, p. 129.

restricted remarks is sufficient to put the reader into an active frame of mind in which his own discrimination does the rest.

As a technician Bage is not consistently in the front rank. He adopts a structure in *Hermsprong*, involving a narrator called Gregory Glen, which is irremediably clumsy and after a while seems to get forgotten. Although *Hermsprong* is actually more tightly constructed than his earlier novels, the action still wanders about, and contains too many inset stories. Even in terms of his own clever concept, the heroine who behaves in accordance with convention, and is yet in the wrong, Bage is to some extent at fault. The reader cannot help feeling conned when he discovers that Hermsprong, Caroline's rational choice, the man of no name, is really (in the worst manner of conventional plotting) the long-lost Sir Charles Campinet. At least Holcroft had the intellectual courage to leave Frank Henley to the last a gardener's son. Besides, Caroline's submissiveness is censured only so far. We cannot help suspecting that Bage partly relies on our sympathy for her gentleness and obedience, and the suspicion is confirmed when he makes Lord Grondale fall ill, so that Caroline's weak-willed conformism merges indistinguishably into her general benevolence.

The plot thus fails to maintain its originality and irony to the end, and the lack of consistency and deficiency in intellectual daring are such serious faults that *Hermsprong* falls short of great satirical comedy. What does not disappoint is the formal innovation, the pointed and dramatic use made of intelligent dialogue. Here, at any rate, is the logical connection with the central inspiration of Godwin. For Bage, too, is writing about individualism, and about liberty, and, in an entirely different genre from Godwin's sombre tragedy, he too has made his characters enact what they stand for. It is perfectly true that Hermsprong himself is a concoction out of place in a realistic novel, suggesting Voltaire's Huron out of Ferguson or Smith. What matters more is that in speech he really does do battle with dictatorial assurance on the one hand, the empty forms of polite address on the other; and that Miss Fluart's lively freedoms support him. This, too, is a drama of consciousness, though it belongs to the comic mode.

And in achieving such a drama, Bage, who is in many ways so old-fashioned, moves towards a novel that speaks for his own time rather than for that of his predecessors.

Here, in fact, is that assault via burlesque on the values of Fanny Burney's world which is sometimes read into Jane Austen.[1] *Pride and Prejudice* especially has been thought of as a disenchanted reappraisal of those plots in which humble heroines aspire to acceptance by the high, mighty, and not self-evidently deserving. But Bage—one of several predecessors of Jane Austen in connecting the words 'pride' and 'prejudice' together[2]—more interestingly anticipates her in challenging the automatic reverence for rank which was an unwritten assumption behind so many stock eighteenth-century fictional situations. The difference between them is that Bage's entire novel sets out to do what is done only by certain scenes and characters in *Pride and Prejudice*—to deflate the swollen pride of the representatives of the State and the Church. Lady Mary Paradyne and Lord Grondale time and again lay claim to pompous dignities, only to have them simply dismissed by their free-minded opponents:

'Should you, Miss Fluart, if I should offer to lay my rank, my title, my person, and fortune at your feet—should you think it worth a serious consideration?'

'Why, my lord, these are very serious things, no doubt; one should like to tread upon some of them.'[3]

To trample upon peers of the realm *ex officio* was never Jane Austen's intention. But recent enterprise by a bibliographical scholar has shown that she possessed a copy of *Hermsprong*.[4] If she acquired it in the year of publication, 1796, that was also the year in which she received her subscription copy of Fanny Burney's *Camilla* (published July), and began work on the early version of *Pride and Prejudice*

---

[1] See below, pp. 198–201.

[2] e.g., ch. xxxii, p. 101. Cf. *TLS*, 29 Dec. 1961, p. 929, and 26 Jan. 1962, p. 57.

[3] *Hermsprong*, ch. xxxv, p. 111.

[4] D. J. Gilson, 'Jane Austen's Books', *The Book Collector*, Spring 1974, p. 31. The copy in question has 'Jane Austen', most probably her own signature, on the front free endpaper of each volume. I am grateful to Mr. Gilson for drawing my attention to his discovery.

(October).[1] Here were seeds for the fertile soil of that great technical intelligence. But it must also be apparent that in *Hermsprong* there was a wholesale and consistent assault upon the idea of inherited authority which Jane Austen showed no sign of repeating.

One device which Bage handed on to his heirs was his form: he mimicked the stale conventions of eighteenth-century fiction in such a manner that he criticized its underlying assumptions, while at the same time availing himself of the popular novelist's power to create an attractive autonomous world. His second contribution was his emphasis on dialogue as an index of value. Here Bage was no doubt influenced by the French philosophic tale, especially Voltaire's and Marmontel's. But he helped to naturalize the convention of a debate on issues of substance, to make it amenable to the full-length romantic plot, and thus to inaugurate one of the most interesting sub-species of the coming generation, the intellectual comedy of Maria Edgeworth, Jane Austen, and Thomas Love Peacock.

Bage was read by three at least of his most important immediate successors: by Jane Austen, who has left no comment on *Hermsprong*, by Maria Edgeworth, who presumably shared her father's approval of it, and by Scott, who wrote a generous appreciation of Bage's work as a whole for the British Novelists' Library. Maria Edgeworth and Jane Austen use conventional plot-motifs much as Bage does. Dialogue which re-enacts a clash of values (though not open debate on national issues) is another corner-stone of their comedy. Of the two, Maria Edgeworth is closer to Bage not only because her novels sometimes also deal frankly with real-life controversial issues, but because she agrees with him in valuing independence above other personal attributes. Even she, however, probably did not write as she did because Bage wrote first. He was not one of the novelists she reread; those were Fanny Burney and Elizabeth Inchbald. It may well be that both Maria Edgeworth and Jane Austen, even if they grasped what he had to teach them, would have felt shy of confessing

---

[1] *'First Impressions* (original of *Pride and Prejudice*), begun October 1796, ended August 1797'. Memorandum by Cassandra Austen, quoted by R. W. Chapman, introductory note to *Sense and Sensibility*, Oxford, 1923, p. xiii.

a debt in this quarter. Bage's politics might not have shocked Maria Edgeworth, or not at first, and not much, but she would have found it hard to take his prurience. The scenes between Lord Grondale and Miss Fluart must have struck a well-bred woman in the period as excessively free, and even a twentieth-century reader is startled to notice how much pleasure the author seems to take himself in Lord Grondale's 'manual operations'.

The point is perhaps merely that from Bage's insights certain formal developments logically followed. In one sense or another he shared his contemporaries' awareness and fear of the power of organized society, which is often most effectively exerted in the moulding of opinion. His humanism takes the form of respect for the mental attributes of people at their best—vitality, independence, humour, and—that old keystone of sentimental optimism—spontaneous sympathy. He is a genuine creator, if a flawed and eccentric one, because the form he develops, his verbal comedy, is a true correlative for what he has to say; his fresh, wry dialogue dramatizes the human characteristic he finds central, which is consciousness itself. Or, at least, the externalized equivalent of it: for it is not the whole consciousness Bage really tries to represent, but that aspect of it which has to do with discriminations about the outside world and about our moral obligations to it. By restricting himself to a stylized comedy, Bage avoids the falsification inherent in other jacobins' would-be naturalistic portrayals of the rational consciousness, and produces a statement of his ideals which is valid after its kind. If it happens that he also anticipates at least one writer of a very different intellectual persuasion—Jane Austen—it is a sign of the common inheritance of jacobin and conservative, and a sign of the times.

CHAPTER 4

THE ANTI-JACOBINS

W HILE the revolutionary novelists constituted a movement only in the heated imaginations of their opponents, the anti-jacobins can scarcely be considered except as a
group. No novelist on the conservative side who matured in
the 1790s had a distinctive talent. Each of them wrote to a
formula and adopted an apparently conscious stance of self-
effacement and personal anonymity. Since they were engaged
in attacking the cult of self in politics, psychology, and ethics,
it was logical for them to belittle the role of personal inspiration in art as well. Novel after novel unashamedly used the
same structure, the same incidents, the same caricatured
figures. Moreover, the worlds imagined by these novelists were
deliberately crude, prosaic versions of the immediately contemporary English, or often London, scene. The idea of
creating a fictional world, of giving so much credence to
personal fancy, was itself anathema.

It was the conservatives who coined the word 'jacobin' for
their opponents. In the last half-decade of the century, and
for some years thereafter, the pursuit of the 'jacobinical'
became a national pastime, a witch-hunt in the course of
which individuals like Charles Lamb, who was largely apolitical, and his friend Charles Lloyd, in most respects an orthodox
moralist, awoke to find themselves branded as a threat to
national security.[1] As reaction became more and more hysterical, 'jacobins' were detected not merely among the self-
acknowledged progressives of the Godwin circle but in writers

---

[1] The formidable caricaturist Gillray, who was enlisted by Canning as an
associate of *The Anti-Jacobin*, featured them in his illustration (of Aug. 1798)
to accompany the satirical poem *The New Morality* (for which see below,
p. 93). With its crowded scene of contemporary political and literary figures—
all worshipping at a Revolutionary shrine which features a hag representing
Sensibility—the caricature is an eloquent example of the contemporary
conservative technique of guilt by association. Other literary victims include
Southey, Coleridge, Godwin, and Holcroft.

whose intentions were sometimes or always politically innocent. But if the persecution of liberals was unpleasantly wholesale, it cannot quite be described as arbitrary. The leading spirits behind *The Anti-Jacobin* of 1797–8 were George Canning, William Gifford, and Hookham Frere, intelligent men who liked at least to claim that their targets were ideas rather than personalities.[1] When they did single out individuals for attack, these *were* as a rule offenders by conservative lights: among creative writers, Southey and, less prominently, Coleridge, Lamb, and Lloyd; the didactic poets Richard Payne Knight and Erasmus Darwin; and the German dramatists Goethe, Schiller, and Kotzebue. Since modern readers do not look at these writers primarily in terms of their ideology, we are inclined to consider perverse the repeated attacks on them (and, later, on Wordsworth) by conservative critics. But an examination of *The Anti-Jacobins*'s charges shows that, whatever else the magazine may have been, it was at least consistent in applying its own principles.

Southey's offence (apart from the dactylic measures of his Sapphics, which Canning in particular took delight in parodying[2]) begins with his choice of subject. He is inclined, for example, to dwell on a figure from low life, as in *The Widow* and *The Soldier's Wife*: in each case society is depicted as indifferent to the poor woman's sufferings, while the poet's attitude is one of identification and compassion. *The Anti-Jacobin* sees this theme as an attempt to dramatize 'the natural and eternal warfare of the POOR and the RICH':

A human being, in the lowest state of penury and distress is a treasure to a reasoner of this cast. He contemplates, he examines, he turns him in every possible light, with a view of extracting from the variety of his wretchedness new topics of invective against the pride of property.[3]

---

[1] Draper Hill, *Mr. Gillray, the Caricaturist*, London, 1965, p. 71.

[2] The dactylics were not easily forgotten: cf. Byron's remark on meeting Southey, '—the best-looking bard I have seen for some time. To have that poet's head and shoulders, I would almost have written his Sapphics.' Letter to Thomas Moore, 27 Sept. 1813; *Letters and Journals*, ed. R. E. Prothero, 1898, ii. 266.

[3] *The Anti-Jacobin*, 27 Nov. 1797, introducing *The Friend of Humanity and the Knifegrinder*, a satire on Southey's *The Widow*.

Interest in the simple rather than the sophisticated in itself carried overtones of Rousseauistic primitivism, and was associated with 'democracy' and 'levelling'. Where Southey's victim of society was actually in conservative eyes a criminal —as in his drama, *Wat Tyler*, or his short *Inscription* on Henry Marten the regicide[1]—his offence was naturally compounded. Here in any case Southey touched upon the familiar Godwinian issues of crime and punishment; while liberals in the period came very close to denying the actual concept of guilt, conservatives became correspondingly severe, and supported their pessimistic view of human nature by recalling some of the blacker crimes. The essence of what the conservatives saw as jacobin ideology is given in a 'letter' from 'Mr. Higgins of St. Mary Axe' (i.e. William Godwin), who is made to define his basic principles as, first, an attack on civil and religious institutions—'social order . . . and regular government and law', and, second, a belief in perfectibility, which is ultimately faith in man and in his potential for continuous improvement.[2] These two fundamental points—hostility to existing forms of society, expressed by a black picture of contemporary hardship, and admiration for Man, expressed by sympathetic treatment of individual sufferers—are what *The Anti-Jacobin* sniffs out as sure symptoms of infidelity.

A deep mistrust of the progressive cult of simplicity lies behind the journal's hostility to Payne Knight, whose primitivist account of the origins and progress of society is satirized;[3] and to Erasmus Darwin, guilty in *The Loves of the Plants*, 1789, of depicting the sexual impulse as an innate and indeed central feature of the natural order. The modern reader may at first wonder how topics like these could stimulate *political* controversy; but in the 1790s they did, and not only among professional polemicists. *The Anti-Jacobin* took particular exception to Payne Knight's didactic poem *The Progress of Civil Society*, 1796. But in 1794 the same author

[1] Satirized in *The Anti-Jacobin*, 20 Nov. 1797, by the *Inscription* on Mrs. Brownrigg, a notorious murderer.

[2] *The Anti-Jacobin*, 16 Apr. 1798, 'letter' introducing *The Loves of the Triangles*.

[3] Knight, 1750–1824, wealthy connoisseur, collector, and authority on classical art, had already acquired some notoriety through his learned but daring *Account of the Remains of the Worship of Priapus*, 1786.

had written a poem, *The Landscape*, in which he opposed the arts of landscape gardeners such as Capability Brown on the grounds that nature was best unadulterated. It is instructive to see how sharply Anna Seward, herself in earlier days a sentimentalist, and not illiberal, reacted to the political subversion she found in *The Landscape:*

Knight's system appears to me the Jacobinism of taste; from its abusing that rational spirit of improvement, suggested by Milton in his description of the primeval garden; and realised and diffused by Brown; which, uniting the *utile* with the *dulce*, has rendered Britain the Eden of Europe. Mr. Knight would have nature as well as man indulged in that uncurbed and wild luxuriance, which must soon render our landscape-island rank, weedy, damp, and unwholesome as the incultivate savannas of America . . . save me, good Heaven, from living in tangled forests, and amongst men who are unchecked by those guardian laws, which bind the various orders of society in one common interest. May the lawns I tread be smoothed by healthful industry, and the glades opened by the hand of picturesque taste, to admit the pure and salutary breath of heaven!—and may the people, amongst whom I live, be withheld by stronger repellants than their own virtue, from invading my property and shedding my blood!!—And so much for politics and pleasure grounds.[1]

By the same token, Erasmus Darwin, the Midlands physician, inventor, and wit, was widely and not unreasonably identified as an opponent by those who believed in the sanctity and permanence of the present civilized order of things; though Darwin's most intellectually subversive poem was not yet published. His posthumous *Temple of Nature*, 1803, versifies 'his belief that life originated as microscopic specks in primeval seas and gradually, under evolutionary pressures and without assistance from any deity, developed its present form'.[2] If his grandson Charles Darwin could cause a convulsion in Victorian society by his successful formulation of the theory of evolution, an outline of the same heresies must have been anathema in the period of the French Revolution. In fact *The Temple of Nature* never had the notoriety of the

[1] Anna Seward to J. Johnson, Esq., *Letters of Anna Seward, 1784–1807*, 6 vols., Edinburgh, 1811, iv. 10–11.
[2] D. King-Hele, *The Essential Writings of Erasmus Darwin*, London, 1968, p. 152.

less far-reaching *Loves of the Plants*, because it never had the popular success. *The Loves of the Plants* (eventually to make Part II of *The Botanic Garden*) emerged at a time when ideas were in ferment, so that it attracted acclaim, as well as criticism. *The Temple of Nature* came out in a period of bleak reaction, and was largely ignored.

The Anti-Jacobin's assault on the German drama is of special interest, since one of these dramas, Kotzebue's *Lovers' Vows*, plays a significant part in Jane Austen's *Mansfield Park*.[1] In the burlesque play *The Rovers*,[2] which never gets beyond the end of Act IV, the group led by Canning and Frere hilariously satirize the leading features of German drama, the principles of which they outline as follows:

. . . a discharge of every man (in his own estimation) from every tie which laws, divine or human, which local customs, immemorial habits, and multiplied examples, impose upon him, and to set them [*sic*] about doing what they like, where they like, when they like, and how they like,—without reference to any law but their own will, or to any consideration of how others may be affected by their conduct.[3]

This rampant individualism is exemplified in *The Rovers*, as the principal characters pursue the objects of their immediate sexual desires, and without the slightest compunction abandon those who no longer interest them. Passion is the guide to conduct, and although the desired one usually belongs to the opposite sex, sentimental friendship between two young girls is also slyly illustrated. 'Let us swear an eternal friendship', 'Let us agree to live together', cry the two heroines, as soon as they meet.[4]

The satirists have two particular targets for burlesque in mind, Kotzebue's *The Stranger*, in which an erring wife is forgiven, and Goethe's *Stella*, in which a man resolves his marital difficulties by deciding to live with both his wife and

---

[1] For the suspect liberalism of German literature, see below, pp. 114–20; and for Jane Austen's use of its dangerous reputation, pp. 233–5.

[2] *The Anti-Jacobin*, xxx (4 June 1798), and xxxi (11 June 1798).

[3] Introduction to the first instalment of *The Rovers*.

[4] Cf. *Love and Friendship:* 'We flew into each other's arms, and after having exchanged vows of mutual Friendship for the rest of our Lives, instantly unfolded to each other the most inward secrets of our hearts.' Jane Austen, *Minor Works*, ed. R. W. Chapman, Oxford, rev. ed., 1963, p. 85.

his mistress. *The Rovers* is thus primarily an attack on the progressives' desire to loosen the marriage tie, but attempts at social levelling are an important lesser theme. The convention by which, in Kotzebue's plays especially, 'the poor man is more virtuous than the prince' receives a glancing blow; so does the tendency of a host of plays to make those in temporal or spiritual authority especially corrupt—'the cruelty of a minister—the perfidy of a Monk'.[1] What perhaps interests us particularly is that *The Rovers* was actually staged in Drury Lane in 1811—a remarkable tribute, since it is manifestly unstageable, to its continued meaningfulness a decade after the vogue for German drama had passed its peak. On that occasion, moreover, George Colman the Younger contributed a Prologue which struck out at *The Stranger* and *Lovers' Vows* in terms which supposed that his audience was still familiar with their plots:

> To make mankind revere wives gone astray,
> Love pious sons who rob on the highway . . .[2]

In discussing the use made of *Lovers' Vows* in *Mansfield Park* (1814), modern commentators sometimes underrate how notorious it was; how critics and satirists from *The Anti-Jacobin* on had made it a byword for moral and social subversion.[3]

The best single poem produced by *The Anti-Jacobin* is probably *The New Morality*, which summarizes in trenchant couplets what it sees as the indiscriminate, easy optimism of the friends of revolution—that quality which it defines as 'candour'. To this habit of easy forgiveness, or unwillingness to scrutinize, it opposes a wary scepticism about human nature; in all contexts, realism is morally preferable to idealism. After reading *The New Morality* it becomes clear that Jane Austen's strong liking for the actual—that virtually moral distaste which she displays, from the juvenilia on, for the romantic gloss on truth—is a characteristic partisan position of the time. Her development of the clever heroine,

---

[1] The 'Minister' is probably a reference to Schiller's *Kabale und Liebe*, translated in 1798 as *The Minister* by M. G. Lewis, who also wrote *The Monk* (1796).

[2] The incident referred to in the first line occurs in *The Stranger*; it is Frederick in *Lovers' Vows* who proves his piety to his mother, Agatha, by committing a robbery in order to buy her food. See below, pp. 234–5.

[3] See below, pp. 232 ff.

who strives, though often fallibly, for a clear-sighted assessment of human weakness, including her own, is also typical, and not the idiosyncratic taste of one original talent. Scepticism about human claims to virtue, however specious, real pessimism about the validity of individual human insights, are the hallmarks of the conservative writer.

If, indeed, a formal creed is required for the conservative literary faction of the post-Revolution era, it is to be found in the Prospectus which *The Anti-Jacobin* issued in November 1797:

> We have not arrived (to our shame perhaps we avow it) at that wild and unshackled freedom of thought, which rejects all habit, all wisdom of former times, all restraints of ancient usage, and of local attachment, and which judges upon each subject, whether of politics or morals, as it arises, by lights entirely its own, without reference to recognised principle, or established practice . . .
>
> Of all these and the like principles—in one word, of Jacobinism in all its shapes, and in all its degrees, political and moral, public and private, whether as it openly threatens the subversion of State, or gradually saps the foundation of domestic happiness, We are the avowed, determined and irreconcileable enemies.

One feature of this passage which would have struck its first readers was that it captured the intonation, just as it echoed the ideas, of Edmund Burke.[1] Although Burke was easily the greatest exponent of the conservative case against the Revolution, this was not the usual tone of anti-jacobin writing. Burke's style was roundly attacked by his opponents earlier in the decade, and to moderate tastes perhaps effectively rebuked by the studied rationality of a reputable opponent like James Mackintosh. Because Burke's appeal to emotion ran against the temper of the times, his style (though not his case) seems to have become discredited. One is reminded of Hazlitt's passing reference to Burke in *The Spirit of the Age*, that beside Godwin he seemed 'a flashy sophist'. Although the suggestion that his gilded, sonorous manner was an embarrassment to his own side cannot be more than speculation, it is surely significant that while his name crops up in revolutionary plays and novels, one finds no direct reference

---

[1] The first paragraph evokes the famous 'We know that we have made no discoveries' quoted above, pp. 38–9.

to it at all in the anti-jacobin novel. In *Douglas, or the Highlander*, 1800,[1] Robert Bisset surveys the English political
scene of 1792, and finds no place in it for the great spokesman
of conservative ideology. Apart from the *Anti-Jacobin*'s
prospectus, deliberate echoes of Burke's style seem almost as
rare. A quite different anti-jacobin manner was evolving,
appropriate above all to satire: it was dry, cynical, detached,
belittling to human greatness and to all rich insights, including
the author's own. A recent critic of Jane Austen has found
her full of allusions to Burke,[2] but he perhaps oversimplifies
the complex intellectual currents of the time. Jane Austen
and Burke had in common their social conservatism, but in
manner they were antithetical. It was so with the lesser anti-
jacobins, whose knowing and worldly demeanour was much
better represented in the body of *The Anti-Jacobin* than in the
prospectus. The rhythms and images of the great partisan of
conservatism seldom recurred in the mass of minor literature
his side produced in the decade following the *Reflexions*.

What the *Anti-Jacobin* gave its side was coherent leadership. It appeared at a time when conservatives were urgent
to define their own intellectual position in terms of the subjective or optimistic writing of their opponents. There was
plenty of anti-sentimental writing from the progressive side
too—but it began by objecting to the passive and irrational
elements in the cult of sentimentality, not by developing a
consistent code in opposition to it. In very general terms the
conservatives knew all along what they were in favour of:
reason, experience, and the Christian religion. Women novelists in particular, concerned to influence the conduct of their
young, impressionable female readers, stressed the importance
of submitting to the guidance of a wise elderly mentor rather
than to the example of books, or, worst of all, to the dictates
of passion. Before the conservative reaction began, many
didactic tales were already being written to advocate discipline and self-denial, often on a nearly superhuman scale. Mrs.
Eliza Parsons, for example, presents a heroine who is reasoned

---

[1] See below, p. 112.
[2] Alistair M. Duckworth, *The Improvement of the Estate*, Johns Hopkins,
Baltimore, 1971.

into marrying a man she does not love, and afterwards, in spite of his ill-treatment and infidelity, heroically makes him a model wife.[1]

Even feminist writers like Elizabeth Inchbald and Mary Hays felt it important for women to govern their passions—though these liberals, like Maria Edgeworth after them, meant government by the woman herself, rather than submission to a mentor or to mere convention.[2] In the ubiquitousness of such propaganda against the passions, it could be argued that not much emerges of a distinctly conservative case. And yet, in spite of the readiness of both sides to denounce Sentiment early in the decade, by 1795 or 1796 it was increasingly seen as a characteristically 'liberal' style or attitude. A study of the career of a conservative moralist like Mrs. Jane West[3] shows how the anti-sentimental theme characteristically developed. Mrs. West begins with an admonitory story about two young girls, making respectively a wise and a foolish choice in marriage (*Advantages of Education*, 1793). Her next novel is a more sophisticated version of the same, with a wider and more explicit intellectual frame of reference (*A Gossip's Story*, 1796). She concludes with a highly coloured drama in which the implications are national and the dénouement even apocalyptical (*A Tale of the Times*, 1799).

The Advantages of Education is a pleasant domestic history, told in an unaffected tone. As so often, the heroine, Maria Williams, is an ingenuous young girl whose formal education has ended, and whose real education in life is just about to begin. Although her mother has now returned to supervise Maria's education, they have been apart for several years, so that Maria begins the novel dangerously impressionable. She meets and is influenced by a new friend, the rich and silly Charlotte Raby, who soon sets her a bad example by marrying for worldly motives. Maria in her turn is wooed by the fashionable rake, Sir Henry Neville, and by the virtuous

---

[1] *Woman As She Should Be; or Memoirs of Mrs. Manville*, 1793.

[2] See above, pp. 54–5.

[3] Jane West, 1758–1852, prolific novelist, dramatist, and poet, was married to a yeoman-farmer in Northamptonshire. She is also known for her literary friendships with Bishop Percy, who wrote of the wholesomeness of her writings in the *British Critic* of 1801, and with the author of edifying tales for children, Mrs. Trimmer.

Edmund Herbert. Neville promises to reform, but is secretive about his past, which Edmund Herbert warns her is a bad indication. When she finds that Neville has kept a mistress, Maria gives him up; later, Werther-like, he shoots himself. Maria begins to outgrow her friendship with Charlotte, while Edmund gains her affection through his steady kindness to Charlotte's neglected elderly father. After a sober courtship, they marry, to settle peacefully in the country at a distance from Charlotte in the town.

Mrs. West's story makes no use of the experiential techniques of the sentimental novel. The plot poses contrasted characters in opposition to one another. The purpose bears no relation to Maria's sensations—which actually in this context are suspect—but to the ethical courses open to her. No English novels before or since have been so unremittingly ethical as the conservative novels of the generation following 1790: no other novels, surely, have consciously rejected emotional experience as a proper field of interest. In choosing between her two suitors, one immediately attractive, the other indifferent, Maria has to lay aside her intuitive first preference for Neville in favour of sounder objective tests: by their deeds shall you know them.

A further contrast in the novel, between the town and the country, does not itself mark the conservative novelist. Primitivists, including those influenced by Rousseau, frequently make the same point. Thomas Day's Harry Sandford grows up more virtuous in the country than Tommy Merton in the town largely because his life is free and simple and more 'natural'. With the classical tradition of Virgil and Horace behind them, all eighteenth-century moralists are liable to agree in finding the town life over-sophisticated, trivial, worldly, and selfish. But progressives and conservatives do differ in the quality of their feeling about the country. The progressive is liable to see it as a place for the individual to expand in freedom, cultivating the self. The conservative, stressing the selfishness of the town, is liable on the contrary to emphasize that the country offers greater opportunities for sober usefulness, both to the family and to the small village community. For Mrs. West, the typical outcome of Charlotte's preference for the town is her neglect of her father;

Edmund in the country fulfils the social obligations that are a traditional aspect of the small community.

Both in feeling for the social virtues of the country as opposed to the selfish virtues of the town, and in recommending objective tests, instead of instinct, as a guide to others' worth, Jane West anticipates Jane Austen. Even the modest, limited scale of *The Advantages of Education*, the restriction of its plot to a few characters in a domestic setting, approximates to the tone of Jane Austen's writing more closely than do the more highly coloured incidents and complex narrative patterns of Mrs. West's next two novels. Not that *The Advantages of Education* is much more than a routine fictionalized conduct-book for young misses; to mention it in the same breath as even *Sense and Sensibility* is infinitely to exaggerate its merit. But in conception Charlotte Raby has something of Isabella Thorpe about her, and the story of the naïve young girl who must choose between two potential husbands, one outwardly attractive, the other really meritorious—the choice respectively of her passions and her moral sense—is the skeleton of Jane Austen's familiar plot. If Mrs. West herself fails to make the best use of her theme, it is partly because the temper of the times encourages her to exaggerate where Jane Austen tones down, to underline and comment on moral contrasts where Jane Austen allows action and character to speak for themselves.

Mrs. West's second attempt, *A Gossip's Story*, is technically more ambitious than *The Advantages of Education*. It is a story set within a narrative framework, the small-town gossip of comic characters led by the narrator, 'Prudentia Homespun'. Although at times laboured, the gossips' scenes become relevant because they sketch in the ordinary daily social world within which the principals have their being. Gossip, even when trivial or false, is a condition of existence with which the flightiest heroine must come to terms. Often the information relayed in the book is misleading or malicious, and yet it is the obverse face of something socially creditable —interest in and concern for others, and the belief that conduct matters. One of the two heroines, Marianne, fails the test imposed upon her by the gossipers: her self-centred conduct first makes enemies, and then, because she has no firmly

rooted, objective principles, adverse comment on her behaviour eats into the very core of her being. In its primitive
fashion, the active use made of the network of comment
within which a principal is enmeshed reminds one of *Middlemarch*.

The plot itself has other reverberations. Following the
death of her mother, Louisa Dudley is brought up by her
father to be thoughtful and considerate. Her younger sister,
Marianne, on the other hand, has been indulged by her grandmother, and her education has consisted largely of romantic
reading. The contrast between the two is that of 'an informed,
well-regulated mind' with a nature 'tremblingly alive to the
softer passions'. Marianne's temper 'rendered her peculiarly
unfit to encounter even those common calamities humanity
must endure'.[1]

The story develops with the appearance of suitors. Marianne
has attracted the attention of Henry Pelham. At first she is
inclined to reject Henry because she fancies that her friend
Miss Milton, to whom she is sentimentally attached, is in
love with him. On being persuaded that this reason is over-
strained, she worries that he is too unromantic. Her father
is pleased with the evidence he finds of Pelham's character—
'I am told he is a kind master, an indulgent landlord, an
obliging neighbour, and a steady active friend.'[2] But Marianne
is disappointed. These, she thinks, are only 'common virtues'.

'He is not, indeed he is not, the tender, respectful sympathizing
lover, which my heart tells me is necessary for my future repose.
He does not love me, at least not with that ardent affection, that
deference, that assiduous timidity—But you smile, Sir?'[3]

Indeed he does. Mr. Dudley has the attitude towards romantic love of all sound anti-jacobin elders—' "Mr. Pelham's
character as a man, is of much greater consequence to your
future peace, than his behaviour as a lover".'[4]

His advice in favour of Pelham goes unheeded, for Marianne is shortly to meet the lover of her dreams in true romantic
circumstances. Mr. Clermont, son of Lord Clermont, saves her

---

[1] Jane West, *A Gossip's Story*, 2 vols., 3rd ed. 1798, i. 18. The phrase 'tremblingly alive' is a favourite cliché picked up by the satirists of sentimentality.
Jane Austen uses it in *Love and Friendship*: see the passage quoted below, p. 168.
[2] *A Gossip's Story*, i. 93.   [3] Ibid., i. 95.   [4] Ibid, i. 96.

from a runaway horse, and immediately the two discover 'a wonderful coincidence of opinion':

'Both were passionate admirers of the country; both loved moonlight walks, and the noise of distant water falls; both were enchanted by the sound of the sweet-toned harp, and the almost equally soft cadence of the pastoral and elegaick muse; in short, whatever was passionate, elegant and sentimental in art; or beautiful, pensive and enchanting in nature.'[1]

Again Marianne's father is ready with sound advice. Clermont's character is not fully formed. She should study the faults from which none of us are free, so that she can make a balanced assessment of him as a friend and husband rather than as a lover. But Marianne is incapable of objectivity. To her Clermont is to be either nothing, or the lover she adores to distraction. Abandoning herself completely to her passion and worried only that Clermont cannot love her as completely as she loves him, she impulsively marries. The result is not catastrophic, but it is sufficiently sad. The waning of passion between the immature young couple is well observed by Mrs. West. In a few years Clermont is busying himself with other pursuits, and Marianne has become broken-spirited and wretched.

Meanwhile her elder sister Louisa has quietly endured her own painful experiences of love. Her real preference is for the steady and dutiful Pelham, whom Marianne has undervalued. But at a time when Pelham is paying court to Marianne, Louisa receives a proposal from the rich and haughty Sir William Milton, and she conceives that it is her duty for her father's sake to marry him. When inquiry establishes that Sir William is as morally unworthy of her as Pelham is worthy —that (like Jane Austen's Willoughby) he has first seduced a girl and then abandoned her—Louisa refuses him and resigns herself to a life of poverty in a cottage with her father. Her conscience clear, she is well contented with her lot. Her father ends his life in a spirit of cheerful Christian resignation, and Louisa looks forward to her eventual quiet reward, a marriage with Pelham.

A Gossip's Story has attracted notice for its obvious simi-

[1] *A Gossip's Story*, i. 205.

larities with Jane Austen's *Sense and Sensibility*. The two sisters, one of them excessively immature and named Marianne, are strikingly like Jane Austen's central pair of sisters. Mrs. West's Marianne makes comments about Pelham which seem to foreshadow her Austen successor's remarks about Edward Ferrars. Her meeting with Clermont, and their ardent single-minded courtship, again seem to find their echo in *Sense and Sensibility*.[1] It does not surprise us to find in Jane Austen's letters that she was familiar at least in general with Mrs. West's work.[2]

What seems more interesting, however, even than so many apparent echoes of a name, a scene, a speech, is the strong generic resemblance between Jane Austen and Mrs. West. The coincidence of outlook is more important than the trivial alleged borrowings. Like other conservative moralists, Mrs. West denigrates the individual's reliance on himself. She shows for example how dangerous it is to trust private intuition or passion in forming judgements of others. Far better in her view to go to the external evidence: Pelham is vindicated by examination of his actions, Milton's façade is destroyed by it, and Clermont is left an unknown quantity, because research into so young a man yields nothing. The same discovery—that objective evidence should be preferred to private intuition—is made by a succession of Jane Austen heroines, Catherine Morland, Marianne Dashwood, Elizabeth Bennett, Emma Woodhouse. And if feeling is an unreliable aid in choosing a husband, it is equally wayward as a general guide to conduct. Instead of the doctrine of cultivation of self, Mrs. West recommends humble, selfless service of others. Moreover, she urges a lowering of expectations, a scepticism about the rewards available in this life. Her Marianne's ardour stems from a half-formulated belief in the nobility of man, a faith that his nature is at least potentially exalted. For survival in Mrs. West's social circles, dominated at all levels by unkind and often mistaken gossips, a girl needs a morality resting on quiet and steady benevolence, a cool eye, and a

[1] See J. M. S. Tompkins, 'Elinor and Marianne', *RES* xiv (1940), and M. Melander, 'An Unknown Source of Jane Austen's *Sense and Sensibility*', *Studia Neophilologica*, xxii (1950).

[2] Jane Austen to Anna Austen, 28 Sept. 1814, and to Cassandra Austen, 8 Sept. 1816; *Letters*, ed. R. W. Chapman, pp. 405 and 466.

clear conscience. Based on a mistrust of one's own nature, and only moderate hopes of others, Mrs. West's assault on the cult of sensibility deliberately goes back to the older traditions of Christianity:

I wish to ask the fair enthusiasts who indulge in all the extravagance of heroick generosity, romantick love, and exuberant friendship, whether they really suppose it possible to improve upon the model which Christianity (our best comfort in this world and sure guide to the next) presents for our imitation . . . It tells us that man is as variable as the world he inhabits, that imperfections mingle with the virtues of the best; and by the fine idea of a state of warfare, urges us to constant circumspection and unwearied attention. From this mixture of good and evil it directs our pursuit after the former, by teaching us to *curb* our passions, and to *moderate* our desires; to expect with diffidence, enjoy with gratitude, and resign with submission.[1]

Mrs. West's opinions manifestly pose problems for the novelist. She is sceptical about the inner life *per se*: and since she holds private judgements to be faulty, the insights of all her characters, even the most sympathetic, are vindicated only when they can be checked by external evidence. She cannot find feeling and suffering interesting in themselves, as they are for most novelists of other periods: Louisa's pain is not dwelt on, and Marianne's is censured as wilfully self-induced. Virtuous behaviour (Louisa's) consists in a stern suppression of inward states of mind; a concentration instead upon action. But although Mrs. West discountenances inward activity of an emotional or experiential kind, she gives a central role to the ethical activity that assesses reality and guides conduct. Her novels are so structured that they throw ethical analysis and the processes of judgement into relief. An inexperienced heroine has to choose her husband. Unlike previous heroines—Clarissa, say, or Evelina—she may not give any credit to her feelings, not even to the extent of allowing them to determine whom she may refuse. The candidates for her hand are as nearly as possible evenly poised; Louisa must judge Sir William Milton, just as Marianne ought to judge Pelham and Clermont (although she fails to do so). The very structure of the novel emphasizes that the central

---

[1] *A Gossip's Story*, i. 48–9.

choices of life, such as the choice of a partner in marriage, ought in ethical terms to be rational and objective—in defiance of the claims of post-Humeian psychology that our thought-processes are naturally irrational and subjective. Minor novelists like Mrs. West express (of course often unconsciously) a deep-seated reaction against the presentation of the workings of the mind as involuntary and hence morally neutral. Appealing to objective Christian morality, they present the unconscious mind in the worst possible terms, as wayward, selfish, and self-destructive. It is in organizing her characters to display right and wrong ethical principles, and in presenting the heroine's inner life in terms of her conscious choices, that Jane Austen most significantly reveals a similarity to Mrs. West.

A third novel by Mrs. West, *A Tale of the Times*, 1799, is exceptionally true to its title. Reference was made at the beginning of this chapter to the impersonal quality of conservative writing in the revolutionary period. Especially after the appearance of the influential *Anti-Jacobin*, which gave definition to the conservative creed, novelist after novelist presents incidents and characters which fit precisely to a pattern. It is strange to see Mrs. West, of the world of country vicarages and fireside gossips, embarking on a plot involving a satanic seducer and rape, and ending in sudden death for both heroine and villain. Mrs. West wrote under the compulsions of the times, and her example illustrates how even the more sensible and domestic of novelists could be coerced by them.

A Tale of the Times advances the heroine's moment of choice to the beginning of the action. Attracted by the superficial good qualities of the Earl of Monteith, Geraldine marries him in preference to the steady Henry Powerscourt; and thereafter she continues to show poor judgement, by trusting her husband's selfish, worldly sister Arabella, and even more disastrously, Arabella's fashionably progressive friend Fitzosborne. As a Christian Geraldine ought to take some notice of the defects in Fitzosborne's value-system which are revealed, for example, in his sneer about Henry—'A very honest, downright soul, with true English notions.'[1] She does

---

[1] Jane West, *A Tale of the Times*, 3 vols., London, 1799, iii. 123.

not, and allows herself to be inveigled from home by Fitz-osborne, to die after he has raped her from shame and remorse.

In one respect only, *A Tale of the Times* resembles Jane Austen's novels even more than its two predecessors, for it has a triple instead of a double arrangement of characters. The central couple, Geraldine and Monteith, are flanked by two contrasting pairs—Fitzosborne and Arabella, Henry Powerscourt and his fincée Lucy—between whom the heroine ought to be able to discriminate. The virtuous friends are Christians, and associated with the countryside; the other pair amoral, and linked with fashionable London. But if the organization of the action is similar to Jane Austen's, the presentation of the ideas is certainly not. Fitzosborne openly canvasses his revolutionary ideology, in the most uncon-vincing jargon imaginable, and his under-motivated scheming is equally implausible. The villain is in fact a relatively new character in the anti-jacobin novel. Mrs. West's earlier heroines, like Maria Edgeworth's Julia (*Letters of Literary Ladies*, 1795), Mary Hays's Emma Courtnay, and Jane Austen's Marianne Dashwood, are their own worst enemies.

From about 1799, the victim in these anti-jacobin novels is no longer a single character in error, but the dupe of a villain; and her mistake is seen as something that affects the community as a whole. Unfaithfulness to a husband is linked with ideological infidelity, and, after allowing herself to be seduced, the betrayed girl is seldom allowed to escape expo-sure, decline, and death. Anything short of tragedy would modify the blackness of the crime. Hysteria can be sensed in the sacrifice of so many despoiled virgins, and in the fact that the authors hint at a scale of catastrophe quite outside the scope of the action they have shown. Mrs. West speaks for all of her kind when she exclaims against the permissive notions Fitzosborne advances in his efforts to seduce Geraldine:

When posterity shall know that these principles characterise the close of the eighteenth century, it will cease to wonder at the calamities which history will then have recorded. Such engines are sufficiently powerful to overturn governments, and to shake the deep-founded base of the firmest empires. Should it therefore be told to future ages, that the capricious dissolubility (if not the absolute nullity) of the nuptial tie and the annihilation of parental authority are among the blasphemies uttered by the *moral* instructors of these times . . . they would not ascribe the annihilation of thrones and altars to the arms of France, but to those principles which, by dissolving domestic confidence, and undermining private worth, paved the way for universal confusion.[1]

Pace Mrs. West, her reference to the successful 'arms of France' has given the larger part of her case away. The immediate events which provoked the reaction headed in 1798 by the *Anti-Jacobin* were surely political and military rather than private or theoretical. Since 1793 England had been at war with France, but within the past two years French power had increased to give her mastery of mainland Europe. Bonaparte had overrun Italy and set up the Italian republics. Austria, its power broken, had been forced to cede the Netherlands to France. Spain also had declared war on Britain, which was therefore almost stripped of effective allies and confronted with a formidable array of power across the Channel. At home in 1797 the Bank of England had suspended cash payments, the Fleet had mutinied at Spithead and the Nore, and Ireland was on the verge of rebellion. In December 1797 Bonaparte attacked Switzerland and set up another puppet republic. His boast at Geneva, that he 'would democratise England in three months', did not seem outside the bounds of possibility.

Bonaparte believed that within Britain, both among intellectuals and among the poor, there was unrest of such proportions that mere token support from France might trigger off a national uprising. His two invasions, in Pembrokeshire in 1797 and in Ireland in 1798, were both launched on the assumption that the countryside was already arming. Of course we know with the wisdom of hindsight that he was wrong. The French who landed in Pembrokeshire were met by hostile peasants armed with scythes and billhooks, and surrendered without a shot being fired. Even in Ireland, the French General Humbert was disappointed not merely by the poor quality of the untrained peasants who rose at the signal given by his landing; he noted how far the rebellion was from being universal. And if the peasants were either loyal to the government, or uncertain, so too were the intellectuals.

---

[1] Jane West, *A Tale of the Times*, ii. 275.

Several years of repression had intimidated most of them; but it was more than that. Bonaparte's invasion of Switzerland had an effect on his British intellectual sympathizers similar to the Soviet invasion of Hungary in 1956. Before that, it was possible (if not always easy) to suppose that the foreign power, whether France or Soviet Russia, appeared hostile and aggressive only because provoked by an international league of reactionaries; that her ultimate intentions were to establish an ideal community at home, and to live at peace with her neighbours abroad. After the invasion of a small country whose crime was to claim freedom, support among British intellectuals fell away so sharply that for a few years only a hard core (men like Holcroft) was left; and even they were partially silenced.

That English society was not being undermined from within in 1797–8 is obvious now. But at the time it was far from apparent, and the sense of crisis generated a formidable witch-hunt. We have seen how systematically the *Anti-Jacobin* rounded up the supposed subversives to hold them up to public obloquy. So little contemporary evidence of real jacobin feeling was available that for their principal targets the patriots had to go back a few years, to the era in fact of *Political Justice*. It is very interesting, for example, that *The Anti-Jacobin* devised the fictional figure of 'Mr. Higgins of St. Mary Axe'—i.e. William Godwin—who was supposed to be the author of such heterogeneous literary works as *The Rovers, The Progress of Man,* and *The Loves of the Triangles.*[1] Apart from its purely comic aspect, the device made Godwin into a powerful bogey, and made him seem as current a force in 1798 as he had been in 1793–4. Robert Bisset used the same sleight of hand in his novel *Douglas, or the Highlander,* which he incidentally revealed was set in 1792—in order, clearly, that he could show revolutionary activity at its most flourishing.[2] Whatever the nominal date, the hysteria, the sense of national danger from without and insecurity within, belonged to the era of composition.

From about 1796, the typical anti-jacobin novel is no longer the feminine female-conduct novel by writers like Mrs.

[1] See above, pp. 90   [2] *Douglas,* London, 1800, iii. 83 ff.

West, with its domestic plot familiar since the days of Richardson—who will a young girl marry? A picaresque variant becomes fashionable, usually though not invariably written by a man, and with a male protagonist. The hero—often, quixote-like, deluded by revolutionary ideas—travels the country, meeting grotesque groups of troublemakers, and eventually learning to see society as it is. With the revolutionary novel, the central impulse of the story is the hero–victim's oppression by society. The anti-jacobin plot leads to a climax in which the hero is made aware of his presumption and learns to take his place in the world as it actually is.

Where Mrs. West's tone is gently ironic, her male counterparts are comic or satiric in the broader tradition of Smollett. Much of the humour comes from burlesque treatment of the Godwin circle. For example, in Isaac d'Israeli's *Vaurien*, 1797, the hero Charles comes to London with an introduction to the democratic peer Lord Belfield, at whose home he meets Mr. Subtile (a butcher's son turned clergyman and thence writer); Dr. Bounce ('a square, squat, sullen and volcanic presbyter[1]);' Mr. Rant, an orator; Mr. Libel, the editor of a newspaper; Mr. Dragon, a politician; and Mr. Sympathy, 'who had invented a new religion'. The satire here is personal, for Subtile is meant to be recognizable as Godwin, Bounce as Richard Price, and so on. A similar group appears in most picaresque anti-jacobin novels of the time, and is amusing or not according to the author's lightness of touch. One of the deftest satires of Godwinian opinions occurs, for example, in George Walker's *Vagabond*, 1799, in which the deluded hero Charles Fenton sets off with his tutor Stupeo and another revolutionary, Dr. Alogos, for a utopian existence in America. Their false expectations about the noble savage are neatly satirized in a series of episodes culminating in the occasion when Stupeo is burnt to death by Indians. ('The Indians . . . perfectly reduced the great philosopher, metaphysician and politician to the idea of a few cinders.')[2] The imaginary state the philosophers try to set up may owe something to Coleridgean ideas of pantisocracy, and more to Godwin's sketch

[1] *Vaurien, or Sketches of the Times*, 1797, i. 51.
[2] *The Vagabond*, 3rd ed., London, 1799, ii. 265. For Walker, see below, p. 111.

of the rational society in *Political Justice*. It fails, and Charles returns home in the classic conservative state of disillusionment:

'Experience has qualified me to judge of learning, whose researches have taught me the *paucity* of the human mind: taught me, that in this age of reason, in the eighteenth century, I may exclaim with the learned and polished Socrates—"*All that I know is, that I know nothing.*" '[1]

But the most amusing of the anti-jacobins is perhaps Mrs. Elizabeth Hamilton.[2] She has a nicely conceived fancy in her *Letters of a Hindoo Rajah*, where in order to demonstrate the all-importance of education, her philosophers earnestly set out to train young sparrows to swarm like bees.[3] Her second anti-jacobin novel, *Memoirs of Modern Philosophers*, 1800, has an unusually good caricature in Bridgetina Botherim (a burlesque of Mary Hays's Emma Courtnay), and some happy touches when Bridgetina and her radical friends discuss their plans to settle in primitive felicity among the Hottentots. Two progressive cults, of the noble savage and of the progress of mind, are neatly spitted when Mr. Glib meets the dumpy Bridgetina as she returns from a walk:

'How d'ye do, citizen Miss?' cried he, as soon as he observed her. 'Exerting your energies, I see. That's it! energies do all. Make your legs grow long in a twinkling. Won't then sweep the street in your gown. All owing to this good-for-nothing state of civilisation. No short legs in an enlightened society. All the Hottentots tall and straight as maypoles.'[4]

When they wax serious the anti-jacobins speak with one voice. Favourite themes are sexual passion (to which they are hostile) and the institution of marriage (which they define in a way that minimizes its connection with the sexual act). According to their opponents, revolutionaries never limit

[1] *The Vagabond*, ii. 274–5.
[2] Elizabeth Hamilton, 1758–1816, sister of the orientalist Charles Hamilton (and thus 'Mrs.' only in accordance with the declining 18th-century convention) wrote didactic fiction on a range of subjects, including education and Scottish peasant manners (*The Cottagers of Glenburnie*, 1808). Maria Edgeworth admired her work, and—despite her present company—it is misleading to think of her as rabidly partisan: she is shrewd and moderate in tone.
[3] *Letters of a Hindoo Rajah*, 1796, ii. 227 ff.
[4] *Memoirs of Modern Philosophers*, 3 vols., 4th ed., London, 1804, ii. 226.

themselves to the political sphere: they are also seducers, of more and more deadly a die as the century nears its close. Charles Lloyd's *Edmund Oliver*, 1798, has advice to give on resisting temptation, and on cultivating the virtuous attachment, which sums up the burden of a host of popular novels of its day.

Edmund Oliver, like so many anti-jacobin protagonists, is a character betrayed by excessive, uncontrolled sensibility. Unlike others, he is not a quixote-type, conceived in a spirit of comedy, but a serious portrait; based, moreover, at least in part, on Samuel Taylor Coleridge, to whose circle Lloyd belonged.[1] The episode in which Edmund runs away and joins the army attracts attention, partly because its connection with Coleridge can be documented, partly because the action itself is so piquant, but in reality the sequence, which occurs early in the second volume, is not typical of the rest of the book. It is as hostile to militarism as any jacobin novel: 'it cannot be that you will wear the garb of systematic and deliberate murder, of carnage by wholesale',[2] exclaims a virtuous character on hearing of Edmund's enlistment. As a whole the action of the book has a very different tendency. Edmund has loved a passionate girl of advanced principles, Gertrude; she is now flinging herself into an affair with a revolutionary who turns out to be a hypocrite and an adventurer. (The resemblance of this relationship to Mary Wollstonecroft's with Gilbert Imlay may be more than coincidence.)[3] Edmund's virtuous friend, the clergyman Charles Maurice, repeatedly exhorts him to master his feelings and submit them to the control of reason: ' "If you marry, marry from serious and well-grounded esteem, and not from love. I view your passion with interest, as eliciting the powers of

[1] Lloyd, 1775–1839, son of a Birmingham banker and philanthropist, met Coleridge in 1796 and helped to support him in 1796–7. In 1798 he was closer to Southey, which accounts for the idealized portrait of the latter in *Edmund Oliver*. Lloyd went on writing novels and poetry, none of it of much merit (though de Quincey admired his conversation and his descriptive powers). His last three decades were shadowed with insanity.

[2] *Edmund Oliver*, 2 vols., Bristol, 1798, ii. 34. Edmund Oliver was taken for Coleridge, Charles Maurice for Southey. Cf. W. Haller, *The Early Life of Robert Southey*, New York, 1917, pp. 189–93.

[3] The only original acknowledged for the character of Gertrude is (as so often) Emma Courtnay. *Edmund Oliver*, i. 40n.

your mind; but Heaven grant that you form no connection while under its influence." '1

Marriage seems valuable to Lloyd because it is essentially a social institution which draws the individual out of himself. Gertrude's love affair does the opposite, and, when it ends unhappily, she kills herself. Instructed by this disaster, Edmund makes a highly rational proposal to Edith, in the course of which he explains that marriage

'. . . implies the constant duty of making another happy . . . It calls each soul out of itself—makes it necessarily extend its compass of hopes, and fears; creates the duties of a parent, and evermore presents objects for the tenderest feelings, and most interesting sympathies.'2

Strong feelings are deplorable if and when they encourage the cult of self. The same arguments that can be used of sexual passion can be applied to the worship of Nature. Maurice condemns life in the city, and advocates the country, with an ardour which recalls Rousseau and reminds the reader of the author's membership of Wordsworth's circle. But, like Cowper and Mrs. West, he expresses a Christian, ethical preference for the simple life, which is traditional and essentially conservative, rather than Rousseau's doctrine of self-cultivation. Life in the city is condemned above all for its egotism. ' "The unnatural flocking together of the species hardens and *unsocializes* the heart more perhaps than uniform solitude." '3 Lloyd departs from Godwin at the point where the latter sees the cultivation of the mind, or perfectibility—a process encouraged by living among an urban intelligentsia—as among the highest of all goods. ' "My criterion . . . of virtue would not be extent of mental dimension, but un-debauchedness, and simplicity of taste, and sincerity of intention . . . We can never be happy till we forget ourselves, and, living in surrounding objects, lose our own individuality in benefiting others.—No sceptic can attain this state of self-annihilation." '4

To find Lloyd among conservatives at all is perhaps surprising. But 1798 was a year to shake the heart of the stoutest liberal, as well as those with less lofty motives. George Walker,

1 *Edmund Oliver*, i. 90.   2 Ibid., ii. 2.
3 Ibid., i. 101.   4 Ibid., ii. 104 and 106–7.

1772–1847, is a convenient barometer of public opinion, for, as a bookseller himself, he evidently knew what sold. He begins his writing career in the early 1790s in the manner of Mrs. Radcliffe; with *Theodore Cyphon, or the Benevolent Jew*, 1795, he is echoing the manner and (mildly) the opinions of Godwin; but his *Vagabond*, 1799, is the epitome of conservatism.[1] Just as Mrs. West is more strident in 1799 than in 1796, so the genial Mrs. Hamilton becomes noticeably severer in tone towards her miscreants. In *Letters of a Hindoo Rajah* she shows mercy towards the romantic novel-reading Julia, who allows herself to be taken in (despite the warnings of a Christian aunt) by a 'hero of exalted sentiment and tender sensibility'.[2] But the heroine of the same name[3] in *Memoirs of Modern Philosophers* is a tragic female quixote to reinforce the perhaps too light-hearted impression made by Bridgetina. Brought up by a father who has an over-individual, personal moral code, the soldierly notion of honour, and by an indolent mother (very much a Lady Bertram), this Julia lacks the backbone Christianity would have given her, and is taken in by the revolutionary scoundrel, Vallaton. When the exemplary Harriet Orwell urges on her the merit of an external rule of conduct, such as Christianity offers, Julia reflects 'how much more noble to be guided solely by the suggestions of reason and virtue in our own breasts'.[4] Yet Julia is able to recognize that in Bridgetina idealistic speculation has led to myopic selfishness and self-delusion. 'Under the idea of cultivating *mind*, she had only been encouraging the mischievous chimeras of a teeming imagination.'[5] Julia falls into the equivalent error herself, is seduced, and dies heart-broken, though, at the last, enlightened. It is the typical anti-jacobin plot—indeed, the typical Jane Austen plot—but painted in the lurid colours of the years of violent reaction.

For an inveterate extremist spirit, however, of a kind that the female domestic novelists never approach, two novels of

---

[1] See above, p. 107.   [2] *Letters of a Hindoo Rajah*, ii. 337.

[3] The name Julia, usually ominous in conservative novels after 1790, of course derives from Rousseau (and perhaps Mackenzie). Both Maria Edgeworth and Jane Austen use it for over-indulged characters. Marianne, another name with similar associations, perhaps goes back to Marivaux's *Vie de Marianne*.

[4] *Memoirs of Modern Philosophers*, ii. 48.   [5] Ibid., ii. 96.

the turn of the century can be taken as typical. Robert Bisset's *Douglas, or the Highlander*, 1800, is interesting chiefly for rooting out its enemies with the wholesale thoroughness of *The Anti-Jacobin*.[1] 'The Object of my attempt is British Society; to draw the intellectual and moral virtues, by the operation of which it is upheld, and to mark the follies and vices by which it is disturbed.'[2] Accordingly, Bisset is not content with extrapolating his philosophers (William Subtle-would, etc.) out of their real social context into a fantasy-land, as George Walker does, or even with the degree of selectivity displayed by d'Israeli. His hero Charles Douglas, first soundly trained in Scottish empiricism, stalks formidably about the sister kingdom, assembling a list of those 'who would annihilate government, order, property and morals'.[3] He includes among his thorough researches the political opponents of the French war, headed by Fox and Sheridan;[4] the notoriously dissipated fourth Duke of Queensberry ('Old Quondam'[5]); and a host of feminine littérateurs, hangers-on of the revolutionary side, among whom he evidently takes Charlotte Smith most seriously.[6] True to the spirit of *The Anti-Jacobin*, which probes deep into the implications of apparently apolitical works, he finds dangerous moral laxity in Sheridan's *The School for Scandal*.[7] Bisset detects behind Godwin, the live philosopher, Hume the dead one—Hume the arch-sceptic and destroyer of systems, Hume the student of the irrational and intuitive mental processes. Even Plato is arraigned, with the aid of Aristotle, the philosopher of experience; for Bisset is bent on rooting out the visionary or theoretical, and on laying the blame for Britain's danger fairly at the door of these intellectuals who 'either weakly or

[1] Bisset, 1759–1805, lawyer, historian, and master of an academy in Sloane Street, Chelsea, was a busy polemicist of the post-revolutionary era. His *Sketch of Democracy*, 1796, aimed to show by a survey of the democratic states of ancient times that democracy is a vicious form of government. He wrote a *Life of Burke*, 1798, and a *History of George III*, 1804. A pamphlet in the British Museum, 'A Defence of the Slave Trade', 1804, has also been attributed to him.

[2] Robert Bisset, *Douglas, or the Highlander*, 4 vols., London, 1800, Introduction, p. xxiv.

[3] Ibid., iii. 33.   [4] Ibid., iii. 36.   [5] Ibid., iii. 116 ff.

[6] Ibid., iii. 37 and iii. 303 ff. The second passage compares Mrs. Smith's novels at length and unfavourably with those of the more conservative Ann Radcliffe and Fanny Burney.

[7] Ibid., iii. 111–14. See above, p. 22.

wickedly erred from not bringing their doctrines to the TEST
OF INDUCTIONS'.[1] It is hard to believe that any other
novel could better exemplify that unprecedented spirit of
bitter partisanship, which so harshly sniffed out subversion
in the work of the unwary or inexperienced, and both cramped
and disfigured literary life for at least a generation.

A more eccentric and if anything more hysterical performance is Charles Lucas's *Infernal Quixote*, 1801.[2] The novel
begins with an awkward pastiche of Sterne, and thereafter
often appears to be borrowing from Bisset, but eventually
Lucas settles down to develop his original central idea. He
has picked out from *Political Justice* that remarkably pregnant
comment by Godwin about Milton's Satan, that he can only
be interpreted as a being of considerable virtue:

'It must be admitted that his energies centered too much in personal
regards. But why did he rebel against his maker? It was, as he
himself informs us, because he saw no sufficient reason, for that
extreme inequality of rank and power, which the creator assumed.
It was because prescription and precedent form no adequate ground
for implicit faith . . .'[3]

Godwin's observation was provocative enough to supply
inspiration to Shelley, and as it stands seems much more
interesting than the strained fantasy which Lucas bases upon
it. Lucas's rather inadequate burlesque of the idea of Satan-
as-hero is contained in the figure of Lord James Marauder,
who catches the contagion of French atheism and at home
sets himself up to be literally diabolical. After the usual
adventures among philosophers and schismatics, and the
equally obligatory seduction of an innocent girl, Marauder
helps to plunge a whole country into chaos by joining the
United Irishmen and fostering the Rebellion of 1798. His

[1] *Douglas*, iii. 33.
[2] Lucas, 1769–1854, miscellaneous writer, was curate of Avebury in Wilt-
shire from 1791, and wrote a descriptive account in blank verse of the pre-
historic monuments there (1795). The rage for ideological novel-writing also
evoked from him *The Castle of St. Donats*, 1798.
[3] *Political Justice*, i. 323–4. Quoted in *Infernal Quixote*, 4 vols., London, 1801,
i. 325–7n. For a discussion of the interest of Godwin and Blake in Milton, and
the possible exchange of ideas between them, see R. Sharrock, 'Godwin and
Milton's Satan', *Notes and Queries*, ccvii (1962), 463–5.

intention, Lucas declares, is 'the introduction of that no-principle of the French, which seeks the gratification of its own interest, without any regard to the laws of God or man, and which has already been so fully defined under the term DIABOLISM'.[1]

Defined like this, diabolism becomes little more than that spirit of self-assertion and self-reliance all along seen by the anti-jacobin side as the converse of pious Christian submission to the existing codes of Church and State. And yet Lucas contributes something by focusing squarely on this increasingly significant figure, the villain who consciously and deliberately serves evil—a composite portrait which means much to the anti-jacobin side between the crisis of 1797–8 and the Peace of Amiens in 1802.

The anti-jacobin villain cannot of course be isolated from other villains of his time; it is odd only to find him flourishing in a picaresque novel, and within the context of an assault upon the world of private imaginings. Mrs. Radcliffe's Montoni or Schedoni seem more convincingly placed, in a setting remote in time and place, and in the course of a story frankly designed to appeal to the emotions rather than to the intellect. The nearest prototype for Lucas's infernal villain is probably Lewis's Ambrosio the Monk. The last-named exerts a powerful hold on the popular imagination from the year of his appearance, 1796; and incongruous though he may be in the would-be rational universe of the anti-jacobins, it is really not surprising to find half-conscious fears of conspiracy, betrayal, the irrational itself, taking on the features of the favourite bogey of the day.

The development of the gigantic, sinister figure, the man of mystery, is one of the most fascinating strands of the literature of the period. He comes into English literature principally in translations from German between 1794 and 1796: Benedict Naubert's *Hermann of Unna*, translated 1794; Schiller's *Ghost-Seer* (with its archetypal Armenian), the first half of which was translated in 1795; Cajetan Schink's *Victim of Magical Delusions . . . a magico-political tale*, translated 1796; and Marquis Grosse's *Genius*, better known in England

[1] *Infernal Quixote*, iii. 182.

under the title of one translation of 1796, *Horrid Mysteries*. The full story of the evolution of these sinister, tormented, and yet at moments attractive figures is too long to be told here.[1] What matters most perhaps is that in their original German context they are generally associated with a secret society—whether this is the repressive Jesuits or Inquisition, or the revolutionary Freemasons or Illuminati, scarcely affects the standardized manner of treatment. Clearly, though, in Germany, where the vogue originated, the theme has profound connotations. On the one hand the *anciens régimes* of Europe are readily seen in terms of a vast conspiracy, maintained in position by the evil engines of a decadent aristocracy and the Catholic Church. Among the most familiar Gothic trappings of these novels are the dungeons of a wicked oligarchy, and much of the power of their sinister figures derives at least indirectly from a sense of fear and repression: the majority of the villains are associated with the old order, and are monks, tyrants, father-figures. Not always, however. After the French Revolution the image of the Bastille is replaced by the even more ghastly image of the guillotine, and the conservative imagination also becomes possessed by the idea of an evil conspiracy. The secret societies of the period become less clearly defined and perhaps even more terrifying, a band of dedicated fanatics bent on drawing the innocent into their clutches as a step towards augmenting their power and influence. The fascination felt by writers of all opinions for secret societies, identified or not identified, contemporary or historical, is a symptom of the instability and political hysteria felt throughout Europe in the 1790s.[2] But if the Society is associated with unadulterated terror, the figure of the powerful individual associated with it is more ambivalent. The Germans especially feel the strong imaginative appeal of human assertion, of greatness for its own sake. With Karl Moor, Schiller launches the figure of the noble robber and outlaw, the evil-doer whose crimes have far more grandeur

[1] See J. M. S. Tompkins, *The Popular Novel in England, 1770–1800*, pp. 278–280.

[2] Scott, whose apprentice work was under German influence, was fascinated by the medieval German secret society, which makes an appearance in two of his plays—*The House of Aspen* (1799–1800) and his translation of Goethe's *Götz von Berlichingen* (1799).

than those of the leaders of society who drove him out.[1]
Goethe's Faust is another emblem of the same heroic rebel.
A generation later Byron makes the figure of the tormented
outcast his own, but in the 1790s the most powerful English
attempt is probably Godwin's. His St. Leon, hero of his second
novel, 1799, is a Faust-figure who has found the secret of
eternal life, and finds himself tragically cut off by his unique-
ness from the rest of human-kind. Godwin is too convinced a
liberal to be in any doubt who is plotting against whom, and
his secret society is the Spanish Inquisition which throws St.
Leon into gaol. And yet his rebel-figure is an extremely pessimistic conception, which conveys the message that his superiority to the rest of his species is in suffering more, and longer,
without the possibility of release by death. Moreover, in the
same novel, the gigantic and misanthropic Bethlem Gabor
who also imprisons St. Leon, embodies many of the ambivalent strands of the mighty villain–hero: at once great
hero and great tyrant, rebel and oppressor, man and monster.

For the English anti-jacobins the issue begins, at least, by
seeming more clear-cut. A rebel cannot be the hero to them
that he represents to German or English liberals. Nor do
they find an intellectual difficulty in seeing cleverness like
Faust's or St. Leon's as a bad thing. It is, after all, an aspect
of the reliance on self, and the anti-jacobins believe that the
wisest of all insights is the discovery of one's own ignorance.
And so they tend in their novels to make villains of their intellectuals, both male and (occasionally) female. They are aided
by the theory, suddenly very popular as Bonaparte swept into
Italy, Switzerland, and the Low Countries in 1797, that there
was a far-reaching and centuries-old conspiracy of liberal
intellectuals to bring revolution throughout Europe.[2] Topi-

---

[1] Schiller's *Robbers* was one of the most influential books of the period,
formative for the plays of the first English Romantics (Wordsworth's *Borderers*
and Coleridge's *Remorse*), and highly significant for Byron's. For the political
adjustments which occur when the robber–hero is translated into English, see
Margaret Cooke, 'Schiller's *Robbers* in England', *MLR*, ii (1916), 170–1.

[2] The Abbé Barruel, *Mémoires pour servir a l'histoire du Jacobinisme* (1797–
1798), maintained that the French Revolution was brought about by an
'interacting conspiracy of the philosophers against religion, the Freemasons
against kings, and Illuminists . . . against society'. J. M. S. Tompkins, *The
Popular Novel in England, 1770–1800*, p. 283. A book on the same theme in
English, John Robison's *Proofs of a Conspiracy against all the Religions and*

cally, the anti-jacobin villain is usually either French or has been to France,[1] but wartime chauvinism contributes less to the portrait than ideology. The philosopher's real crimes are his impiety in setting himself above law and custom, and his cynical cruelty in wishing to mislead innocent youth.

And yet, such is the intractable capacity of imaginative insight once it takes on form, that even the anti-jacobins, with their relatively simple row to hoe, become nearly as ambivalent as their opponents. It is true that the rebel is for them *per se* an evil-doer; but at that point the period's love of a villain begins to manifest itself.[2] The anti-jacobins, most of them too trivial to make real use of their borrowed tools, nevertheless betray signs of the contemporary fascination for a great energy bent on destruction. D'Israeli's Vaurien is easily the most attractive character in the book named after him; Lord James Marauder eclipses everyone else in *The Infernal Quixote*.

But the chilling figure of a demon-philosopher backed by a revolutionary conspiracy is one thing; the literal presence of William Godwin and the London Corresponding Society quite another. Incongruity comes perilously near to comedy on the issue of sex. Mary Wollstonecraft first provoked her opponents with her *Vindication of the rights of Woman*, and then, in her *Letters written during a short residence in Sweden, Norway and Denmark*, 1796, she alluded fairly plainly to her relations with Imlay and to the illegitimacy of their child. In the same year her friend Mary Hays brought out *The Memoirs of Emma Courtnay*, which was read as condoning sexual licence for women, and as such attracted more remonstrance than any other individual revolutionary novel. Godwin set the seal on his circle's notoriety by publishing his *Memoirs of the author of a Vindication of the Rights of Woman,*

Governments of Europe, carried on in the Secret Meetings of Free Masons, Illuminati and Reading Societies (1797) supplied Godwin with material for *St. Leon* and Maria Edgeworth for her unpublished play *Whim for Whim* (for which see below, p. 138).

[1] e.g. d'Israeli's Vaurien (a French spy), D'Oyley in Charles Lloyd's *Edmund Oliver*, Fitzosborne in Mrs. West's *Tale of the Times*, and Vallaton in Mrs. Hamilton's *Memoirs of Modern Philosophers*. Henry James Pye's *The Democrat*, 1795, is an earlier specimen of the novel about a French libertarian who visits England.   [2] See above, p. 15.

1799, in which he described the liaison with Imlay, and also gave details of how he and Mary decided to live together before marriage.[1] The emancipated girl convinced of her right to pre-marital sexual intercourse becomes the second standard target of the conservative novelist; she appears as Gertrude in *Edmund Oliver*, Julia (and Bridgetina) in *Memmoirs of a Modern Philosopher*, Maria Cloudley in *The Infernal Quixote*,[2] and, later, as Amelia Opie's Adeline Mowbray and Maria Edgeworth's Olivia.[3] She is, of course, the obvious partner for the hypnotic philosopher, as most of these examples illustrate; and from 1799 it must have seemed providential to the conservative propagandist that the nation's leading radical philosopher and its leading feminist had made public their contempt for the sacred institution of marriage. The anti-jacobins' usual manner, a rather flat naturalism, coupled with their too ready habit of annotation from real life, ensures that the Godwin–Wollstonecraft scandal is never far from their readers' minds. The image of Mary, with her woes, her wrongs, and her deeply pathetic (or retributive) death in childbed, is no bad one for the imaginative writer to conjure with.[4] Her husband, 'Mr. Higgins of St. Mary Axe', has rightly or wrongly other reverberations. It is more than once belittling to these feverish productions at the turn of the century, that, superimposed upon their vast and shadowy demons, there appears the small figure of a

[1] Godwin's *Memoirs* are referred to by Robert Bisset as 'his history of the life, literary and amorous adventures of his spouse' (*Douglas*, iii. 94n.); and by Charles Lucas as 'The History of the Intrigues of his Own Wife' (*Infernal Quixote*, i. 171). Godwin's passage describing why he and Mary did not marry is a favourite one for quotation by his opponents: 'Nothing can be so ridiculous . . . as to require the overflowing of the soul to wait upon a ceremony, and that which, wherever delicacy and imagination exist, is of all things most sacredly private, to blow a trumpet before it, and to record the moment when it has arrived at its climax' (pp. 154–5). (The syntax of this passage cannot easily be defended. See above, p. 74.)

[2] After her elopement, Mrs. Cloudley confesses that her children, who have names like Brutus, Voltaire, and Tom Pain (*sic*), are all the offspring of different fathers. (*Infernal Quixote*, iii. 205.)

[3] In *Leonora*. See below, pp. 149 ff.

[4] Death in childbed is a convenient punishment for a female lapse from virtue, and is much invoked by the popular novelist. See above, p. 104. The Rev. R. Polwhele found Mary Wollstonecraft's own death singularly appropriate. (*The Unsexed Females*, 1798, cited J. M. S. Tompkins, *The Popular Novel in England, 1770–1800*, p. 316.)

retiring man of letters known to live a frugal and well-ordered life in the St. Pancras district.

Like most lesser artists in all periods, the anti-jacobins could not resolve the conflicting literary pressures upon them. Just as their opponents earlier in the decade wished to exalt the nature and powers of man, but were involuntarily swept along by an irresistible suspicion of sentiment,[1] so the anti-jacobins, who wished to recommend common sense and conformity, paid unwilling tribute to the power and fascination of the superhuman individual. The predominant subconscious literary and intellectual fashion proved stronger than the partial needs of a faction. For this reason, revolutionary and conservative literature shared common features between 1798 and 1802, as between 1791 and 1794. Afterwards a misconception spread abroad—accepted for example by Scott—that *The Anti-Jacobin*'s parody, *The Rovers*, had at once succeeded in killing the vogue for German drama.[2] On the contrary, the German drama, like the German ballad, reached the peak of its mushroom popularity precisely in the period, 1798–1802, when the conservative campaign was most frenzied.

In this upheaval of popular taste one general truth emerges. While a weakness for the feverish appears everywhere, the form it took in the provinces and in Scotland was more liberal than in London. This was largely a continuation of a discernible tendency throughout the second half of the eighteenth century. The English provincial centres—Manchester, Liverpool, Derby, Lichfield, Birmingham, Norwich, Bristol—all had their coteries of littérateurs, or their Literary and Philosophical Societies, and, especially where the manufacturing interest predominated, they tended to be liberal in tone. From the 1760s to the end of the century, provincial writers were noticeably more free-thinking than run-of-the-mill contemporaries in the capital: Bage and Erasmus Darwin in the Midlands; the most knowledgeable of all the German translators, William Taylor, in Norwich; the Coleridge–Southey circle which settled in Bristol. The same hardy strain of

[1] See above, pp. 32 ff.
[2] Advertisement to *The House of Aspen*, 1829: *Poetical Works*, Edinburgh, 1880, xii. 367.

liberalism held out for a while in Scotland. Between 1798 and 1802, the vogue for Kotzebue raged north of the border as it did south,[1] and, although cautious doubts were certainly heard in Edinburgh about German morality, the more bipartisan intellectual atmosphere of the Scottish capital allowed clever young men an open mind. M. G. Lewis was in Scotland putting together his collections of translations from German ballads, and among those whose enthusiasm he stimulated was the young Walter Scott. The latter's conservatism—at the same time he was training diligently as a Volunteer to defend the country from invasion—did not operate until later to curb his admiration for Goethe and Herder. By then the first important fruits of this admiration had appeared—his own brilliant collection of native ballads, *The Minstrelsy of Scottish Border*, 1802, and his apprentice efforts at historical writing, the plays based on German models such as Goethe's *Götz von Berlichingen*.[2] Scott's mature work evolved naturally out of German progressive writing; that of his great English contemporary, Jane Austen, belonged squarely to the reaction against it.

On the whole the novel falls sooner and more decisively into the counter-revolutionary camp than poetry or drama. There are a number of reasons for this. Novels are written to sell on a substantial scale, whereas poetry, a more private activity, can afford to reflect its author's personal imaginative insights. Therefore the novel is likely to be more sensitive than other forms of writing to a strong tide of public opinion. Furthermore, the setting of the novel in contemporary society more or less forces it into sensitive areas. Conventional eighteenth-century fictional issues, like the conflict between child and parent, especially over the choice of husband or wife, could hardly steer clear of the key controversies of the day. A poem on a lesser celandine might pass as politically and morally neutral (although, as we have seen, some critics thought Simplicity and Nature subversive concepts,

[1] Especially in 1799 and 1800. See David Lindsay, 'Kotzebue in Scotland', *Proceedings of the English Goethe Society*, no. xxxiii (1962–3), 56 ff.

[2] Scott translated various ballads, including *William and Helen*, from Burger's *Lenore*, and four plays, including *Götz* (for the others, see Duncan M. Mennie, 'Sir Walter Scott's unpublished Translations of German plays', *MLR* xxxiii (1938)).

at least when conjoined). A novel could hardly avoid overtly taking sides. Before the critics or the public even had a chance to scrutinize it, it had to win the approval of a book-seller, and the great majority of novels were published in the politically cautious capital. No manifestly jacobin novel had appeared in London since 1796. It was a sign of the nervous times that in 1798–9 Joseph Johnson, the publisher of God-win, Mary Wollstonecraft, and, among others, Blake and the Edgeworths, spent ten months in prison for publishing a so-called seditious pamphlet against the conservative Bishop of Llandaff. Other publishers were unwilling to risk the same fate. The pressures that led to censorship of the novel were greater than for any other art-form. Apart perhaps from the courageous Godwin, no novelist eventually resisted them.

A striking example of the insidious spread of reaction is supplied by Amelia Opie. Mrs. Opie, wife of the painter John Opie and friend in the 1790s of Godwin, published in 1804 a novel called *Adeline Mowbray, or Mother and Daughter*, which demonstrates how fully liberals now came back into the con-formist fold. After an indulgent education, its heroine, Ade-line, becomes an enthusiastic reader of Glenmurray, a philo-sopher writing against marriage. She meets him, falls in love with him, and insists not on marriage but on cohabitation, in keeping with the principles of his book. Glenmurray tries to dissuade her, since, as he foresees, their friends, and even her own mother will not receive her when she is his kept mistress. Adeline, who wishes to 'act independently of society, and serve it by our example even against its will',[1] survives all its cruel challenges, but is at last abashed by the rebuke of a Quaker lady: ' "Thou art one of those wise in their own conceit, who disregarding the customs of ages, and the dictates of experience, set up their own opinions against the hallowed institutions of man and the will of the Most High." '[2]

Glenmurray's death leaves her wretchedly exposed, and at last, in extreme misery, she pines away in her mother's arms. It is, in short, the usual cautionary tale of the anti-jacobins, with the full cast-list of emancipated female and seductive philosopher; and only the relative amiability, the real if wrong-headed idealism of the principals, reveals that the

---

[1] Amelia Opie, *Adeline Mowbray*, 3 vols., 1805, ii. 83.   [2] Ibid., ii. 113.

author was once a friend of Godwin's, and something near to a prototype of Adeline.

For Jane Austen it was different. The daughter and sister of clergymen of the Established Church, she began life in the conservative fold, and even as a teenager was the author of a satire on sensibility, *Love and Friendship*. Two of her first completed novels, *Sense and Sensibility* and *Northanger Abbey* (both of them in draft by 1798), display broadly the typical attitudes of the feminine type of conservative novel. Of the two, *Northanger Abbey* has the Gothic concern fashionable from 1794 to 1798, though it manages to avoid its period's hysteria. *Pride and Prejudice*, written as *First Impressions* between October 1796 and April 1797, has many of the same formal features as its contemporaries. These three novels are constructed, like Mrs. West's, around the contrasted characters of two or three young women. The key issue on which virtue is distinguished from vice is the choice of a marriage-partner. The key virtues are prudence and concern for the evidence; the vices are romanticism, self-indulgence, conceit, and, for Jane Austen, other subtle variations upon the broad anti-jacobin target of individualism.

Significantly, Jane Austen seems not to have conceived new work in the years in which her fellow-conservatives were at their most hysterical: she was silent from 1799 to 1802, and there is no Austen equivalent to Mrs. West's *Tale of the Times*. In a work of uncertain date, *Lady Susan*, she does attempt a villain, a cruising shark in her social goldfish pond.[1] With her charm and irresistible air of up-to-date fashion, Lady Susan is the female counterpart of the male seducers of the later anti-jacobin period. Interestingly, the first of Jane Austen's novels which seems to have originated wholly after the anti-jacobin period has the most numerous echoes of its motifs. In *Mansfield Park* the fascinating and fashionable Crawfords bring a threat of anarchy to the English country house, as Fitzosborne brought subversion to

---

[1] Family tradition has *Lady Susan* as 'an early production'. The manuscript, a fair copy, includes two leaves watermarked 1805, and Dr. Chapman suggests that it may have been composed about that date (*Facts and Problems*, Oxford, 1948, p. 52). B. C. Southam inclines to a much earlier date, perhaps 1793–5: *Jane Austen's Literary Manuscripts*, Oxford, 1964, pp. 45–6.

the Monteith household, or Lord James Marauder to the country as a whole. This novel contains what for Jane Austen are unusually clear allusions to the ideological background of the period: Fanny's Christianity is explicitly opposed to the Crawfords' cynical materialism, and, for once, in the inclusion of Kotzebue's radical play, there is a direct association between the villains and the new philosophy.[1] *Emma* and *Persuasion* present their issues in more idiosyncratic terms, and yet their central ethical insights remain those of the distinctive anti-jacobin kind. Perhaps, above all, these last three novels reveal a sense of a hazard to the larger community which distinguishes them from the earlier group: the heroine's ethical choices no longer solely affect her private happiness in life, but are subtly interlinked with the stability and well-being of her society. In this too they reflect the broadening and deepening of range given to the conservative cause in the years 1797–8 by the critical turn in the war, and by the articulate leadership of *The Anti-Jacobin*. Whatever their actual date of composition, they belong generically, like all Jane Austen's works, to a movement that defines itself by its opposition to revolution.

[1] See below, pp. 232–6.

CHAPTER 5

MARIA EDGEWORTH

N OT always successfully, the so-called Jacobin novelist seeks to dramatize and give value to the individual. He believes in the reality of the external social world, but he views it with hostility, and presents it angled through a single consciousness: it is an environment which at best puts pressure on his hero, at worst imprisons him. His opponents are, at first, insignificant artists, and even less inclined to experiment to find a format; but, from existing types of novel, they take devices which best give effect to a conservative philosophy. Their social panoramas are broader, more objective: although the same central character surveys each scene, there is seldom a hint that the impression the reader receives has been modified by the idiosyncrasies of the hero's vision. In the conservative novel, society itself is the real hero. The most typical plot has the central character, gradually schooled to objective reality, renouncing the private delusions that once tempted him to see the world other than it is.

Judged by these criteria, Maria Edgeworth is unquestionably a jacobin. And yet, in spite of her opinions, and the unusual clarity with which they are presented, her novels do not belong unequivocally to one side. She is far more nearly bi-partisan than Jane Austen, who begins to write about the same time. We think of Maria Edgeworth, and Walter Scott, as more 'political' than Jane Austen, because one is obviously serious-minded, the other known in life to have been an active Tory. The fact remains that neither wrote novels as typical of one side or the other as Jane Austen's are. In Maria Edgeworth's case this certainly does not mean that the novels are untouched by the current controversies. It was impossible to be untouched by them: it was possible only to avoid fixed preconceptions about the answers. A more dedicated intellectual than Jane Austen, and through a combination of circumstances largely cut off from prior conditioning by her class, Maria Edgeworth found her own route to the contemporary battle-ground.

Her father, Richard Lovell Edgeworth, was the main intellectual influence in her life. After a flirtation with the writings of Rousseau, he had moved into a circle of Midlands industrialists and inventors, one which also included Bage, and his ideas had taken a characteristically practical, empirical turn. In politics he was a liberal, in all intellectual matters an individualist: and the mind of the daughter he educated inevitably took on the same colouring as his.

Away at Edgeworthstown in Ireland during the 1790s, the family took the liberal, rather scientific *Monthly Magazine*, and latterly the even more scientific *Nicholson's Journal*. Edgeworth had no intellectual friends in London, and in 1795 he was still telling correspondents in the provinces of his general sympathy with the French Revolution. 'America is a dreary unsociable puritanical abode—When peace permits if it ever will permit everybody who can speak French and who loves Freedom will go there.'[1] Later, however, with the rise of Bonaparte and the threat to national security, Edgeworth, like almost all English liberals, ceased to approve of France. The danger of invasion was far more real in Ireland than anywhere else. In December 1796 a small French fleet arrived off Bantry Bay, and in 1798 General Humbert's army actually landed near Galway. Edgeworth responded to the alarms with typical ingenuity and energy, by offering the government his invention of a telegraph, and drilling a corps of yeomanry on his estate. However, at the news that the French were approaching, the Catholic peasantry of County Longford rose, and, like the other gentry, the Edgeworths had to flee for their lives into the Protestant town of Longford. There the danger was so real that the French campfires could clearly be seen from the walls.

Here, then, was the very situation that so haunted the feverish imagination of the anti-jacobins. Edgeworth's reaction was coolly detached: he had contributed (or tried to contribute) to Ireland's defence, but he was publicly critical of an incompetent, corrupt Administration,[2] and he considered

---

[1] RLE to Erasmus Darwin, 2 Mar. 1795; see M. Butler, *Maria Edgeworth*, Oxford, 1972, p. 111.

[2] In his pamphlet *A Letter . . . on the Tellograph and on the Defence of Ireland*, 1797. See *Maria Edgeworth*, p. 122.

that the agrarian unrest of the past few years had been severely provoked by Orange petty tyranny. In fact, his refusal to share the loyalist hysteria was so noticeable that the Protestant mob of the town of Longford concluded Edgeworth was a traitor. The day that the French were decisively beaten, a few miles away near Granard, a drunken crowd tried to lynch him.

It was the decisive experience of the crisis for Maria Edgeworth. She was certainly not disloyal to her own class, the Protestant Anglo-Irish: her father considered himself first and foremost an Englishman, and Maria was more timid and more conventional than he. Nevertheless, she took the real lesson of 1798 to be the evil of mob feeling. She had seen with her own eyes how a rational, well-intentioned individual could be browbeaten by a tyrannical majority. The individualism she had been taught as a creed was reinforced by the experience of seeing a hysterical reaction at work. Her early fiction has a common theme, of opposition to that upper-class herd-instinct that expects unthinking conformism to a received view. The fiction she published in the period of active controversy, from 1795 to 1801, entitles her to be called the most thorough-going individualist writing outside the jacobin movement.

Maria Edgeworth's first published work, *Letters for Literary Ladies*, came out in 1795 just as the anti-jacobin reaction was beginning. It includes three pieces, the first of which (*A Letter from a Gentleman to his friend upon the birth of his daughter, with the answer*) touches—though innocently—on some of the most hotly disputed issues of the day. A debate on the merits of feminism, it is based on a twelve-year-old exchange of letters between R. L. Edgeworth and his friend Thomas Day.[1] The topic under discussion had been whether Maria should be an authoress. Day, an ardent disciple of Rousseau, shared his master's opinion that women should be soft and passive, in accordance with what he took to be 'natural' femininity; whereas Edgeworth, like Bage and afterwards the feminists of the early 1790s, strongly advo-

---

[1] The date of this correspondence was probably 1783. See *Memoirs of Richard Lovell Edgeworth*, 1820, ii. 342, and *Maria Edgeworth*, p. 149.

cated the right of women to self-realization. The reply based on Edgeworth's letter—which Maria obviously agreed with—defends female education and argues that it should be in all essentials the same as men's. In her first published piece of writing, therefore, earnest and stiff as it is, Maria Edgeworth sketches out an ideological position based on the rights of individuals, and the value of the conscious mind.

Edgeworthian feminism has occasionally in recent times been misunderstood and even denied.[1] A woman like Mary Wollstonecraft, of the middle classes and financially dependent, spent much of her energy as a feminist arguing against the economic injustices suffered by women: the terribly limited opportunities for employment, the low wages of governesses, the wife's loss of property rights. The Edgeworths were of the relatively wealthy landed gentry, and they were probably insufficiently aware of the importance of the economic discrimination against women. But it is certainly not out of any desire to limit feminine scope that Maria Edgeworth makes her model women daughters, wives, and mothers rather than wage-earners; except, that is, when she consciously sets her story in a class well below her own.[2] She takes the domestic setting of her upper-class female characters for granted, just as in these early social comedies she makes their brothers, husbands, and fathers landed gentlemen rather than members of a profession. She is not, after all, campaigning for female rights, but attempting to make through fiction certain moral discriminations of a more personal and inward kind. The gentry as she sees them face a choice of role. They may be content to be social parasites, the mindless slaves of pleasure and fashion. Alternatively they can choose to live as active, rational beings, bent on ordering and leading their own small sphere. Rightly or wrongly, she believes the parent can determine the character of the child. Like other progressives in the period, she wants

---

[1] eg. by Claire Tomalin, *Mary Wollstonecraft*, London, 1974, p. 243.
[2] Where she writes about tradespeople and farmers, as for example in *Popular Tales*, she stresses the need for women as well as men to learn a trade in order to be morally independent. The same point is made about workpeople in *Madame de Fleury* (one of the *Tales of Fashionable Life*, 1st series, 1809). Her refusal to consider women as requiring in any sense special treatment or protection is in fact strikingly liberated for the period.

to see the assertion of the conscious will, and a planned programme of education is a method of mastering the all-important element of the environment.[1] But, as well as leading their family and household, her men and women are also landlords and heads of the local community. In all these roles, where they govern instead of being governed in their turn by a fashionable ambiance, the husband and wife are equal. Or rather, Maria Edgeworth wants them to be equal, and she sees nothing to prevent it but women's inadequate education. Her father taught her to accept the irrational in human behaviour as an observed fact. Only education can overcome the strength of habit, or the unthinking acceptance of common goals: and women, because they are not educated, are commonly the slaves of fashion. More subtly, they play on a cunning intuitive knowledge of human nature to get their own way, not realizing that in giving themselves over to irrationality it is they, rather than their husbands, who become enslaved. Feminine irrationality in argument is satirized in the last of the three component parts of *Letters for Literary Ladies, An Essay on the Noble Science of Self-Justification*.[2] It is an amusing burlesque of feminine stupidity, built on a well-concealed foundation of serious reading. The female sophists are slyly allowed to adorn their arguments with references to a passage of Rousseau on involuntary habits, and to a passage of Hume on association.

But in relation both to her thinking, and to her later development as a novelist, Maria Edgeworth's most interesting early work is the remaining part of *Letters for Literary Ladies, Letters of Julia and Caroline*. Very much a product of its time, this novella in letters could easily at a superficial glance have emanated from the anti-jacobin school. One correspondent is Julia,[3] beautiful, ardent, well-meaning, but a great reader of sentimental literature, and an opponent of all kinds of rational analysis—'Dear Caroline, is it not enough

---

[1] See above, pp. 52–3.

[2] The *Essay* afterwards became the basis for a tale, *The Modern Griselda*, 1805, in which there is a fully developed portrait of a female sophist.

[3] For the associations of this Christian name, see above, p. 111n. Maria Edgeworth has a particularly strong sense of the significance of names, using the same ones again and again. Her Helens and Carolines are all rational, for example; and Percy, Percival, Temple, and Russell are promising surnames.

that I *do* feel?' Not nearly enough, of course, for Maria Edgeworth. But as soon as Julia's friend Caroline sets out to
reason with her, the story diverges from more conservative
treatments of sense-and-sensibility.

Essentially, Julia's sensibility is a form of passivity. Her
object in life is to please, and, as Caroline points out, she is
undiscriminating about whom she pleases. In admiring sentimental literature, with its play upon pity and other involuntary emotions, she indulges a *'passive sensation'*, disconnected
from 'the active desire to relieve'.[1] When the crucial choice
arrives, that of a husband, she proves incapable of ordering
her life in the way that will make her happy. Caroline puts
the issue before her forcibly (if, one may think, rather un-
equally). She must decide between Lord V—— and a fashionable life in town, and Caroline's brother Mr. Percy, with
whom she would have a retired domesticated existence. The
fashionable life is seen as a pursuit of externals, involving
the loss both of self-sufficiency, and of the opportunity to
cultivate inner resources—'You must renounce all the
pleasures of the heart and of the imagination.'[2] With Caroline's brother, on the other hand, 'The regulation of your
time and occupations would be your own ... you might
follow your own judgement, or yield to the judgment of one
who would never require you to submit to his opinion, but
to his reasons.'[3]

What follows employs a typical plot, though with an
economy and poise most untypical of the period. There are
only four more letters, all from Caroline and all in response to a new situation. In Letter IV, dated some five years
after Letter III, Caroline advises Julia to think long before
leaving her husband, Lord V——. In Letter V, she rebukes her
for her behaviour since her separation from Lord V——, and
gives her fresh advice. Letter VI is a last appeal to Julia before
she goes to France with her lover. Letter VII, addressed to
Lord V——, describes how a sick and exhausted Julia arrived at
Caroline's house, and, after a pathetic last meeting with her
daughter, whom Caroline is bringing up, died the same evening.

[1] *Letters of Julia and Caroline*, Letter II: *Collected Works*, London, 1833,
xiii. 328.
[2] Ibid., Letter III: xiii. 333.   [3] Ibid., Letter III: xiii. 334.

The key letter is the fifth, for it is there that Caroline identifies Julia's intellectual error. When they last met,

the boundaries of right and wrong seemed to be no longer marked in your mind . . . some unknown, wayward power seemed to have taken possession of your understanding . . . You appeared peculiarly averse to philosophy . . . you asked, 'Of what use philosophy could be to beings who had no free will, and how the ideas of just punishment and involuntary crime could be reconciled?'[1]

Julia has in short adopted an extreme form of the new psychology. Her belief that man's actions are involuntary has wholly destroyed both the idea of external (i.e. religious) sanctions, and of critical analysis by the conscious mind. It is on the latter that Maria Edgeworth lays most stress. For her very next point is the deplorable blow struck at the conscious moral life of the individual by Julia's mechanistic physiology:

. . . in speaking of the striking difference between the conduct and understanding of the great Lord Bacon, you said, that 'it by no means surprised you; that to an enlarged mind, accustomed to consider the universe as one vast *whole*, the conduct of that little animated atom, that inconsiderable part *self*, must be too insignificant to fix or merit attention. It was nothing,' you said, 'in the general mass of vice and virtue, happiness and misery.' I believe I answered, 'that it might be *nothing* compared to the great *whole*, but it was *every thing* to the individual.'[2]

Like jacobins and anti-jacobins alike, Maria Edgeworth baulks at the involuntary psychology of Hume and the more mechanistic mid-century physiologists. But her positive is an insistence on the personality and powers—if exerted—of the individual, and it is at this point that she diverges from conservative advocates of Sense. For the characteristic recourse of the conservative—Burke, Jane West, Jane Austen—is to remind us ultimately of the insignificance of individual insights and even individual concerns when measured against the scale of 'the universe as one vast whole'.

Although in obvious ways still very inexperienced, Maria Edgeworth's handling of form in this her first published

[1] *Letters of Julia and Caroline*, Letter III: xiii. 342–3.
[2] Ibid., Letter V: xiii. 343.

work of fiction reveals real promise. Most of the models of letter-novels available to her—such as *Julia de Roubigné,* which she admired[1]—were sentimental. *Letters of Julia and Caroline* develops its potential in quite different directions, first for rational debate, afterwards for considered, ethical analysis of situations as they arise. From Mackenzie's naturalistic, non-moralizing presentation of psychological experience, the reader steps on to a much more philosophical and moralistic plane. As though aware of how unusually ethical her interests are, Maria Edgeworth defends them as, significantly, a concern peculiarly central in the lives of women:

Speculative opinions, I know, have little influence over the practice of those who act much and think little; but I should conceive their power to be considerable over the conduct of those who have much time for reflection and little necessity for action. In one case the habit of action governs the thoughts upon any sudden emergency; in the other, the thoughts govern the actions. The truth or falsehood then of speculative opinions is of much greater consequence to our sex than to the other; as we live a life of reflection, they of action.[2]

In the first half of her career, especially, Maria Edgeworth consciously develops a form of novel she thinks especially relevant to women readers. Nearly all her early tales for adults have heroines rather than heroes, and nearly all focus on the manners and morals of women. But there is more in it, as this passage reveals. Maria Edgeworth considers that the educated woman leads 'a life of reflection': and her early 'women's tales' are written both to reveal and to extend that inner life of continuous discrimination and ethical choice.[3] Though much more 'natural' to outward seeming than the ideological novelists of the era of her first published work, she really resembles them in seriousness of purpose. In a

[1] It is listed in the Advertisement to *Belinda* among a small minority of works she approved of.

[2] *Letters of Julia and Caroline,* Letter V: iv. 328.

[3] Her awareness that her goal was different from that of most other novelists is betrayed in words she puts in the mouth of the model teacher in *The Good French Governess* (see below, pp. 132–3). Madame de Rosier, in praising John Moore's *Zeluco*, agrees that a name ought to be devised for 'philosophical novels' to distinguish them from 'trifling, silly productions'. (*Moral Tales: Works,* 1832, iii. 113). From the first ME's own works aimed at the higher category.

later phase of her writing, her tales *Ennui*, *The Absentee*, and *Ormond* attempt broad and much more masculine sketches of national life, and thus become her best-known contribution to literary history, since they are an influence on Scott. At first glance her earlier novels are less ambitious. This, after all, is a format, the 'feminine novel', which she and many others inherited from Fanny Burney; and most modern literary historians have assumed that Jane Austen went to the same source without needing an intermediary. This modern belief, however, overlooks Maria Edgeworth's peculiarly sharp perception of the ethical content of feminine lives; and what follows will try to show how critical an omission it is.

During the height of the conservative reaction, identified in the previous chapter as belonging to the years 1797 to 1801, only part of Maria Edgeworth's attention went to novel-writing. She thought of the treatise *Practical Education*, 1798, as her most significant publication in those years: in comparison, the book many modern readers would identify as her masterpiece, *Castle Rackrent*, 1800, was a *jeu d'esprit*. The following year, 1801, she did indeed produce a standard three-volume novel, *Belinda*. Otherwise the period was spent in turning out a substantial body of fiction for children and young people. Some of these are frankly pedagogic in character: the *Harry and Lucy* series of 1801, for example, and at least one of the collection of stories for adolescents which appeared in the same year as *Moral Tales*. *The Good French Governess*, about an inspired teacher's rescue of four spoilt, bored children, is a readable and in its way brilliant appendix to *Practical Education*, and hardly pretends at all to be fiction. Yet there are other tales of the same series which by virtue of their approach to character and to value in character may be considered in the same context as the tales for adults.

The simpler stories for adolescents tend to follow a single pattern: a brave and rational child, backed by a wise mentor, is contrasted with an irrational and would-be fashionable one, foolishly indulged.[1] Maria Edgeworth shares with most

[1] The same form occurs in *The Good French Governess*, *Mlle Panache*, and *The Good Aunt*.

conduct-writers of the period a dislike of superficial education, which for girls might typically be an education in
accomplishments, for either sex an emphasis on the types of
cleverness which can best be shown off in society. The last
volume of *Practical Education*, written (unlike Edgeworth's
more technical early chapters) by Maria herself, deals in full
with the topic of mere 'wit', and mere information, so often
instilled at the expense of the reasoning process. The point is
more lightly dealt with in the portrait of the fourteen-year-
old Isabella, who sounds like a sketch for Maria Bertram in
Mansfield Park:

. . . her countenance was intelligent, but rather too expressive of
confidence in her own capacity, for she had, from infancy, been
taught to believe that she was a genius. Her memory had been
too much cultivated; she had learned language with facility, and
had been taught to set a very high value upon her knowledge of
history and chronology. Her temper had been hurt by flattery, yet
she was capable of feeling all the generous passions.[1]

Although they have their dislike of vanity and worldliness
in common, Maria Edgeworth's positives are very different
from Jane Austen's, as an examination of the two most
ambitious of the *Moral Tales* shows.

Angelina, or *L'Amie Inconnue*, has been the best-known
tale in the collection, at least since Miss Lascelles identified
it as a story of 'The Female Quixote' type, comparable with
Northanger Abbey.[2] Anne Warwick, or, as she prefers to be
called, Angelina, has been so intoxicated by some high-flown
sentimental novels published under the pseudonym 'Araminta'
that she has conducted a literary correspondence with the
author. Now, disillusioned by the empty fashionable life of
her guardian, Lady Diana Chillingworth, she has impulsively
run away to seek poverty in a cottage with her unknown
friend. Her journey leads her to an inn at Cardiff and to the
Welsh cottage where they are to live idyllically together, but
'Araminta' is away from home. Accompanied only by a
comically ignorant Welsh servant girl called Betty Williams,
Angelina goes to look for her in Bristol, and eventually, after

[1] *The Good French Governess, Moral Tales: Works*, iii. 94–5. See below, pp.
220–1.
[2] *Jane Austen and her Art*, Oxford, 1939, pp. 55 and 57.

a series of embarrassing, prosaic failures, she finds her sentimental friend—a coarse, stout, middle-aged woman, loud-
voiced and smelling unmistakably of brandy. Cured of her
illusions, Angelina agrees to return, not to Lady Diana's
household, but to the more rational companionship of Lady
Diana's sister, Lady Frances Somerset.

The Quixotic form is strongly marked throughout, and
indeed underlined by the heroine herself, when she reflects
that her Welsh companion is a veritable Sancho Panza, and
as destructive of romance. However, *Angelina* is very different from other stories of quixotic young girls led astray by
romantic reading. The difference lies in the placing of the
author's (and hence the reader's) sympathy: the story is not
primarily or essentially opposed to sentimentalism. Most
quixotic heroes and heroines are more or less attractive:[1]
their warmth and idealism makes us love them, despite their
folly. But Angelina differs significantly from the common run.
It would be wrong to call her more sympathetic than Catherine
Morland, since she is far less effectively characterized; but
her attitude of mind comes much nearer to being judged right
by the author than is usual in a form apparently dedicated
to burlesquing romance.

At the beginning of the story, Angelina's elopement is
discussed by Lady Di Chillingworth and her rational sister,
Lady Frances:

'You remember you used to tell me, that Anne Warwick had
such great abilities——!'
'That I thought it a pity they had not been well directed,' said
Lady Frances.
'And such generosity of temper, and such warm affections!' said
Lady Di——.
'That I regretted their not having been properly cultivated.'[2]

Angelina's search for 'Araminta'—or to use her real-life
name, Rachael Hodges—gives the plot its forward impetus.
But her true quest is obviously for something else, for a
sanity of judgement based ou her own idealism, but informed

---

[1] e.g., Charlotte Lennox's Arabella, in *The Female Quixote*, 1752, and Eaton
Stannard Barrett's Cherubina, of *The Heroine*, 1813.
[2] *Angelina, or L'Amie Inconnue, Moral Tales: Works*, iii. 2.

with a little more knowledge of life. In this real quest Miss
Hodges plays only a small part, as the arrangement of
characters makes clear. The story introduces three young
girls, all at the threshold of entry to the world. One is the
heroine Angelina, one a good-hearted Scots girl, Clara Hope,
whom she meets at a Bristol dancing class; one Miss Burrage,
Lady Di's companion, who, it turns out, originally haled
from a fairly low life in Bristol. At Lady Di's house, before
the elopement, Miss Burrage was a false friend to Angelina;
in Bristol, at her time of need, Clara Hope extends her the
hand of true friendship out of instinctive good nature. Each
girl has an adoptive parent, an older mentor whom she has
chosen—and the choice reveals everything about the values
of the girls. Clara's mentor is the rational Lady Frances. Miss
Burrage, motivated by a desire to rise in the world, has
rejected her good Quaker aunt, a cheesemonger's widow
called Dinah Plait, and attached herself to the fashionable
Lady Di. Angelina, having rejected *her* first guardian, Lady
Di, is now looking for another. Of course her choice of an
unknown sentimental friend was folly; yet her quest for something better than her fashionable guardian showed, as Lady
Frances hints, the innate rightness of her mind. Once exposed
in Bristol to life as it actually is, Angelina succeeds in discriminating between false and true. She perceives the goodness of Dinah Plait, whom Miss Burrage snobbishly rejected,
and of the apparently quaint little Scots girl Clara. The scene
in which she at last meets Araminta is uncomfortably broad
and farcical, but this is partly because a satire of sentiment is
far from Maria Edgeworth's purpose. Angelina was deceived
by Araminta's letters because they spoke the language of
idealism, and her travels have taught her to judge people by
their deeds rather than their words; without, however, modify-
ing the ideals themselves. The real significance of the scene
with Araminta is that—counterpointing the broad farce of
Araminta's theatrical behaviour, the unromantic appearance
of her fiancé, Nat, and the brandy in the teapot—Angelina's
thought-processes develop a new, sober realism. 'Everything
appeared to her in a new light.' Earlier, on her arrival at the
inn at Cardiff, her language and thought-processes were
inflated and romantic. Now she speaks, as she thinks, with

precision, and in marked contrast with the sentimental style:

'Yes, my Angelina: so end "The Sorrows of Araminta"—Another cup?—do I make the tea too sweet?' said miss Hodges, while Nat handed the bread and butter to the ladies officiously.

'The man looks like a fool,' thought miss Warwick.

'Set down the bread and butter and be quiet, Nat.—Then, as soon as the wedding is over, we fly, my Angelina, to our charming cottage in Wales:—there may we bid defiance to the storms of fate——

"The world forgetting by the world forgot." '

'That', said Angelina, ' " is the blameless vestal's lot:"—but you forget that you are to be married, my Araminta; and you forget that, in your letter of three folio sheets, you said not one word to me of this intended marriage.'[1]

The contrast between Angelina's clear perception of truth and Araminta's vague one is realized here in their respective tones of speech, in anticipation of Maria Edgeworth's maturer work, and of Jane Austen's. Nevertheless, Angelina's story does not centre on this scene of broad comedy. The moral process Maria Edgeworth wants to chart is from Lady Di's household to Lady Frances's, and Araminta is merely an aberration along the way. The real anti-heroine is Miss Burrage, who forsook the true parent-figure for the false. Miss Burrage's unmasking—when she denies the good Dinah to her face—is a serious counterpart to the merely comic unmasking of Araminta. Vice in the story is identified not with sentimentalism, but with cold-hearted worldliness, vanity, self-seeking, hypocrisy—the vices of the rich and their parasites. Virtue is illustrated by those who stand aside from the 'world', in the sense of the fashionable world, or who never aspire to be part of it: decent good-natured people of the working class, like the Irish driver and the Quaker tradesmen. Angelina is always looking for goodness, and she finds it, in various homely disguises, and ultimately in Lady Frances. Somehow it seems no accident that one of the 'pattern' characters in the story speaks broad Scots. The moral belongs to an earlier era of sentimentalism, for it conveys faith in human goodness: Angelina is forgiven her folly because of

[1] *Angelina:* iii. 69–70.

her goodness of heart, while Miss Burrage is cast out because she is cold, and these are both motifs of sentimentalism. But mingled with them is the flavour of a practical, downright, anti-aristocrat, Midlands world—the same world as Bage's— where the intellectual affinities are with Scotland rather than with London.

Had Maria Edgeworth not lived so far from London, in the household of a father whose real education took place in the Midlands between 1765 and 1780, she could never have made unselfconscious use of so many properties of sentimental optimism about human nature. Many of her stories contain a character who is a pure, good-hearted child; and this is really nothing but the eighteenth century's child of nature trans- lated into the terms of the naturalistic novel. A good-hearted, simple, faithful little black boy, loved by the hero and loving him in return, recurs three times in rapid succession: in the unpublished play *Whim for Whim*, written in 1798; in *The Good Aunt* (where the boy is admittedly not Negro but Creole): and in *Belinda*. Sometimes, as a variant, the good child of nature is Irish: the purest example is Little Dominick in *Irish Bulls* (1801), but the figure recurs as late as *Patronage*, 1814. The naturally good representative of a race too often sneered at in over-sophisticated English society was a staple of English sentimental drama of two decades earlier.[1] One difference, though, and an important one, is that Maria Edgeworth is not content with mere intuitive good nature, as in earlier, irrational sentimentalism. Her black boys and Irish boys are associated with more important characters than themselves, whose benignity is blended with rationalism. The fact that her heroes befriend types who would otherwise be despised is intended only incidentally to prove their good nature. The crucial characteristic of her heroes is their willing- ness to make judgements independent of prejudice or fashion.

Maria Edgeworth thus shares the optimistic view of man of the earlier sentimental generation, while rejecting—like Bage, Godwin, Holcroft, and the feminists—the irrational psychology of that movement. She believes in the individual man's capacity for great virtue, but conceives that he realizes his potential by a conscious exercise of reason, and not by

[1] See above, p. 18.

the so-called 'moral instinct'.[1] The play *Whim for Whim*, for example, satirizes intellectual fashions of various kinds, but its sentimentalists, Opal and Mrs. Fangle, are let down remarkably lightly. Opal has already proved his kindness by freeing the slave-boy Quaco, and the sensible heroine Caroline resolutely defends his fundamental kindness and good sense against the criticism of her guardian, Sir Mordent Idem:

'But he has so much enthusiasm.'
'Tis the enthusiasm of virtue, sir.'
'He'll be a dupe sooner or later.'
'But never a knave—and if ever he is made a dupe, it will be by the appearance of virtue.'[2]

Although *Whim for Whim* exploits the whole hysterical paraphernalia so typical of 1798, of foreign philosophers, a secret society, and a world-wide conspiracy,[3] it never implies that sincere sentimentalism will undermine society. On the contrary, it is clear that Maria Edgeworth believes that vice occurs more among the haves than among the have-nots, that she sympathizes with the poor, and remains in favour of social reform. In the most substantial of *The Moral Tales*, *Forester*, her liberalism is stated explicitly.

Forester is a companion-piece to *Angelina*, and much better done. Again, the youthful protagonist is the victim of his own quixotic idealism: for Forester, wholly imbued (like Thomas Day, who was the original of the portrait)[4] with Rousseau's hatred for fashionable society, leaves the home of his kindly guardian Dr. Campbell (based on the Scottish moralist and empiricist, Dugald Stewart), and attempts to live 'naturally' by the toil of his own hands. Like Bridgetina's circle, he has read Le Vaillant's *Travels in Africa*, and he admires the simplicity of the Hottentots[5] as much as he despises the superfluities of fashionable society and the hypocrisies entailed in polite manners. But his first effort

---

[1] Maria Edgeworth reveals her poor opinion of the moral instinct in her treatment of two characters who trust in it, Mr. Vincent in *Belinda* and Olivia in *Leonora*. See below, pp. 142–3 and 149.

[2] *Whim for Whim*, Bodleian Library, M.S. Eng. misc. d. 684.

[3] See above, p. 116n. Maria Edgeworth read Robison's book as research for *Whim for Whim*.

[4] See *Maria Edgeworth*, p. 164n.   [5] See above, p. 108.

to support himself, in the most 'natural' employment, gardening, ends disastrously because the people around him are ignorant and stupid. His next job, as a clerk in a brewery, is little better, for here his companions are would-be sophisticates, the parasites of an urban society. It is only when Forester goes to work in a printing-house as a compositor that he once more encounters educated people whose conversation gives him any satisfaction. His career proves that Dr. Campbell was right when at the outset he mused tolerantly on his ward's intellectual fallacies—'education creates the differences between men, more than riches or poverty'.[1]

All the same, what Forester learns far from completely reverses his earlier radicalism. As in *Angelina*, there are three youthful characters—Forester himself, Dr. Campbell's son Henry, and the young laird Archibald Mackenzie. Henry Campbell is the true son of his father, moderate, genial, liberal, and practical. Mackenzie, who like Forester is being brought up in Dr. Campbell's household, is immediately perceived by Forester to be the villain of the piece, for he is snobbish, selfish, and inhumane, his misdeeds including carelessness with vitriol, by which a cat is killed, and an attempt to have an honest washerwoman charged with theft. Like most youthful Edgeworth villains, Mackenzie bullies his inferiors while toadying to acquaintances of higher rank. Forester begins by detesting him, and the outcome of the story proves him quite right. All that Forester needs to learn, in fact, is the lesson acquired by Tom Jones: that in order to live with society as it is, we need not shed our generosity, provided we can learn the prudence necessary for self-preservation.[2] As a compositor he falls in with the young radical, Tom Random, and is inclined to adhere to him until he discovers that for all his democratic talk, Tom will brook no disagreement from a mere compositor. But this is not satire of the reformist position: on the contrary, it is a complaint that Tom does not understand the liberty and equality that should prevail among thinkers and scientists, in the world of the mind. Tom is piqued because an essay of his own has been judged inferior to Henry Campbell's 'Essay on the

[1] *Forester, Moral Tales: Works*, ii. 6.
[2] Cf. Fielding, *Tom Jones*, Bk. xviii, ch. x.

best method of reforming abuses'. Forester, reading Henry's piece, at once recognizes that its tendencies are really more liberal (and therefore more admirable) than Tom's high-sounding words. 'Henry had written on the question with . . . moderation and yet with . . . unequivocal decision had shown himself the friend of rational liberty.'[1]

Belinda, Maria Edgeworth's first full-length novel, deploys the plot of a young girl setting out in life, the well-tried format of Fanny Burney. In different ways it resembles all three Burney novels published by the time it was written, but perhaps the most interesting relationship is with the most recent—*Camilla*.[2] Although a Tory, Fanny Burney was never a consistent reactionary in her novels, since she carried with her far too many techniques learnt from her own senti-mental generation. But in *Camilla*, published after the Revo-lution and after her own marriage to an émigré, she used a thorough-going conservative theme, that of the good-natured but impulsive heroine who needs to learn to school her own judgement and to submit it to the superior authority of her parents and her future husband. Camilla is regaled with long earnest letters of advice, notably from her clergyman father, whose precepts are unimpeachably lofty. Belinda's much more entertaining correspondence with *her* guardian, Mrs. Stanhope, is surely offered in conscious contrast.

Mrs. Stanhope is a notorious matchmaker, who has already got five nieces successfully off her hands. Before coming to London, Belinda, the sixth, has had the misfortune to be 'as well advertised as Packwood's razor strops'.[3] Mrs. Stanhope (like Camilla's parents) has done her utmost to bring her niece up in accordance with her own values. 'Her aunt had endeavoured to teach her that a young lady's chief business is to please in society, that all her charms and accomplish-ments should be invariably subservient to one grand object— the establishing herself in the world.[4] After Belinda leaves home for a wealthier patron and a wider world, Mrs. Stanhope

---

[1] *Forester:* ii. 93.
[2] Like Jane Austen, Maria Edgeworth was a subscriber to *Camilla*. Her annotated copy of it still survives.
[3] *Belinda*, ch. ii: *Works*, 1833, xi. 28.　　　　[4] Ibid., ch. i: xi. 1.

feels the need to remind her at intervals of the principles of her upbringing. She does so in letters solemnly echoing the usual language of moral exhortation (including the Edgeworths' own). Considering the dire possibility that her 'education' will fail, for example, she conjures up a future for her young charge in terms that could be paralleled in many a conduct writer of the time, except for the ironic variation at the end: 'She finds herself at five or six and thirty a burden to her friends, destitute of the means of rendering herself independent (for the girls I speak of never think of *learning* to play cards).'[1]

The theme of the novel is precisely the opposite of *Camilla's*: instead of learning to submit to authority, Belinda learns to escape it, and to rely instead on her own judgement. Her new mentor, Lady Delacour, is no more dependable than Mrs. Stanhope, for like all fashionable women she is a 'slave to the world'.[2] Belinda does afterwards find refuge with a model family, the Percivals of Oakley Park, and while she is with them 'reasoning gradually became as natural to her as wit'.[3] But there is no question of the Percivals' directing her. They merely help her to achieve her goal in the novel, to stand on her own feet.

The point is made through the kind of elaborate pattern of contrasting characters already made familiar in the ethical novel of the 1790s.[4] Belinda is compared with two very different women. The simple Virginia has been educated in total retirement, because the hero, an admirer of Rousseau, considers that this training should render her wholly innocent.[5] In society Belinda meets the fashionable 'dasher' Mrs. Harriott Freke, who loves to dress up as a boy, and proclaims the cause of female liberty. Belinda wholly rejects her example, but at the same time she disagrees with the West

[1] Ibid., ch. i: xi. 3–4.   [2] Ibid., ch. iii: xi. 52.
[3] Ibid., ch. xvii: xi. 328.   [4] See above, e.g. pp. 102–3.

[5] The Virginia subplot, although partially based on the real-life experiment by Thomas Day, also makes frequent reference to another popular novel of the period, Bernardin St. Pierre's *Paul et Virginie*. Translated into English by Helen Maria Williams in 1795, *Paul et Virginie* is a sentimental classic about two beautiful, ideally virtuous young lovers, brought up in seclusion on Mauritius. In *Belinda* Maria Edgeworth thus rejects both *Camilla*'s doctrine of submission to authority, and *Paul et Virginie*'s of innate virtue, and makes out a case for the individual who is mature and rational.

Indian Mr. Vincent, when he praises by contrast the passivity and languor of Creole women. For Maria Edgeworth, the truth about the Creoles, as about Virginia, is that ignorance cannot be identified with innocence; nor is lack of opportunity to sin the same thing as positive virtue. Belinda's reflections on Mrs. Freke read prudishly to the modern reader, but they are to be taken as a rider on female liberty, not a denial of it. Maria Edgeworth considers that the rational Belinda is more and not less free than the passionate, unrestrained Harriott Freke.

The point is underlined by the trio of young men who parallel the young women. As usual, the fashionable one, Sir Philip Baddely, is affected, ignorant, and contemptible. The second, Clarence Harvey, is a typical Edgeworth hero, innately virtuous, capable of rationality, but temporarily caught up first in his flirtation with worldliness, afterwards in his unrealistic experiment with pastoral simplicity. The third young man, Mr. Vincent, is sufficiently appealing for Belinda to contemplate marrying him when she thinks Clarence Harvey is lost to her.[1] From the ethical point of view, Mr. Vincent proves an interesting study, since his typical sentimental virtues prove his undoing. 'Social spirit, courage, generosity all conspired to carry our man of feeling to the gaming table.'[2] At times the intuitions by which he is wholly governed prompt him to behave badly. 'The acuteness of his feelings was to his own mind an excuse for dissimulation; so fallacious is moral instinct, unenlightened or uncontrolled by reason or religion.'[3] It is not any kind of religion, but only reasonable religion, that might have made a sound guide. Lady Delacour becomes a convert to Methodism when she believes she is dying, and of her state at this time Maria Edgeworth says drily 'Lady Delacour was governed by pride, by sentiment, by whim, by enthusiasm, by passion—by anything but reason.'[4] It is clear that when she refers to a steady

[1] The plot was modified for a later edition (of 1810). In the revised version Mr. Vincent's courtship made less headway than originally in 1801. See *Maria Edgeworth*, Appendix C, pp. 494–5.

[2] *Belinda*, ch. xxviii: xii. 276.

[3] Ibid., ch. xxviii: xii. 279.

[4] Ibid., ch. xxvi: xii. 53. Afterwards Lady Delacour appoints a chaplain after the model of Chaucer's 'poor persoune', and becomes converted to a 'mild and rational piety', evidently of a middle-of-the-road Church of England variety.

standard, it is that of right reason, independently arrived at by the individual, rather than the external wisdom of any authority whatsoever. It is for want of the rational habit that Mr. Vincent founders, and in the process loses Belinda. 'His most virtuous resolves were always rather the effect of sudden impulse than of steady principle. But when the tide of passion had swept away the landmarks, he had no method of ascertaining the boundaries of right and wrong.'[1]

Anti-jacobin female novelists, Mrs. West and Mrs. Hamilton, previously deployed their characters neatly according to their respective ideologies, and set a heroine to choose a husband among them. Maria Edgeworth achieves something more detailed and distinctive by putting language, and especially dialogue, to full use in this process of assessment: her characters act out the people they are by their manner of using words. They have no need (most of the time) to proclaim a series of beliefs, as in the doctrinaire novel of the nineties. Their respective value-systems are sufficiently revealed by the way they talk. Lady Delacour, the best character (especially in the first volume: and she is not alone in losing vitality in the second), has a splendid, nervous style of delivery that fully conveys her intelligence, her wit, and her touch of daring. She is herself conscious about style in speech, and will comment, for example, that the note she once sent challenging a woman to a duel had more elegance than her opponent's reply.[2] She is always rapid and lively, and sometimes verbally inventive, as in her observation about her friendship with Harriott Freke: 'we were mutually agreeable to each other— I as starer, and she as staree'.[3] Her conversations with Clarence Harvey breathe a perfume of agreeable cleverness and literary allusion, reminding one that Maria Edgeworth's own real-life conversation was once said by Sydney Smith to breathe a perfume of wit.[4] Belinda's conversational tone

[1] *Belinda*, ch. xxix: xii. 295.
[2] Ibid., ch. iv: xi. 71–2.
[3] Ibid., ch. iii: xi. 55.
[4] Another witness of Maria Edgeworth's conversation remarked that there was some resemblance to Lady Delacour's in it. See *Maria Edgeworth*, p. 416. Francis Jeffrey remarked that with Lady Delacour Maria Edgeworth excelled other novelists in the 'faithful but ffattering representation of the spoken language of persons of wit and politeness of the present day'. *Edinburgh Review*, xx (1812), 103.

is quieter, and consequently more serious and sincere: but it has the precision that is always the hallmark of Edgeworth characters who know how to think. In strong contrast are the breathless confusions of Virginia, or the clichés of fops like Sir Philip Baddely and his friend Mr. Rochfort. The latter's description of the rational Dr. X—— as a 'quiz', and his refusal to understand Belinda's disagreement with him, perfectly express the absence of Mind which is the symptom of the character Maria Edgeworth disapproves of:

> 'I never argue, for my part,' cried Mr. Rochfort. ''pon honour, 'tis a deal too much trouble. A lady, a handsome lady, I mean, is always in the right with me.'[1]

Bage's comedy similarly lets virtue and vice emerge through contrasting verbal mannerisms, which reveal wholly different levels of intellectual freedom and originality in the characters that use them. But Maria Edgeworth is far more subtle and natural in the range of types she introduces, and the unselfconscious way in which she lets them betray themselves. Bage organizes his stories like ideological tournaments; Maria Edgeworth is writing naturalistically, in the Burneyesque comic genre of love and marriage. But in fact her choice of action gives the discrimination she shows in dialogue greater, not less, significance: for her heroes and heroines, going about their very human business of choosing a partner in marriage, are themselves listening to the other characters, and discriminating between them by virtue of their speech, as Bage's are not. In a world more commonly of reflection than of action, they know that what people are emerges in words and not in deeds. Belinda as a heroine is above all a listener: her real education in the world begins when she overhears a conversation about Mrs. Stanhope, and afterwards her discriminations and discoveries are made through conversations, relayed to us, as readers, through her consciousness. Comparison with *Hermsprong* and even more with *Camilla* points to Maria Edgeworth's achievement. In *Belinda* she has conceived an appropriate plot and appropriate narrative techniques to make the conscious mind central, as it had never so naturally been before.

---

[1] *Belinda*, ch. ix: xi. 161.

Maria Edgeworth's social comedy must surely have made a contribution to Jane Austen's, where values are also revealed through contrasting a whole range of character and deploying in the comparison every nuance of speech. Although Jane Austen writes subtle, revelatory dialogue in a juvenile performance like *Catharine*, probably composed in 1793, she does not yet link this technique for dramatically representing values in speech with a growth in her heroine's understanding. That particular connection is not stressed in any of the novels begun before 1800. The verbal styles of minor characters are not made an index of moral value even in so verbally asured a novel as *Pride and Prejudice*.[1] Style, or verbal evidence, is not what Elizabeth has to go on. In *Northanger Abbey* the reader is very aware of contrasting styles, but Catherine is not: her consciousness is not brought into active relationship with the outer world of speech. Good and bad characters are not evaluated by their mannerisms at all in *Sense and Sensibility*. It is only in the later novels that Jane Austen fully dramatizes the process of judgement and intimately involves the reader in it through his relationship with the heroine. To most modern critics this technique of engaging heroine and reader in a game of ethical detection is a characteristic of Jane Austen's novels, and of hers alone. But before any of Jane Austen's work appeared, Maria Edgeworth had completed her *œuvre* in the 'feminine' novel—domestic comedy, centring on a heroine, in which the critical action is an inward progress towards judgement.

In form and in original conception, *Leonora* is the odd one out among Maria Edgeworth's novels. It was planned after her visit to Paris during the Peace of Amiens in 1802–3, and it is touched by the sophistication she picked up then from French intellectuals. The stories Maria Edgeworth wrote in Ireland before 1802 (all those so far considered) were in many ways provincial. They were insulated from London literary warfare of the 1790s. They made a virtue of sturdy provincial independence, with its suspicion of fashionable metropolitan attitudes. They also had the thinness of an upper-class scene drawn from books and from report, rather

[1] See below, pp. 223–4.

than from life. Paris gave her first-hand experience, and it also exposed her to some at least of the intellectual crosscurrents of the day.

The literary *cause célèbre* during the Edgeworths' Paris visit was Madame de Staël's *Delphine*. Appearing two months after the Edgeworth family party arrived there, in December 1802, it immediately attracted attention as a strikingly libertarian book, flouting convention not so much by the characters' behaviour, as by the author's sense of values. Like *Werther*, *La Nouvelle Héloïse*, and *Julia de Roubigné*, *Delphine* is the story of a triangle of lovers. Delphine falls in love with Léonce de Mondoville, the fiancé of her cousin Matilde de Vernon, and he with her. They are well matched in nobility of character although Léonce (who, like Montauban in *Julia de Roubigné*, was brought up in Spain) has a fatal disposition to overvalue honour. Disregarding his instincts about Delphine, he is misled by appearances into thinking her unchaste. The mistake is nourished by the false Madame de Vernon, whom Delphine thinks of as a friend, and Léonce marries Matilde after all. When it is too late, Léonce discovers that Delphine was true, and an agonizing, protracted, but platonic *affaire* begins, a hopeless imbroglio which ends only with Léonce's death and Delphine's suicide.[1]

As usual in romantic triangles by progressives in the period, the reader's sympathies are with the lovers and against the formal marriage.[2] Delphine, in what conventional people would regard as the disgraceful role of the Other Woman, has the loftiest motives of any of the characters. Guided by 'la morale et la religion du cœur',[3] impatient of

[1] Mme de Staël later changed the suicide for a natural death: the new ending appears in her *Complete Works* (1820). In her *Reflections on Suicide* (1813) she explains her changed attitude on the subject. See J. Christopher Herold, *Mistress to an Age*, Charter edition, 1962, p. 235n. The suicide in the first edition, which is implicitly condoned, must have contributed greatly to the novel's notoriety, just as Werther's suicide coloured the reputation of Goethe's novel.

[2] In the three comparable novels by Rousseau, Goethe, and Mackenzie, the marriage is seen as somewhat cold and formal compared with the generous, irresistible passion of the unmarried lovers. The latter are innocent because their feelings are involuntary. They are even superior to more conventional people, because they act according to their 'true', i.e. intuitive, natures, rather than in obedience to forms imposed from without. See above, pp. 24–6.

[3] *Delphine*, 3 vols., Paris, 1803, i. 21.

'les convenances arbitraire de la societé',[1] she is Madame de Staël's self-portrait, though very much idealized. Compared with this free, generous, 'natural' creature, her bigoted (though sympathetically realized)[2] cousin and her cousin's worldly mother are morally lesser figures, the slaves, in their different ways, of convention and received ideas.

Maria Edgeworth discussed *Delphine* more than once, but her most stimulating source of ideas about it must have been Talleyrand. It was common knowledge that Talleyrand himself was intended by one of the most cutting of several excellent character-sketches from life, that of the outwardly charming but unscrupulous Madame de Vernon. In referring to the portraits of himself and Madame de Staël in the novel, Talleyrand drily remarked 'Oui, elle nous a tous deux déguise en femme.' More seriously, he condemned, as others did, the strikingly libertarian code of values revealed by the treatment of character. 'Le livre ne manque que d'être abregé épuré et éclairci.' Referring perhaps to the sympathy shown not only towards Delphine and Léonce's extra-marital passion, but to that of a minor character, Thérèse d'Ervins, he concluded 'On y trouve une métaphysique galante.'[3]

In view of Talleyrand's own less than exemplary private life, the high moral tone he adopted may strike us as hypocritical. But his was evidently the common view; and he was responding, as contemporary English critics of *Delphine* did,[4] to its implicitly private, subjective morality, its defiance of external authority. His view must have been echoed by the man

---

[1] Ibid., i. 19.

[2] Again, in the three other triangular novels with which *Delphine* has been compared, the 'third party', i.e. the husband or wife, is invariably handled with tact and sympathy; for this is essentially a world of victims rather than of villains.

[3] Manuscript notes in the hand of Harriet Butler, Maria Edgeworth's stepsister, on the inside cover of her family's copy of *Delphine*. The notes scattered through this edition, most of them by R. L. Edgeworth, disprove the belief of the Swiss scholar H. W. Häusermann that Maria Edgeworth was prejudiced against Mme de Staël. (See his *Genevese Background*, London, 1952.) Although improprieties are certainly noted, most of the comments register admiration.

[4] 'To us it appears rather an attack against the Ten Commandments, than the government of Bonaparte, and calculated not so much to enforce the rights of the Bourbons as the benefits of adultery, murder, and a great number of other vices.' Review of translation of *Delphine*, *Edinburgh Review*, ii (1803), 172.

Maria Edgeworth most wanted to please in Paris, the Swedish Chevalier Edelcrantz, who in November 1802 had asked her to marry him. Specifically in order to appeal to Edelcrantz, generally in response to the criticisms she had heard in Paris, Maria Edgeworth set herself on returning to England to compose a novel that would answer *Delphine*.

Like *Delphine* (and like so many other sentimental novels, from *Clarissa* to *La Nouville Héloïse* and *Julia de Roubigné*), *Leonora* is a novel in letters. The central situation is the same romantic triangle, but with a very different emphasis. Mr. L—— and his wife, Lady Leonora L——, are happily married until the arrival at their English country home of Leonora's friend, Lady Olivia. Olivia has been living apart from her husband, and has travelled abroad for some years; and, especially from her stay in Paris, scandal attaches to her name. Against the advice of her mother, a duchess of great wisdom and propriety,[1] Leonora deliberately countenances Olivia in order to ease her re-entry into English society.

Olivia has been reading German philosophy and literature, and for her the test of any feeling is its intensity. Her attitudes are unsympathetically summarized by Leonora's sprightly friend Helen:

Certain novels are the touchstones of feeling and *intellect* with certain ladies. Unluckily I was not well read in these; and in the questions put to me from these sentimental statute-books, I gave strange judgments, often for the husband or parents against the heroine. I did not even admit the plea of destiny, irresistible passion or entrainement, as in all cases sufficient excuse for all errors and crimes. . . . I was further disgraced by the discovery, that I am deplorably ignorant of metaphysics, and have never been enlightened by any philanthropic transcendental professor of humanity.[2]

In a letter to her Parisian confidante Madame de P——, Olivia gives her own account of her philosophy. Her theory that the moral sense is innate, and 'proportioned to the

---

[1] The Duchess is of course Maria Edgeworth's exemplary counterpart to Mme de Staël's brilliant character, the devious, hypocritical, falsely conforming Mme de Vernon. This is one of Maria Edgeworth's dullest model portraits, but a mild piquancy is added by the link with Talleyrand.

[2] *Leonora*, Letter XII: *Works*, xiii. 41–2.

delicacy of our sensibility', is a deft Edgeworth burlesque of
the sentimentalist's linking of 'natural' human virtue with a
high and not very natural degree of personal refinement.
Olivia goes on to propose a physiological 'seat' for the moral
sense which would in effect take so-called morality out of the
sphere of the rational consciousness:

In my opinion it [the moral sense] resides primarily and principally in the nerves, and varies with their variations. Hence the
difficulty of making the moral sense a universal guide of action,
since it not only differs in many individuals, but in the same
person at different periods of their existence, or (as I have often
experienced) at different hours of the day. All this must depend
upon the mobility of the nervous system: upon this may *hinge* the
great difficulties which have puzzled metaphysicians respecting
consciousness, identity, etc. If they had attended less to the nature
of the soul, and more to the system of the nerves, they would have
avoided innumerable errors. . . . Nothing is wanting but some great
German genius to bring this idea of a moral sense in the nerves
into fashion. Indeed if our friend madame *** would mention it
in the notes to her new novel, it would introduce it in the most
satisfactory manner possible to all the fashionable world abroad;
and we take our notions in this country implicitly from the
continent.[1]

These are thorough-going satires of the progressive position, containing pointed and barely disguised references to
Madame de Staël. In fact, when it burlesqued sentimental
excesses, *Leonora* seemed to echo earlier anti-jacobin writing so
faithfully as to give a sense of being somewhat old-fashioned
in 1806.[2] Olivia is a feminine equivalent of the dangerous
foreign-trained interloper who breaks up domestic happiness
in Mrs. West's *A Tale of the Times*, or Lucas's *Infernal
Quixote*. As a character, however, she is much more psychologically sophisticated: when she tells herself that she is

[1] Ibid., Letter XXXIX: xiii. 126–7. Olivia is allowed to claim originality for
her 'system', but Maria Edgeworth must have been aware that similar
mechanistic theories had been proposed half a century earlier by Scottish
physiologists and medical writers such as William Cullen.

[2] 'The affectation or the indulgence of excessive sensibility, is no longer the
vice of our countrywomen; they have been pretty well laughed out of it; and,
we believe, no tolerably well-educated young woman of eighteen would feel
anything but contempt and derision for such effusions as fall from the pen of
Lady Olivia.' [Francis Jeffrey], 'Miss Edgeworth's *Leonora*', *Edinburgh Review*,
viii (1806), 207.

justified in proceeding with her campaign of seduction, since first Mr. L——, and then Leonora, are colder and coarser-grained than she, her self-deception is more acute than anything in a previous portrait of revolutionary subversion. Although Maria Edgeworth is hardly at home in a tale of sexual passion, jealousy, and betrayal, she manages an adventuress who at least bears comparison with Jane Austen's Lady Susan—though in Jane Austen's version of the plot, the ideological debate is characteristically left implicit.

At times Maria Edgeworth certainly does better in *Leonora* than the common anti-jacobin level of satire, but she does not rise to the level of the best writing in *Delphine*. It is partly on account of the form. Madame de Staël is at home with letters, since it is a record of experience that she is after, and different characters' private, subjective accounts of themselves. Maria Edgeworth, interested above all in ethical analysis, is relatively hamstrung by the epistolary convention. The fact that she is limited to a series of monologues destroys the best device of her habitual moral ·drama, the use of apparently natural, revelatory speech.

An exception, and the best character in *Leonora*, is Olivia's French correspondent, Gabrielle de P——. An intriguing political hostess, a blend of amorousness, affectation, and power-seeking, she is a vignette in Maria Edgeworth's best-observed vein. In fact, she is one of a series of French vignettes, for Maria Edgeworth was plainly fascinated by the triviality and superb complacency that she detected in fashionable Parisian females.[1] Madame de P—— is one of those articulate Edgeworth women who, without proclaiming their creed as their predecessors in the 1790s would have done, unconsciously betray a philosophy of life with every word they utter. She is the one real survival into the letter-form of Maria Edgeworth's comic sketch, for, with little or no part to play in the serious business of the plot, she has nothing to do but reveal herself:

Do you know, it is said, we shall soon have no wood to burn. What can have become of all our forests? People should inquire

[1] Among her witty portraits presumably from Parisian life are the ineffable Mme de Coulanges in *Emilie de Coulanges* (1812), and the Irish–French Mlle O'Faley in *Ormond* (1817).

after them. The Venus de Medicis has at last found her way down the Seine. It is not determined yet where to place her: but she is at Paris, and that is a great point gained for her . . .[1]

So lively a portrait begins subtly to modify our conception of the novel's target. Madame de P—— is carefully distinguished from her friend Olivia: she has *affaires*, and a taste for sensibility as a current vogue, but her real interest lies merely in remaining with the fashion, and her ultimate goal is the cold-hearted one of wielding power and influence. Olivia, with a more genuine and reckless surrender to her senses, and the will to possess Mr. L—— beyond the point where it actually serves her own interest, nevertheless ends by proving as selfish and cold-hearted as Madame de P——. When Mr. L—— is sick, she feels (like Sophia in Jane Austen's *Love and Friendship*[2]) that she could never sustain the shock of seeing him—'I speak not of the danger of my catching the disease.'[3] Whether it is sincere frailty, or egotism, Maria Edgeworth does not think much of it; and she compares it with Leonora's hasty journey from a sick-bed to her husband's side. In arguing to gain admittance, Leonora uses the idea of wifely duty, but Maria Edgeworth makes it very plain that she is motivated by simple strong feeling. Throughout the novel, she has shown English and, in this period, feminine inhibitions in discussing Leonora's marriage; yet she leaves the attentive reader unusually little doubt that Leonora is supposed to have experienced physical fulfilment with Mr. L—— before Olivia appeared.[4] Leonora is in love in precisely the sense of 'passion' mouthed so readily, but not deeply felt, by Olivia.

It is very true that Maria Edgeworth conceives that something else in addition to passion is meant by happy, stable marriage. The Duchess, dispenser of wisdom in the book, at the end advises her daughter not to indulge all year her penchant for retirement; and to develop all those common tastes and pursuits which will ensure that the marital relationship is made up of friendship as well as love. Although this is not the union of souls aimed at by Olivia and other sentimental heroines, nor is it the prudential social contract

---

[1] *Leonora*, Letter XVIII: xiii. 60.   [2] See below, p. 169.
[3] *Leonora*, Letter CII: xiii. 247.   [4] e.g. ibid., Letter XXV: xiii. 80–1.

which marriage had become in conservative novels.[1] For the partisan of orthodoxy, passion is either subsumed in, or replaced by, 'esteem' and 'rational attachment'. The relationship of the happy couple is as little private as it could well be. What appears to matter is the social significance of their union, the contribution they are about to make as the stable keystone of the community.[2] There is no word in *Leonora* about the social implications of the L——s' marriage, whether it succeeds or fails. Theirs is a very intent private relationship, an extension of the inner life which encompasses two people. *Leonora* is not against passion but for it.

Thus, having begun as a familiar-looking attack on the new philosophy, *Leonora* turns along the way into some typically liberal Edgeworthian by-paths. There is something more idiosyncratic still in the fact that the central crux of the plot becomes the process by which Mr. L—— makes up his mind between his mistress and his wife. Early in the story, when Leonora becomes jealous, she asks her mother what she should do, and the Duchess advises her to behave with dignity and restraint. She should not betray jealousy of Olivia. She should not exert any kind of emotional pressure on her husband. The modern reader may simply conclude that the Duchess gives bad advice, since both Mr. L—— and Olivia justify going ahead with their *affaire* on the grounds that Leonora does not care. But it is clear from the way she handles the dénouement that Maria Edgeworth approves of the Duchess's reasoning. Mr. L—— is a man with a choice to make. He should be given all possible objective evidence— it is the Duchess herself who sends him Leonora's letters,

[1] e.g. see above, pp. 109–10. In his review of *Emma* Scott whimsically rebuked conservative novelists for their habitual treatment of marriage: 'One word . . . we must say in behalf of that once powerful divinity, Cupid, King of gods and men, who in these times of revolution, has been assailed even in his own kingdom of romance, by the authors who were formerly his devoted priests . . . Before the authors of moral fiction couple Cupid indivisibly with calculating prudence, we would have them reflect, that they may sometimes lend their aids to substitute more mean . . . motives of conduct, for the romantic feelings which their predecessors perhaps fanned into too powerful a flame.' *Quarterly Review*, xiv (1815), 200.

[2] Typical conservative marriages occur at the end of Charles Lloyd's *Edmund Oliver*, Elizabeth Hamilton's *Memoirs of Modern Philosophers*, and Jane Austen's *Sense and Sensibility* (Marianne–Colonel Brandon), *Pride and Prejudice*, *Mansfield Park*, and *Emma*.

so that he may know his wife's real state of mind. That done, he must work out his own destiny for himself. The Duchess (and her creator) in fact believe that the educated, rational mind must *necessarily* arrive at the truth. If unsuborned by emotion, and uncoerced by external authority, Mr. L—— must in the end perceive the difference in human value between a Leonora and an Olivia.

The modern reader may feel that the Duchess and her daughter take a considerable gamble. Only a dedicated rationalist chooses to put a man's objectivity to the test just when he is in the grip of a sexual infatuation. In fact, Maria Edgeworth is unable to show that Mr. L——'s return to reason is entirely self-generated. She has to lean on an improbable sequence of accidents, whereby he discovers the secrets of Olivia's private correspondence in the nick of time. Even if not convincing, however, Maria Edgeworth's dénouement at least gives the tale of the philosophic seducer a twist all her own. The debate she inaugurates between Leonora's principles and Olivia's turns into a struggle in Mr. L——'s mind: and the human value of the two women in his life is equated with their respective scheme of values. In this way, against the grain of both theme and format, *Leonora* turns into another drama of evolving consciousness with Mr. L—— as the key figure. The dénouement of this initially conservative novel conveys a faith in the human mind and in its capacity to achieve Right Reason comparable with Holcroft's in *Anna St. Ives*. Strangely enough, its ending is even akin to the faith Madame de Staël expresses through the character of Delphine—a faith in the nobility and larger capacity for love of men and women who assert their right to choose.

In this acutely partisan period, Maria Edgeworth's individualism might well have been enough to attract the hostile notice of critics. Yet despite her vein of modest liberalism on a number of issues (including, later, the Irish question), Maria Edgeworth attracted conservative censure on only one of them. The subject of religion is omitted from *Practical Education* entirely; typically, when the Catholic Madame de Rosier is hired to teach the Protestant English family in *The Good French Governess*, the question of what religion she is to

instil is dismissed in a paragraph.[1] Several critics made unfavourable reference to the absence of religious education in
an otherwise comprehensive treatise, and vestiges of the
controversy clung to Maria Edgeworth in later life.[2] Especially in the conservative *Quarterly Review*, for example, the
question of Miss Edgeworth's religion recurs, however inappropriate the context; and when Richard Whately[3] comes
to compare her novels with Jane Austen's, he seizes upon it as
the intellectual issue that divides them:

> With regard to the influence of religion, which is scarcely, if at all,
> alluded to in Miss Edgeworth's novels, we would abstain from
> pronouncing any decision which should apply to her personally
> . . . but, as a writer, it must still be considered as a blemish, in the
> eyes at least of those who think differently, that virtue should be
> studiously inculcated with scarcely any reference to what they
> regard as the main spring of it; that vice should be traced to every
> other source except the want of religious principle; that the most
> radical change from worthlessness to excellence should be repre-
> sented as wholly independent of that agent which they consider
> as the only one that can accomplish it . . .
>
> Miss Austin [*sic*] has the merit (in our judgment most essential)
> of being evidently a Christian writer . . .[4]

Maria Edgeworth was irritated that the charge should
linger on to be applied to her social comedy, where she
thought it irrelevant. In fact, Whately's diagnosis was not
unfair: the heroes of Edgeworth novels do indeed find their
own road to salvation, along a route that is rational rather
than religious, and owes nothing to external guidance. Maria
Edgeworth ought instead to have thanked her good fortune
that in spite of an *œuvre* which was distinctly progressive
for the period, she was benignly reviewed—above, we now
think, her deserts—by conservatives and liberals alike.
    The explanation for her critics' indulgence—indeed, for

---

[1] *Moral Tales: Works*, iii. 98.   [2] See *Maria Edgeworth*, pp. 341–2.

[3] Whately, 1787–1863, was a Fellow of Oriel College, Oxford, at the time
of writing this review. From 1831 to 1863 he was Archbishop of Dublin. In
Church and Irish matters he was a moderate, but an eccentric and often
abrasive personality impaired his usefulness as a conciliator in these two highly
contentious spheres. See below, pp. 162–5.

[4] [Richard Whately] 'Northanger Abbey and Persuasion', *Quarterly Review*,
xxiv (Jan. 1821), 359. For the remainder of the comparison, as it affects Jane
Austen, see below, p. 162.

Francis Jeffrey's noticeable partisan approval[1]—lies, surely, in the safety of her tone. There was something about Maria Edgeworth's demeanour that effectively neutralized such dangerous examples as Forester's democratic sympathies, Belinda's decision to act independently of her guardian, or, later, the steady stream of criticism directed at Irish absentees and their agents. This something is connected with a sober realism of presentation, which tends to imply commitment to the world as it is. For all the anti-jacobin novelists, 'empiricism' is the true philosophic answer to the abstract idealism of the revolutionaries; only not one of those practising in the 1790s has the creative intelligence to find the literary equivalent. Maria Edgeworth is not Jane Austen, but she has a far sounder literary instinct than any other contemporary writer of prose fiction, until Scott. Even her early novels, and especially the children's tales of *The Parent's Assistant*, have an air of literal, prosaic reality that is at once, implicitly, opposed to the sense-created, sense-centred, imagined world of sentimental fiction. Her literalness increases: the Irish Tales are often so stuffed with fact as to read like travel-literature, or blue books. It is a seeming paradox that the same novels can be at once dramas of the consciousness, and to an unprecedented degree 'realistic' in terms of the external world.[2] Maria Edgeworth, like Jane Austen, wastes few words describing a setting, but, again like Jane Austen, she strains every nerve to command the reader's acceptance. The sense of contemporary actuality is fortified by street-names in real towns; consistent dates, culled from almanacks; journeys, timed with atlases and time-tables; lawsuits, carefully checked with legal experts.[3] Not all realists, in all periods, have been conservative. But in the era after Hume, simultaneous stress on the conscious mind and on an objective, prosaic external

---

[1] Jeffrey admitted that he favoured Maria Edgeworth, on account of what he considered to be the peculiarly wholesome influence of *Popular Tales* (see below). 'Miss Edgeworth's *Leonora*', *Edinburgh Review*, viii (1806), 212.

[2] Darrel Mansell has recently noted the same paradox in Jane Austen's novels. *The Novels of Jane Austen: An Interpretation*, London, 1973, pp. x–xii and *passim*.

[3] The concern for literal accuracy of this kind became characteristic in the nineteenth century. The intricacies of the Statute of Limitations, for example, drove both Maria Edgeworth and George Eliot to seek professional guidance: the former for *Patronage*, the latter for *Felix Holt*.

scene, suggests only one thing: the dismissal of doubts about the material world; the demotion of the wayward senses.

What is more, although her physical settings are not by Victorian standards specific, Maria Edgeworth is literal to a degree about the economic circumstances of people's lives. We nearly always know about their incomes, their jobs or professions (if any), their precise class status, their appropriate daily pursuits. The salvation of Edgeworth characters tends to be worked out in explicitly material terms. We are left knowing the routine stretching indefinitely into the future, and (in the case of poorer characters) the source of income too. It is a materialism also to be conveyed by Jane Austen's novels, and the effect is reassuringly stabilizing. Much more than Jane Austen, Maria Edgeworth avoids the typically conservative, institutional view of marriage; but her individualism is anything but rebellious, since she equates moral independence with financial independence within a free-enterprise system. It is a view she might have justified by quotation from her father's favourite Adam Smith. When she urges rich and poor to do an honest day's work, she imagines them as a result both happier and freer. But, as Francis Jeffrey shrewdly discerns in writing of her *Popular Tales*, the effect if they obeyed her would also be to keep the present system going:

It is for this great and most important class of society [that great multitude who are neither high-born nor high-bred] that the volumes before us have been written . . . to fix [their attention] upon those scenes and occurrences which have an immediate application to their own way of life; and in this way to fix upon their minds the inestimable value and substantial dignity of industry, perseverance, prudence, good humour, and all that train of vulgar and homely virtues that have hitherto made the happiness of the world, without obtaining any great share of its admiration.

This is an attempt, we think, somewhat superior in genius, as well as utility, to the laudable exertions of Mr. Thomas Paine to bring disaffection and infidelity within the comprehension of the common people, or the charitable endeavours of Messrs. Wirdsworth [*sic*] & Co. to accommodate them with an appropriate vein of poetry. Both these were superfluities which they might have done very tolerably without; but Miss Edgeworth has undertaken . . . to bring them back from an admiration of pernicious absurdities, to a relish for the images of those things which must make the happiness of their actual existence.[1]

Nothing could demonstrate more clearly that to Jeffrey's mind a literal, naturalistic treatment of the economic and social world induced the reader to accept the existing order of things. No wonder, then, that Maria Edgeworth did not frighten him.

[1] 'Miss Edgeworth's *Popular Tales*', *Edinburgh Review*, iv (1804), 329–30.

PART II

JANE AUSTEN

In MORALS We are equally old-fashioned. We have not yet learned the modern refinement of referring in all considerations upon human conduct, not to any settled and preconceived principles of right and wrong, not to any general and fundamental rules which experience, and wisdom, and justice, and the common consent of mankind have established, but to the internal admonitions of every man's judgment or conscience in his own particular instance.

Prospectus of The Anti-Jacobin, 1797.

CHAPTER 6

SEEING A MEANING

OF all the truisms about Jane Austen, the favourite for the past century at least is that she take no interest in the broad concerns of national life. It is a proposition which has seemed as obvious to the general reader as to the professed critic. Winston Churchill exclaimed, 'What calm lives they had, those people! No worries about the French Revolution, or the Napoleonic Wars.' Chesterton wrote of 'a story as domestic as a diary in the intervals of pies and puddings'. Frederick Harrison visualized Jane Austen with more severity, as 'a rather heartless little cynic . . . penning satirettes about her neighbours while the Dynasts were tearing the world to pieces and consigning millions to their graves'.[1] Among rather more recent critics, H. W. Garrod makes her limitation of scope a central point in his celebrated *Depreciation*, and the Marxist Professor Arnold Kettle, although more sympathetic to the novels, has also felt the need to grapple with it— 'the limitation must not be ignored or glossed over'.[2] The commonest modern solution is probably Ian Watt's, that Jane Austen dodges the charge because she is a moralist rather than a realist. 'Many readers had mistaken the novels for a complacent mirror of that limited world, but they were really Jane Austen's mode of mastering it.'[3] The narrow range is admitted, but modern criticism has become reconciled to it. Indeed J. Christopher Herold, comparing *Pride and Prejudice* with *Delphine*, actually implies that it is precisely because Jane Austen *did* ignore the partisan battles that her novels have survived as current classics, while Madame de Staël's have not.[4]

[1] Churchill, Chesterton, and Harrison all quoted by F. B. Pinion, *A Jane Austen Companion*, London, 1972, pp. 24–5.

[2] *An Introduction to the English Novel*, New York, 1960, p. 101.

[3] *Jane Austen: A Collection of Critical Essays*, ed. Ian Watt, Englewood Cliffs, N.J., 1963, p. 6. (Watt makes the observation while summarizing sympathetically the views of the Victorian critic, Richard Simpson.)

[4] *Mistress to an Age*, Charter ed., 1962, p. 236.

For good or ill her twentieth-century readers seem agreed that Jane Austen stands aside from the ideological convulsions that accompanied and followed the French Revolution. But detachment is not the quality that evidently strikes her contemporaries. Her first critics may be aware of her unusual tact in handling her didactic content. Richard Whately, noting this, compares her very favourably with Maria Edgeworth. It is a well-known passage of criticism, shrewd, sensible, and in line with twentieth-century conceptions. Whately is not saying, however, that Jane Austen has less didactic content than Maria Edgeworth: merely that she manages it better. It is clear from the development of his argument that he does not look upon Jane Austen's unobtrusiveness as an admirable quality in any final sense. It is a virtue because it gives additional effect to her impeccable orthodoxy:

Miss Austen has the merit (in our judgment most essential) of being evidently a Christian writer; a merit which is much enhanced, both on the score of good taste, and of practical utility, by her religion being not at all obtrusive. She might defy the most fastidious critic to call any of her novels (as *Coelebs* was designated, we will not say altogether without reason) a 'dramatic sermon'. The subject is rather alluded to, and that incidentally, than studiously brought forward and dwelt upon.[1]

Whately's association of Jane Austen with the Evangelical Hannah More—for he makes no overt theological difference between them—raises the issue of what *kind* of a Christian Jane Austen was taken by her contemporaries to be. Her attitude to Evangelicalism cannot easily be defined, since her two direct comments on the movement are contradictory. 'I do not like the Evangelicals', was her reply in 1809 when her sister urged her to read *Coelebs*;[2] but in 1814, the year of

---

[1] 'Northanger Abbey and Persuasion', *Quarterly Review*, xxiv (Jan. 1821), 359. For Hannah More's *Coelebs* (1808), see below, p. 219. Whately is engaged in a comparison between Jane Austen and Maria Edgeworth as equals: two naturalistic novelists, and also, to use Maria Edgeworth's phrase, two 'philosophic' novelists, one rationalist and one Christian. For the other half of the comparison, see above, p. 154.

[2] JA to Cassandra Austen, 24 Jan. 1809: *Letters*, ed. R. W. Chapman, 2nd ed., Oxford, 1952, p. 256. This letter, and a reference probably to *Practical Piety* (1811) (*Letters*, p. 287), both suggest that Hannah More was read and liked in the Austen circle, even if not by JA herself.

Mansfield Park, she was declaring. 'I am by no means convinced that we ought not all to be Evangelicals, & am at least
persuaded that they who are so from Reason and Feeling,
must be happiest and safest.'[1] A later reference to her acquaintance Dr. Edward Cooper's *Two Sermons Preached at Wolver-
hampton* (1816) refines the matter still further. 'We do not
much like Mr. Cooper's new Sermons;—they are fuller of
Regeneration & Conversion than ever—with the addition of
his zeal in the cause of the Bible Society.'[2] Evidently she had
a theological dislike of Calvinism, coupled with an aesthetic
distaste for that wing of the Evangelical cause which was permeated by Methodism.

But taken as a whole Evangelicalism meant an influence for
religion and morality, rather than a particular dogma. In the
first two decades of the nineteenth century it became effective
as a powerful upper-middle-class pressure group directed towards reforming abuses and combating vice. Long before 1814
its parliamentary successes, and above all its publicists (Wil-
berforce, Zachary Macaulay, Hannah More) had brought the
movement to the attention of all educated Christians—and,
through cheap tracts, to vast numbers of the poor as well.
Changing social conditions—of which in truth the Evangelical
movement was the symptom rather than the cause—prepared
the ground in 'good' society for the most generalized of its
crusades: that which urged more decent and pious living, a
stricter sense of social decorum (or what Byron in *Don Juan*
characterizes as 'cant'). For the hostile remark in *Persuasion*
about Mr. William Walter Elliott's 'Sunday travelling' surely
tells us that a changed climate of opinion was abroad by 1816,
the year of *Persuasion*'s composition.[3] The world of the last
novel reflects the moral influence of the rising middle class, and
is subtly different from the laxer, more permissive social
atmosphere of the three novels Jane Austen began before
1800.[4]

[1] JA to Fanny Knight, 18 Nov. 1814: *Letters*, p. 410.
[2] JA to Cassandra Austen, 8 Sept. 1816: *Letters*, p. 467.
[3] See below, p. 284.
[4] For evidence of how different *The Anti-Jacobin*'s tone and style was
from the Evangelicals', see F. K. Brown, *Fathers of the Victorians*, Cambridge,
1961, pp. 15–20, which is especially amusing about the most un-Evangelical
freedom of language *The Anti-Jacobin* permitted itself in 1797–8. The tone of

The detail of Jane Austen's opinions, and her style of expressing them, were both no doubt subject to fashion, as these things usually are. Jane West and Elizabeth Hamilton wrote as avowed Christians in the 1790s: they were light and satirical in tone, they placed their emphasis on good works rather than on the more inward 'faith', and they entirely avoided displays of 'enthusiasm'. During the first two decades of the nineteenth century, numbers of Christian novels of a much more pietistic, crusading, and emotional spirit appeared. The avowedly Evangelical *Coelebs* was followed, for example, by the well-regarded religious novels of Barbara Hofland (*Son of a Genius*, 1812) and Mary Brunton.[1] Children's fiction also began to pass out of the rationalistic phase of Thomas Day and the Edgeworths, who were serious-minded and instructive, but cheerful, into the gloomier era of Mrs Sherwood (*The History of the Fairchild Family*, 1818–47), harbinger of the death-bed religiosity of so much early-Victorian children's literature. Because in very general terms they reflect 'established' ideas, Jane Austen's novels share society's growing seriousness of tone during the period of her writing life.

However, the purpose of this study is not to follow every clue to her religious opinions. It is to show that her manner as a novelist is broadly that of the conservative Christian moralist of the 1790s;[2] that she continues to write as a Christian, with minor modifications only to accord with the prevailing manner; and that before the disputatious sectarianism of the next generation, it is still possible to draw a critical divide where Whately puts it: between the advocates of a Christian conservatism on the one hand, with their pessimistic view of man's nature, and their belief in external authority; on the other hand, progressives, sentimentalists, revolutionaries,

---

an unreformed upper class peeps out in JA's first three novels. *Mansfield Park* and *Persuasion* each contains much more social criticism of aristocratic self-indulgence, a theme that was increasingly typical of the Evangelicals in the period (see below, pp. 242–5 and 284–90). The idea that a gentleman ought to be socially useful does not appear at all in *Northanger Abbey* or *Sense and Sensibility*, whereas it is crucial in all of the last three novels.

[1] See above, p. 55, and below, p. 219 ff.

[2] Jane Austen's modern critics, notably Q. D. Leavis and B. C. Southam, have established the essential continuity of her work. Their field of interest has been primarily her evolving technique, but their demonstration applies equally to her ideas and to her form.

with their optimism about man, and their preference for spontaneous personal impulse against rules imposed from without.
It is important to recognize that this great distinction in
dogma dwarfs lesser ones, interesting in themselves though
these may be. As it happens, Richard Whately himself was an
opponent of Evangelicalism, and his 'chaste, clearcut, unimpas-
sioned, argumentative style' of preaching was unpalatable to
enthusiasts for that cause.[1] His anxiety to make the point that
one entertaining novelist at least was an impeccable Christian
may have been due to his desire to score off the Evangelical
philistines. Equally, it could be argued that without the undiscriminating Evangelical suspicion of *all* fiction, he could
still make the kind of distinction regularly drawn by *The
Anti-Jacobin*. His belief that Maria Edgeworth was too free-
thinking was shared by critics at various points of the religious spectrum, writing in the Anglican and Tory *Quarterly
Review*, the Nonconformist *Eclectic Review*, and the Evangelical *Christian Observer*.[2]

Just as the nuances of Jane Austen's religious position are
not central to the scope of this inquiry, so the finer points of
her outlook on class must be left to others. Certainly she
shows no love for the great aristocracy (as represented in
Darcy's family) or for the very rich (the Rushworths); and
pride of rank, whether in an earl's daughter or a baronet, is
evidently anathema to her. Jane Austen's attitude to social
distinctions in the upper reaches of society has been called
that of a 'Tory radical':[3] which is accurate provided we recognize that over all in the novels her Toryism carries more
weight than her radicalism. For a novelist during the revolutionary era, form and manner are decisive indices to partisanship, and an analysis of Jane Austen's characteristics in the
light of contemporary practice reveals, unarguably, the linea-
ments of the committed conservative.

Study of the novel of the 1790s shows how the two types of
partisan differ in placing the hero in his environment. One
test of allegiance is the degree of sympathy with which a
novelist views the feelings of his hero. Another, whether the

---

[1] 'Richard Whately', *DNB*. See above, p. 154n. From the description of
his own style we may guess that JA was a writer peculiarly to his taste.
[2] See above, pp. 153–4.   [3] See above, p. 2, and below pp. 284 ff.

plot, broadly, suggests a victim suffering at the hands of society, or a misguided individual rebelling against it. The first issue arouses real differences of interpretation among readers of Jane Austen, and is best left to an examination of the individual novels. But on the second, the question of her plot—or, for the two are hardly separable, her form—some preliminary generalization is possible.

Jane Austen moves turn and turn about between two plots, which can be crudely characterized as built about the Heroine who is Right and the Heroine who is Wrong. The first type, the Heroine who is Right, acts as spokesman for conservative orthodoxy. Elinor, Fanny, and Anne advocate principle, duty, and the sacrifice of private inclination to the service of others. The Heroines who are Wrong arrive at this state of true understanding only late in the day: they begin in intellectual error, brought about in Catherine by immaturity and false lights, but in Elizabeth and Emma by the more spiritual-looking errors of pride and presumption. In these three novels the dénouement follows the heroine's discovery of her mistake, and Elizabeth's exclamation is representative. 'I have courted prepossession and ignorance, and driven reason away . . . Till this moment, I never knew myself.' The moment of self-discovery and self-abasement, followed by the resolve in future to follow reason, is the climactic moment of the majority of anti-jacobin novels.

But of course the same moment occurs in the other three novels: in essence the *action* of all six Jane Austen novels is the same. In *Sense and Sensibility, Mansfield Park,* and *Persuasion,* however, it is a character other than the heroine, or more typically at least two characters, not only a lover but a parent-figure, who must perceive how far they have been deluding themselves. The difference between the two types of plot does not lie in the action, but in the relationship of the central character to the action. In the one case the heroine herself makes the moral discovery, in the other she brings it about in someone else. Where the heroine is fallible, the novel as a whole can be said to enact the conservative case; where the heroine is exemplary, she models it.

The great nineteenth-century novelists changed the reader's relationship to the consciousness of the central character, so that we are trained to involve ourselves more sympathetically than critically in the inward experience a novel has to offer. We do not look primarily to the plot to convey a meaning, and we may have to be cajoled, as a conscious exercise in historicism, into seeing that earlier novels may be about general and ethical rather than personal and emotional truths. Jane Austen's achievement is to naturalize a didactic tradition; but she relies on our sharing her beliefs, or at least identifying what they are. Her subtlety is such that, from the first, inattentive readers might be misled—as Maria Edgeworth was when she found *Emma* merely trivial. ('One grows tired at last of milk and water, even tho the water be pure and the milk sweet.')[1] But Whately saw more clearly, and Scott, and others too, or Jane Austen would not have been reviewed so seriously and approvingly as she was. The language of partisan writing was there in her novels for the alert to read: the day-to-day realism, the sceptical treatment of inward 'lights', and above all the chastisement that her plots meted out to presumption. Christians or moralists, or philosophers of the Victorian era might still see her meaning, but already they were competing with new assumptions, a new language of fiction, as an encounter between the backward-looking Mrs. Grote and the forward-looking George Sand neatly epitomizes:

She [Mrs. Grote] said to Madame Sand that it was a pity she did not employ her great powers for the leavening and mellowing of mankind, as Miss Austen had done. 'Madame', said Madame Sand, 'je ne suis pas philosophe, je ne suis pas moraliste, et je suis romancière.'[2]

Jane Austen was at least George Sand's equal as a novelist. But, like Mrs. Grote, she would have drawn the boundaries of that sphere somewhat differently.

[1] Quoted by ME from Mrs. Marcet: *Maria Edgeworth*, p. 445.
[2] Augustus J. C. Hare, *The Story of My Life*, 6 vols., London, 1896–1900, iv. 428. Harriet Grote, *née* Lewin (1792–1878), wrote two biographies and the privately printed *Philosophic Radicals of 1832*. Together with her husband, George Grote the historian, she belonged to the circle of Ricardo and J. S. Mill, and knew many French liberals. Although odd in her appearance ('Sydney Smith . . . said she was the origin of the word grotesque'), she was intelligent: 'De Tocqueville pronounced [her] the cleverest woman of his acquaintance.' (Hare, ii. 26.) Her perception of Jane Austen's serious meaning is telling evidence.

CHAPTER 7

THE JUVENILIA AND *NORTHANGER ABBEY*

W E are often told that Jane Austen's original satirical
inspiration was fed by dislike for a literary manner,
rather than for a moral idea. The juvenilia are, according to
this view, 'burlesques': though definition and re-definition
tends to surround the word, since it is by no means easy to see
what, precisely, is being burlesqued. Goldsmith's history-
writing, in 'The History of England . . . by a partial, prejudiced and ignorant Historian'? Surely not. The conventions of
the sentimental novel, variously in 'Volume the First'? The
great majority of these short fragments seem meant for
nothing more ambitious than to raise a laugh in a fireside
circle by that favourite eighteenth-century comic recourse,
extreme verbal incongruity. The heroine Alice 'has many rare
and charming qualities, but sobriety is not one of them'.[1]

Love and Friendship is another matter. Here there is an
unequivocal relationship with the sentimental novel, a tilt at
both form and content. Mackenzie had used the letter-novel
not as a means of contrasting different characters, but in order
to indulge his heroine's propensity for narcissistic self-
examination.[2] *Love and Friendship* presents an uninterrupted
stream of letters from the heroine, Laura, who dismisses the
occasional criticisms of others in favour of a complacent view
of her own character. 'A sensibility too tremblingly alive to
every affliction of my Friends, my Acquaintance, and particularly to every affliction of my own was my only fault, if a fault
it could be called.'[3] But though this may be parody, it is
directed not at manner but at substance: Laura (and Mackenzie's Julia) pretend to a virtue which Jane Austen wishes to

---

[1] *Minor Works*, ed. R. W. Chapman, Oxford, rev. ed., 1963, p. 23. But for
the argument that literary burlesque is pervasive in the juvenilia, cf. B. C.
Southam, *Jane Austen's Literary Manuscripts*, Oxford, 1964, p. 9 and *passim*.

[2] See the account of *Julia de Roubigné*, above, p. 26–7.

[3] *Minor Works*, p. 78. See above, p. 99.

deny them. The capacity to feel was presented as the trans-
cendent merit of every sentimental heroine from Julie to
Delphine, enough in itself to lift them above the common run
of mortals. Laura is placed in a numerous company when she
is made to applaud her own refinement and dismiss the more
utilitarian or extrovert qualities of others:

She [Bridget] could not be supposed to possess either exalted Ideas,
Delicate Feelings or refined Sensibilities——. She was nothing
more than a mere good-tempered, civil and obliging Young
Woman; as such we could scarcely dislike her—she was only an
Object of Contempt.[1]

The intention in satirizing Laura is above all to expose the
selfishness of the sentimental system. Here is a heroine
governed by self-admiration, and aware only of those others so
similar in tastes and temperament that she can think of them
as extensions of herself. Her rejection of the claims of the rest
of humanity arises either from hostility to those who try to
thwart her, or from unawareness of the claims of anyone outside the charmed circle of sentimental friendship. The co-
heroine, Sophia, cannot even visit her beloved, Augustus, in
Newgate—' "my feelings are sufficiently shocked by the *reci-
tal,* of his Distress, but to behold it will overpower my Sensibility" '.[2] Laura remembers to mention the death of her parents
only because it is a factor in making her destitute.[3] Rather
more subtle, perhaps, is Jane Austen's mocking observation
of the solipsism which may lie behind the sentimentalist's
paraded sensitivity to nature:

'What a beautiful sky! (said I) How charmingly is the azure varied
by those delicate streaks of white!' 'Oh! my Laura (replied she
hastily withdrawing her Eyes from a momentary glance at the sky)
do not thus distress me by calling my Attention to an object
which so cruelly reminds me of my Augustus's blue satin waistcoat
striped with white!'[4]

Although Jane Austen's sentimentalists act in a way that
is at the very least equivocal, for in practice they appear ruth-
lessly self-interested, it is no part of her intention to suggest

[1] Ibid., pp. 100–1.
[2] Ibid., p. 89. Cf. *Leonora*, in the passage quoted above, p. 151.
[3] *Minor Works*, pp. 89–90.   [4] Ibid., p. 98.

that they are insincere. In her view the contradiction is inherent in the creed: she wants to show that the realization of self, an apparently idealistic goal, is in fact necessarily destructive and delusory. As a formal burlesque rather than a novel, *Love and Friendship* is quite apart from Jane Austen's later career. Thematically, however, it makes the first chapter of a consistent story.

Of the early work, *Catharine, or the Bower* is the nearest attempt at true fiction: in fact it is the first recognizable effort at the classic Jane Austen form of novel. As in so many works of the period, an inexperienced young girl is on the threshold of life. One source of interest for the reader was clearly to have been Catharine's assessment of 'the world': her eventual discriminations about Camilla Stanley, the girl who offers her false sentimental friendship, and Camilla's brother Edward, who, as a lover, threatens her peace more substantially. In dramatizing this process of growing discernment Jane Austen achieves a technique which already belongs to the era of Maria Edgeworth rather than of Fanny Burney. The dialogue offers the reader direct evidence about the character of the two girls:

'You have read Mrs. Smith's Novels, I suppose?' said she to her Companion——. 'Oh! Yes, replied the other, and I am quite delighted with them—They are the sweetest things in the world ——' 'And which do you prefer of them?' 'Oh! dear, I think there is no comparison between them—Emmeline is *so much* better than any of the others——' 'Many people think so, I know; but there does not appear so great a disproportion in their Merits to *me*; do you think it is better written?' 'Oh! I do not know anything about *that*—but it is better in *everything*—Besides, Ethelinde is so long——' 'That is a very common Objection, I believe, said Kitty, but for my own part, if a book is well written, I always find it too short.' 'So do I, only I get tired of it before it is finished.'[1]

The characteristic of Camilla's mind as revealed here is carelessness, a habit of exaggeration and inaccuracy. She is not interested in the books they are talking about, though Catharine is. The striking feature of the conversation is its implicit moral frame of reference. Catharine is right to take the issue seriously, because it is a test case, a trial attempt at defining

[1] *Minor Works*, p. 199.

the good, which is the process upon which the moral life depends.

Dialogue of this kind is developed in *Northanger Abbey*, and in far subtler forms in the later novels, beginning with *Pride and Prejudice*. It is always associated with a narrative prose which so closely tracks the heroine's consciousness that it often approximates to 'free indirect speech'. Jane Austen never gives up her option of insinuating comments into her heroine's thought-process that in fact could have emanated only from the author, but in *Catharine* she is still clumsy about such interventions. Catharine's introduction to Camilla is spoilt by the superfluous observation that Camilla 'professed a love of Books without Reading, was lively without Wit, and generally goodhumoured without Merit'. But in the passage that follows, the author's comment, though officious, shows a kindly insight into the heroine's dangerous intellectual isolation:

... and Catharine, who was prejudiced by her appearance, and who from her solitary Situation was ready to like anyone, tho' her Understanding and Judgement would not otherwise have been easily satisfied, felt almost convinced when she saw her, that Miss Stanley would be the very companion she wanted. . . .[1]

Here is the first example of Jane Austen's technique of comparing the evidence given to the mind with the mind's insidious habit of perverting evidence: two planes of reality, the objective and the subjective, respectively presented in dialogue and in a form which approaches internal monologue. Catherine Morland's thoughts about Isabella, Elizabeth's about Mr. Wickham, and Emma's about Frank Churchill, are anticipated in Catharine's self-deceiving trains of thought about Camilla and afterwards about Edward:

The Evening passed off as agreably as the one that had preceded it; they continued talking to each other, during the chief part of it, and such was the power of his Address, & the Brilliancy of his Eyes, that when they parted for the Night, tho' Catherine had but a few hours before totally given up the idea, yet she felt almost convinced again that he was really in love with her. . . . The more she had seen of him, the more inclined was she to like him, & the

[1] Ibid., p. 198.

more desirous that he should like *her*. She was convinced of his
being naturally very clever and very well disposed, and that his
thoughtlessness & negligence, which tho' they appeared to *her* as
very becoming in *him*, she was aware would by many people be
considered as defects in his Character, merely proceeded from a
vivacity always pleasing in Young Men, & were far from testifying
a weak or vacant Understanding.[1]

If Jane Austen was no more than sixteen when she wrote
this, it is something of a *tour de force*; and what makes it more
remarkable is that the resourceful use of language supports
other appropriate narrative techniques. Catharine's situation
is well prepared in the opening pages of exposition. We are
shown that she is especially vulnerable because she is solitary:
her childhood friends, the Wynnes, have gone away, and she
is left in the company of her aunt, Mrs. Percival, who is fussy
and prosaic. Catharine likes to indulge her sentimental regret
for the Wynnes alone in her 'Bower', a romantic spot which,
as the sub-title indicates, was to have been given special
symbolic significance. Mrs. Percival, a prototype perhaps for
Mrs. Jennings or Miss Bates, objects to her habit of going
there, but for valetudinarian reasons which at the moment
Catharine finds it easy to dismiss. The real threat offered by
the Bower was clearly to have been to her moral health, for it
encourages her in a dangerously solipsistic reverie; and it is
there, appropriately, that Edward Stanley appeals to her
emotions by seizing her hand. It is clear even from these short
beginnings that the story was to have encompassed both the
natural evolution of Catharine's error, and its moral implications, so that in conception and, primitively, in technique, it
belongs to the series that culminates with *Emma*.

The first of Jane Austen's novels to be completed for publication, *Northanger Abbey*,[2] makes use of all the same impor-

---

[1] *Minor Works*, pp. 235–6. Cf. the passage from *Emma* cited below, p. 255.

[2] To discuss *Northanger Abbey* before *Sense and Sensibility* is a somewhat
arbitrary decision. In conception *S. & S.* is the earlier: the letter-version,
'Elinor and Marianne', dates from 1795, while the novel as we know it was
begun in Nov. 1797. In structure and theme *S. & S.* is a typical novel of
1795–6, while *N.A.*, which in part reacts to the rage for Gothic of 1796–8,
belongs historically a little later. And yet *N.A.*, which was accepted for
publication by Cadell under its title of *Susan* in 1803, was probably ready by

tant features. A naïve, inexperienced heroine stands at the threshold of life and needs to discriminate between true friends and false. The evidence she is given are words and the system of value they express; so that the reader, cleverer or at least more cleverly directed than Catherine, is able to make the correct discriminations for himself as the action unfolds. In one important respect the second Catherine is a coarser conception than the first, for she has been crossed with the burlesque heroine of the 'female quixote' variety, so that many of her intellectual errors are grosser and far more improbable. Yet although *Northanger Abbey* is often remembered for its sequence at the abbey, when Catherine is led by her reading of (presumably) Mrs. Radcliffe's *Romance of the Forest*[1] into fantastic imaginings, the central impulse of *Northanger Abbey*, and its serious achievement, has nothing to do with burlesque. Like *Catharine*, it uses the literary conversation not for the sake of the subject, but in order to give an appropriate morally objective ground against which character can be judged.

Catherine Morland has five important conversations about the Gothic novel: with Isabella Thorpe (vol. i. ch. vi); with John Thorpe (i. vii); with Eleanor and Henry Tilney (i. xiv); with Henry Tilney, in his phaeton on the way to Northanger Abbey (ii. v); and with Henry Tilney again, when he uncovers her suspicions of his father, the General (ii. ix). In all of these conversations, as in *Catharine*, the reader is not asked to criticize certain novels, nor the habit of novel-reading,[2] but rather to consider the habits of mind which the different speakers reveal. For example, when Isabella and Catherine first discuss horrid novels together, in chapter six of the first

then in substantially its present form. Cf. Alan D. McKillop, 'Critical Realism in *Northanger Abbey*', *From Jane Austen to Joseph Conrad*, ed. R. C. Rathburn and M. Steinmann, Jr., Minneapolis, 1958; and B. C. Southam, *Jane Austen's Literary Manuscripts*, 1964, p. 62.

[1] It was Adeline, heroine of that novel, who stayed at a ruined abbey and found a secret chamber behind the arras, containing a rusty dagger and a roll of paper which told the story of the man kept prisoner there.

[2] One of the commonest misconceptions about *Northanger Abbey* is that Isabella leads Catherine astray by introducing her to a world of horror and make-believe. But Catherine's worst error, to be taken in by Isabella, occurs before she has begun to read popular novels. Cf. Kenneth L. Moler, *Jane Austen's Art of Allusion*, Nebraska, 1969, pp. 19–20.

volume, Isabella's knowledge proves superficial: she is dependent on her friend Miss Andrews for all her information, and
Miss Andrews knows what is current, but not *Sir Charles
Grandison*. From this conversation it emerges that Isabella's
mind is not held by novels, for it continually runs after young
men, whereas Catherine's comments are characterized by
extreme, if naïve, interest. 'I do not pretend to say that I was
not very much pleased with him [Henry Tilney]; but while I
have *Udolpho* to read, I feel as if nobody could make me
miserable.'[1] Again, when Catherine raises the subject 'which
had long been uppermost in her thoughts' with John Thorpe,
it is to discover that despite his assurance he does not know
Udolpho is by Mrs. Radcliffe, and that he has got less than half-
way in the first volume of the five-volume *Camilla*. On the
other hand, the characteristic of the Tilneys which emerges
when Catherine raises the subject with them is informed
interest. 'I have read all Mrs. Radcliffe's works,' says Henry,
'and most of them with great pleasure.'[2] The mild qualifica-
tion is important, for the proper attitude of the person who
reads is a discriminating exactness—the quality Henry shows
when he challenges Catherine's word 'nice', and Eleanor when
she emends it to 'interesting'.[3]

After discussing novels the Tilneys move on to the subject
of history, just as the earlier Catharine of the juvenilia did.
Both topics, together with the Tilneys' choice of landscape,
enable Jane Austen to illustrate character at a light and
amusing level without imputing triviality. Choice of these as
subjects for conversation already implies a certain degree of
thoughtfulness and rationality—unlike John Thorpe's topics
of horses, curricles, drink, and money, and Isabella's of 'dress,
balls, flirtations and quizzes'.[4] Thus far at least the conversations about Gothic novels in *Northanger Abbey* belong to the
over-all strategy of the novel, which is concerned first to reveal
the character of the heroine, second to contrast the minds of
her two sets of friends, the Thorpes and the Tilneys.

The clarity of Jane Austen's conception appears to waver in
the second volume. Henry's teasing conversation with
Catherine during their drive to the abbey is, as earlier dia-

---

[1] *Northanger Abbey*, ed. R. W. Chapman, Oxford, 3rd ed., 1933, p. 41.
[2] Ibid., p. 106.   [3] Ibid., p. 108.   [4] Ibid., p. 33.

logues were not, a series of observations directed *at* the
Gothic mode. What Henry invents is a burlesque Gothic story,
compounded of various clichés—ancient housekeeper, isolated
chamber, secret passage, instruments of torture, hidden manuscripts, and extinguished candle—though it should also be
noticed, since it is typical of the discriminating reader in the
period, that he puts as much stress upon verbal blunders as
upon extravagances of plot. He imagines Catherine surmount-
ing an *'unconquerable'* horror of the bed, and discovering a
secret door through 'a division in the tapestry so artfully
constructed as to defy the minutest inspection'.[1] Henry's
lively and critical approach to his Gothic material is thus
contrasted with Catherine's selection of precisely the wrong
aspect to comment on. 'Oh! Mr. Tilney, how frightful!—This
is just like a book!—But it cannot really happen to me. I am
sure your housekeeper is not really Dorothy.'[2]

The memory of Henry's intelligent detachment in this conversation lingers as an unspoken commentary on Catherine's
series of interior monologues at Northanger—while she
searches her room, or lies terror-stricken in bed, or concocts
wild fantasies concerning the General and the death of Mrs.
Tilney. Typically, it is in the 'objective' form of dialogue,
where we are equally detached from both parties, and not in
subjective thought-processes, that we hear, reliably, the note
of rationality. And it is through another speech from Henry
that Catherine is brought at last to an understanding of the
'real' world of long-lasting social and religious institutions:

'What have you been judging from? Remember the country and
the age in which we live. Remember that we are English, that we
are Christians. Consult your own understanding, your own sense
of the probable, your own observation of what is passing around
you—Does our education prepare us for such atrocities? Do our
laws connive at them? Could they be perpetrated without being
known, in a country like this, where social and literary intercourse
is on such a footing; where every man is surrounded by a neighbourhood of voluntary spies, and where roads and newspapers lay
everything open? Dearest Miss Morland, what ideas have you been
admitting?'[3]

[1] Ibid., p. 159.   [2] Ibid., p. 159.
[3] Ibid., pp. 197–8.

There is clearly a difference in Jane Austen's use of dialogue in the first volume and in the second. In the first, it is the reader alone who is enlightened, by comparable dialogues between Catherine and the Thorpes, and Catherine and the Tilneys. During the same period the heroine neither learns to discriminate between her two groups of friends, nor to be discriminating about them. Although Henry Tilney has been setting her a good example for virtually a full volume, Catherine returns from her walk with him and Eleanor nearly as unenlightened as when she set out:

It was no effort to Catherine to believe that Henry Tilney could never be wrong. His manner might sometimes surprize, but his meaning must always be just:—and what she did not understand, she was almost as ready to admire, as what she did.[1]

In the second volume the impact on Catherine of Henry's remarks and, negatively, of Isabella's letters, is far greater. Aided no doubt by prosaic external evidence at the Abbey, she is brought sharply to a sense of reality:

The visions of romance were over. Catherine was completely awakened. Henry's address, short as it had been, had more thoroughly opened her eyes to the extravagance of her late fancies than all their several disappointments had done. Most grievously was she humbled. Most bitterly did she cry.[2]

When she becomes more tranquil, Catherine continues soberly to recognize that 'it had been all a voluntary, self-created delusion, each trifling circumstance receiving importance from an imagination resolved on alarm, and everything forced to bend to one purpose by a mind which, before she entered the Abbey, had been craving to be frightened'.[3] This, then, is the typical moment of *éclaircissement* towards which all the Austen actions tend, the moment when a key character abandons her error and humbly submits to objective reality.

During the period of *Northanger Abbey*'s evolution, before its near-appearance as *Susan* in 1803, Maria Edgeworth was experimenting with similar devices. *Belinda* has precisely the same stylized arrangement of characters, according to their contrasting philosophies of life, and perhaps an even more

---

[1] *Northanger Abbey*, p. 114.   [2] Ibid., p. 199.   [3] Ibid., pp. 199–200.

fully developed sense of the relationship between verbal style and quality of mind. What is very different in *Northanger Abbey*, however, different even from Maria Edgeworth's rather undistinguished execution in *Angelina*, is Jane Austen's reluctance to commit herself to her heroine's consciousness. It is not merely Catherine's emotional distress after she discovers her errors that receives hurried treatment; her actual mental processes are also summarily dealt with. From the consistent *naïveté* of her earlier thinking to her final state of enlightenment is a long step, but Jane Austen is not really concerned to examine it. Ultimately this is because, unlike Maria Edgeworth, she does not value the personal process of learning to reason as an end in itself. What is required of Catherine is rather a suspension of a particular kind of mental activity, her habit of romantic invention; at the moment Jane Austen is not concerned to define positively what kind of regular mental process it is that will keep Catherine sensible. For the naturalistic treatment of an individual's inner history which was promised in the first *Catharine*, here we have to make do with facetious stylization, and allusion to a ready-made inner world acquired from reading other people's books. We are shown that Catherine has learnt a significant general rule, that human nature is worse than she first thought: for, apart from her aberration over the General, she has successively overrated the Thorpes, Frederick Tilney, and perhaps even Henry, with all the sentimentalist's optimism about human nature. The reader is asked to take it on trust that henceforth she will apply more caution, more scepticism, more concern for the objective evidence. Of the actual change in her habits of mind that would make such a revolution possible he sees little or nothing.

Jane Austen was slower to handle the inner life confidently than to deploy dialogue: her next novel with a similar format, *Pride and Prejudice*, also fails to give Elizabeth's train of thought with the same clarity and brilliance with which it presents the dialogue.[1] Yet *Northanger Abbey* is consistent and ingenious in dramatizing the author's point of view, like all Jane Austen's novels to employ a fallible heroine. It establishes the antiphonal role of dialogue and free indirect speech which is

[1] See below, pp. 215–17.

to be so important in Jane Austen's career. It deploys characters around the heroine with the kind of antithetical precision
that is typical of Mrs. West, but much more amusingly and
naturally. Even if Catherine's mind is a somewhat implausible
blank, the arrangement of the two pairs of brothers and sisters,
the Tilneys and the Thorpes, virtually forces the reader into a
series of ethical comparisons between them on the author's
terms. However strong his training and his inclination to involve himself uncritically in the heroine's emotions, he is
manipulated into undertaking an unfamiliar kind of intellectual activity. Stylistically the novel induces him to value
sincerity and accuracy, rather than those emotions which are
harder to account for or specify. Formally it requires him to
use his judgement and not his feeling.

At the same time *Northanger Abbey* is very much a novel,
which is to say that it succeeds in creating and maintaining an
autonomous fictional world. The story is not a parody of a
novel story, but actually, like *Pride and Prejudice*, employs
the common novelist's fantasy of the poor girl who meets, and
after a series of vicissitudes marries, the rich young man.
Catherine may not be a 'heroine' in the idealized mode of
sentimental fiction, but she is a very good heroine at the level
which matters. She invites and keeps our sympathy, and she
makes us feel that what happens to her matters to us. No
wonder, indeed, that in the famous passage in chapter five
Jane Austen ironically refuses to condemn the novel: for
Northanger Abbey is quite as much a novel as *Udolpho* is.

It is perhaps because Catherine is so pleasing, even when
she blunders, that some recent critics have felt that Jane
Austen ends *Northanger Abbey* by reversing its whole moral
tendency; that she turns her irony on the good sense advocated
by Henry Tilney, and at least in part vindicates Catherine's
intuition. The central piece of evidence cited is that the
General, Montoni-like, turns Catherine out of Northanger
Abbey, and thus proves to be a villian after all. But an act of
rudeness is not villainy. It is not even, to use Andrew Wright's
term, 'violence'.[1] It arises from the ill-tempered pique of a

---

[1] Professor Wright is one of the most influential critics to hold that
Catherine's view of the General is not altogether illusory (*Jane Austen's
Novels: A Study in Structure*, London, 1954, pp. 106–7). Among others who

snobbish man who has just discovered that Catherine is a person of no social account. There is plenty of evidence throughout the novel that Henry and Eleanor are aware of their father's bad temper, as well as of his snobbery and formality: Eleanor's instant obedience on all occasions, for example, suggests that she has learnt to fear the General's anger. His treatment of Catherine comes nearer to confirming their view of him than hers, although it is perhaps not fully in keeping with either.[1]

Again, after Catherine returns home her romantic feelings are opposed to Mrs. Morland's worthy moralizing, and here at least Jane Austen appears to be on Catherine's side: 'There was a great deal of good sense in all this; but there are some situations of the human mind in which good sense has very little power; and Catherine's feelings contradicted almost every position her mother advanced.'[2]

But it is only by taking this observation out of context that we can read into it a serious meaning which relates to the whole book. The nice little vignette of Catherine's relations with her mother after her return home is surely yet another literary borrowing, this time from Fanny Burney's *Camilla*. Camilla's parents think that Camilla has been spoilt by high life, when really she is pining for the loss of her lover, Edgar Mandlebert; and Mrs. Morland is mistaken in just the same way. Had she really tried to cure a case of true love by fetching down a volume of *The Mirror* (containing 'a very clever Essay . . . about young girls that have been spoilt for home by great acquaintance'[3]), the incident might indeed suggest that Jane

---

have taken the same line, with incidental variations, are John K. Mathison, 'Northanger Abbey and JA's Conception of the Value of Fiction', *ELH* xxiv (1957), 138–52; Lionel Trilling, *The Opposing Self*, 1955, p. 217; Frank J. Kearful, 'Satire and the Form of the Novel: the Problem of Aesthetic Unity in Northanger Abbey', *ELH* xxxii (1965), 511–27; Henrietta Ten Harmsel, *Jane Austen: a Study in Fictional Conventions*, The Hague, 1964, pp. 25–6; and A. Walton Litz, *Jane Austen: A Study of her Artistic Development*, London, 1965, p. 63. But cf. Kenneth L. Moler, op. cit., pp. 38–40.

[1] The General's behaviour was so out of line with gentlemanly standards in the period that early readers found it incredible. Maria Edgeworth called it 'out of drawing and out of nature' (letter to Mrs. Ruxton, 21 Feb. 1818: Mrs. Edgeworth, *Memoir of Maria Edgeworth*, privately published, 1867, ii. 6). Hitherto we have thought of him as over-formal, and there is no room to modify his character sufficiently.

[2] *Northanger Abbey*, p. 241.   [3] Ibid., p. 239.

Austen was after all merely balancing the merits of feeling and sense. In fact Mrs. Morland's error is no more than a joke designed to reintroduce the hero in the lightest and least emotional manner possible.

Northanger Abbey is a novel, and it works as a novel, while at the same time it subjects the conventional matter of the merely subjective novel to consistently critical handling. Ideologically it is a very clear statement of the anti-jacobin position; though, compared with other anti-jacobin novels, it is distinctive for the virtuosity with which it handles familiar clichés of the type. Very pleasing, for example, is the cleverly oblique presentation of the subject under attack.

Most anti-jacobin novels include characters who profess the new ideology, and are never tired of canvassing it in conversation. In *Northanger Abbey* there is no overtly partisan talk at all. ('By an easy transition [Henry] . . . shortly found himself arrived at politics; and from politics, it was an easy step to silence.')[1] But in *Northanger Abbey* Jane Austen develops, perhaps from the prototypes the Stanleys in *Catherine*, her version of the revolutionary character, the man or woman who by acting on a system of selfishness, threatens friends of more orthodox principles; and ultimately, through cold-blooded cynicism in relation to the key social institution of marriage, threatens human happiness at a very fundamental level. Isabella Thorpe, worldly, opportunist, bent on self-gratification, is one of a series of dangerous women created by Jane Austen. Lucy Steele, Lady Susan, Mary Crawford, all like Isabella pursue the modern creed of self, and as such are Jane Austen's reinterpretation of a standard figure of the period, the desirable, amoral woman whose activities threaten manners and morals. Moreover, already in *Northanger Abbey* the opportunists find allies where they should properly be most vigorously opposed—among those who uphold only the forms, and not the essence, of orthodoxy. The pompous but mercenary General is as much implicated as John Thorpe in the pursuit of Catherine's mythical fortune. In the same vein, Henry and Mary Crawford meet no resistance, but encouragement, when they threaten to introduce anarchy into Mr. Rushworth's ancestral estate. And William Walter Elliott finds an easy

[1] *Northanger Abbey*, p. 111.

dupe, even an ally, in the empty figure-head he despises, Sir Walter.

That Jane Austen is perfectly clear what she is doing can be demonstrated by identifying the same cluster of themes and characters in *Sense and Sensibility*. Inheriting a set of conservative dogmas, and some impossibly theatrical characters—notably the revolutionary villain—already in her first two full-length novels she produces a more natural equivalent, on a scale appropriate to comedy. Her villains are not only better art than her rivals'; they are also better propaganda. The tendency among the routine anti-jacobins was to create Satanic demon–villains who were dangerously close in the temper of the times to being heroes.[1] Jane Austen's intelligence, like Burke's, is more subtle. Her selfish characters are consistently smaller and meaner than their orthodox opponents, the heroines; they are restricted within the bounds of their own being, and their hearts and minds are impoverished. Jane Austen's achievement, the feat of the subtlest technician among the English novelists, is to rethink the material of the conservative novel in terms that are at once naturalistic and intellectually consistent.

[1] See above, pp. 114–17.

CHAPTER 8

SENSE AND SENSIBILITY

OF the novels Jane Austen completed, *Sense and Sensibility* appears to be the earliest in conception. An uncertain family tradition suggests that its original letter-version, 'Elinor and Marianne', may have been written in 1795:[1] before the publication of Mrs. West's similar *Gossip's Story*, and in the same year as Maria Edgeworth's *Letters of Julia and Caroline*. The didactic novel which compares the beliefs and conduct of two protagonists—with the object of finding one invariably right and the other invariably wrong—seems to have been particularly fashionable during the years 1795–6. Most novelists, even the most purposeful, afterwards abandon it for a format using a single protagonist, whose experiences can be handled more flexibly and with much less repetition.[2] On the whole, therefore, all Jane Austen's other novels are more sophisticated in conception, and they are capable of more interesting treatment of the central character in relation to her world. But there is a caveat. Catherine in *Northanger Abbey* is dealt with, as we have seen, in an inhibited manner. A rather mindless character, of somewhat undefined good principles, she matures in a curiously oblique process that the reader does not quite witness. The format of the contrast-novel, with all its drawbacks, at least obliges Jane Austen to chart the mental processes of her heroines directly, and to locate the drama in their minds.

By its very nature *Sense and Sensibility* is unremittingly didactic. All the novelists who choose the contrast format do so in order to make an explicit ideological point. Essentially they are taking part in the old argument between 'nature' and

[1] W. Austen Leigh and R. A. Austen Leigh, *Jane Austen, her Life and Letters, A Family Record*, London, 1913, p. 80.

[2] Maria Edgeworth does not completely discard the contrast-novel, which recurs in one of the *Popular Tales*, *The Contrast*, 1804, and in *Patronage*, 1814. Jane Austen does not quite discard it either—for *Mansfield Park* is a contrast-novel, of the consecutive rather than the continuous type. See below, p. 220 ff.

'nurture': which is the more virtuous man, the sophisticated, or schooled individual, or the natural one? Obviously there is a total division on the issue between the type of traditional Christian who takes a gloomy view of man's unredeemed nature, and the various schools of eighteenth-century optimists, whether Christian or not. Although a Catholic, Mrs. Inchbald is also a progressive: of the two brothers in her *Nature and Art*, the sophisticated one stands for greed, self-seeking, worldly corruption, the 'natural' one for primal simplicity, honesty, sympathy, and innate virtue.[1] Maria Edgeworth, although in a sense favouring 'nurture' in her *Letters of Julia and Caroline*, does so on idiosyncratic terms which take her out of rancorous current controversy. But Mrs. West, in preferring her disciplined, self-denying Louisa to her self-indulgent Marianne, is entirely relevant to the contemporary issue, and entirely conservative. So, too, is Jane Austen.[2]

Jane Austen conscientiously maintains the principle of a didactic comparison. Her novel advances on the assumption that what happens to one of the central characters must also happen to the other; at every turn the reader cannot avoid the appropriate conclusion. The motif of the first volume is the attitude of each girl towards the man she hopes to marry. When the novel opens Elinor already knows Edward Ferrars. Her views about him are developed in conversation with Mrs. Dashwood, and the reader is also given Marianne's rather qualified opinion. When Edward and Elinor have to separate, Mrs. Dashwood invites him to visit them at Barton, but Edward seems reluctant. Thereafter Elinor's endurance of uncertainty about Edward's feelings becomes a factor in her character, and in our response to her.

Shortly after the family's arrival at Barton Cottage, Marianne's lover, Willoughby, enters the novel. His dramatic arrival is in keeping with his more flamboyant character; his

[1] *Nature and Art* appears to borrow its format from Thomas Day's Rousseauistic *Sandford and Merton*, 1783–9, with its spoilt little aristocrat Tommy Merton, and its robust, simple farmer's son, Harry Sandford.

[2] The very terminology adopted by some of the titles is revealing. Mrs. Inchbald sees the issue in terms of 'nature' versus 'art', art in this context having the connotation of artificiality. 'Sense' gives nurture a very different bearing. By the mid-nineties sensibility is commonly a pejorative word. See E. Erämetsä, *A Study of the Word 'Sentimental'*, etc., Helsinki, 1951.

appearance, too, is contrasted with Edward's; but the manner in which the sequence of his courtship is developed shows Jane Austen's concern to enforce a similarity of situation in order to bring out a dissimilarity of character. Again, Mrs. Dashwood gives her enthusiastic approval, while the other sister, in this case Elinor, expresses her reservations. When Willoughby leaves, Mrs. Dashwood once more issues her invitation, which is inexplicably not accepted, and Marianne, like Elinor, is left to a period of loneliness and anxiety.

When in the second volume the two heroines go to London they are placed, again, in a similar predicament. Both expect to meet the loved one there, both are obliged uneasily to wait; cards are left by each of the young men; each is lost, or seems lost, to a rival woman. In all the embarrassments and worries of the London visit, the reader's developing knowledge of the sisters is based on a substructure which demands that he adjudicate between them. And they leave London, as they entered it, still similarly placed, travelling towards the county, Somerset, where each believes her lover to be setting up house with his bride.

The parallels can be taken further, for example to the influence first of upbringing, later of idleness, on the characters of the two young men. The entire action is organized to represent Elinor and Marianne in terms of rival value-systems, which are seen directing their behaviour in the most crucial choices of their lives. It is an arrangement which necessarily directs the reader's attention not towards what they experience, but towards how they cope with experience, away from the experiential to the ethical.

In the two contrasted opening sequences the emphasis is on each girl's scale of values as she applies it to both young men. Edward Ferrars's attractions are not external. 'Edward Ferrars was not recommended to their good opinion by any peculiar graces of person or address. He was not handsome, and his manners required intimacy to make them pleasing.'[1] But even Marianne, who has reservations about Edward as a lover, has 'the highest opinion in the world of his goodness and

---

[1] *Sense and Sensibility*, ed. R. W. Chapman, Oxford, 1923, p. 15.

sense. I think him everything that is worthy and aimiable.'[1] For Elinor, this is commendation so high that she does not know what more could be said. As for herself, she admits that she 'greatly esteems' and 'likes' him: words which define the state of her understanding rather than her feelings, and, as such, seem to Marianne inappropriate.

But Marianne hesitates because in addition to Edward's lack of physical grace (what we might call physical attractiveness), he does not act like a lover with Elinor. In Marianne's language, he wants fire and spirit. His passionless temperament is further illustrated in his attitude to literature and to matters of 'taste' generally. When set by Marianne to read Cowper, he was, as she complains to her mother, tame and spiritless:

'To hear those beautiful lines which have frequently almost driven me wild, pronounced with such impenetrable coldness, such dreadful indifference!———'
'He would certainly have done more justice to simple and elegant prose. I thought so at the time; but you *would* give him Cowper.'
'Nay, Mama, if he is not to be animated by Cowper!—but we must allow for difference of taste. Elinor has not my feelings, and therefore she may overlook it, and be happy with him. But it would have broke *my* heart had I loved him, to hear him read with so little sensibility!'[2]

Marianne's objection is that Edward does not give free rein to the intuitive side of his nature. She equates lack of 'taste' with lack of response, an inability to enter subjectively into the emotions of a writer, or to attempt *rapport* with the spirit of a landscape. Again, as in *Northanger Abbey*, the reader is certainly not supposed to draw a moral distinction between characters concerned with literature, and characters concerned with life: for Elinor likes books and drawing, and Edward, who has views about both, and about landscape too, would do justice to 'simple and elegant prose'. But he, like Elinor, approaches the arts differently from Marianne. He would be likely to concern himself more than she with the intellectual content; when he looks at a landscape, he considers questions of utility—such as whether the terrain would be good for

1 Ibid., p. 20.　　　　2 Ibid., p. 18.

farming—and practicality—such as whether a lane would be too muddy for walking.

Edward's tastes can be considered aesthetically, as Augustan and thus in terms of contemporary landscape art old-fashioned: he has more in common with Pope than would please Marianne. But, and this is more to the novel's purposes, they are also the tastes of a self-effacing man, who likes to apply objective criteria, independent of his own prejudices and the limitations of his knowledge. His objective approach to art resembles Elinor's way of evaluating him. She knows enough of his background to see beyond the defects of his manner to the enduring qualities of his mind and spirit, his 'sense' and 'goodness', and both these words imply that Edward's virtues are those of a given code of value, namely the Christian. Edward's character, Edward's aesthetic opinions, and Elinor's method of assessing Edward, all have this much in common—that they are based on prescribed standards, not on subjective impulse.

With all this Marianne's choice of Willoughby is carefully compared. His entrance, like that of the 'preserver' of the heroine in a romantic novel, at once gives him a superficial glamour. He is 'uncommonly handsome' and his manner 'frank and graceful', so that not merely Marianne, but Mrs. Dashwood and Elinor,[1] are struck with admiration on his first appearance. His beauty encourages an intuitive response from Marianne, and receives it. She reacts to Willoughby with the same whole-hearted impulsiveness with which she reacts to books, and indeed before long she is reacting to books and Willoughby together, in a style that suggests all feeling, little or no intellectual detachment:

The same books, the same passages were idolized by each—or, if any difference appeared, any objection arose, it lasted no longer than till the force of her arguments and the brightness of her eyes could be displayed. He acquiesced in all her decisions, caught all her enthusiasm; and long before his visit concluded, they conversed with the freedom of a long-established acquaintance.[2]

---

[1] *Sense and Sensibility*, p. 42. Elinor's involuntary admiration of Willoughby is important in the light of their last interview together. See below, pp. 190–2.

[2] Ibid., p. 47. Cf. the courtship in *A Gossip's Story*, quoted above, p. 100.

When Elinor teases Marianne for running so recklessly through the beauties of Cowper and Scott, Jane Austen clearly means no criticism of two poets who were among her own favourites. But she does mean to criticize, through Elinor, the way Willoughby and Marianne read, and to show that, when they abandon themselves to their reading together, the result is grossly self-indulgent. Everything they do follows the same pattern of shared selfishness. Wholly absorbed in one another and in their exclusive pursuits, they rudely ignore the rest of their social circle, and, on the day of the cancelled outing, drive off together to Allerton in Willoughby's phaeton. As it happens, Sir John Middleton and Mrs. Jennings cheerfully tolerate the lovers. They in their turn are less tolerant; indeed, their self-sufficiency has an unattractive arrogance about it, which is displayed when they mount their unreasonable joint attack on Colonel Brandon. Willoughby's irrationality is as apparent here—'he has threatened me with rain when I wanted it to be fine'[1]—as it is later, when he begs that no alteration be made to Barton Cottage because he has pleasant associations with it as it is.[2] That Marianne has gone far along the same subjective path is demonstrated after her visit to Allerton. Elinor argues that she has been guilty of serious impropriety in going there in Mrs. Smith's absence. Marianne relies on her usual criterion, intuition: ' "If there had been any real impropriety in what I did, I should have been sensible of it at the time, for we always know when we are acting wrong, and with such a conviction I could have had no pleasure." '[3]

She believes in the innate moral sense; and, since man is naturally good, his actions when he acts on impulse are likely to be good also. Just as Marianne has no doubts about herself, so she can have none about her *alter ego*, Willoughby. Neither can Mrs. Dashwood, who, proceeding according to the same intuitional method as her second daughter, is wholly convinced of the goodness of Willoughby. When Elinor tries to argue with her, and to check instinct with the objective test of Willoughby's behaviour, her mother protests. She rightly sees that a broader question is at issue: Elinor's sense (stemming from the Christian tradition that man's nature is fallible) has come into conflict with the sentimentalist's tendency to

[1] Ibid., p. 52.　　　[2] Ibid., p. 73.　　　[3] Ibid., p. 68.

idealize human nature. From Elinor's caution, Mrs. Dashwood draws a universal inference. 'You had rather take evil upon credit than good.'[1]

So far, then, the issue between the two contrasted sisters is presented according to the view of the nature–nurture dichotomy usually adopted by conservatives. The contrast, as always, is between two modes of perception. On the one hand, Marianne's way is subjective, intuitive, implying confidence in the natural goodness of human nature when untrammelled by convention. Her view is corrected by the more cautious orthodoxy of Elinor, who mistrusts her own desires, and requires even her reason to seek the support of objective evidence.

It is in keeping with Elinor's objectivity (and also typical of the feminine variant of the anti-jacobin novel) that she should advocate a doctrine of civility in opposition to Marianne's individualism. Elinor restrains her own sorrow in order to shield her mother and sister. By her politeness to Mrs. Jennings she steadily makes up what Marianne has carelessly omitted. She respects Colonel Brandon for his activity in helping his friends long before Mrs. Dashwood and Marianne have seen his virtues. Civility is a favourite anti-jacobin theme, which does not appear in *Northanger Abbey*, although it is present in Jane Austen's later novels. Its objective correlative, the sketch given in *Sense and Sensibility* of society at large, is impoverished compared with the solid worlds of *Mansfield Park*, *Emma*, and *Persuasion*: the Middletons and Colonel Brandon, even supported by Mrs. Jennings, hardly stand in for a whole community. Yet this is a judgement arrived at by a comparison with Jane Austen's later work. If *Sense and Sensibility* is compared with other novels of the same genre, and originating at the same time, it can be seen to move in innumerable small ways towards fullness and naturalness. A conception of civility illustrated by gratitude to Mrs. Jennings is more natural, for example, than portraying a similar concept in terms of prayers beside a dying father, or fidelity to the death-bed advice of an aunt.[2]

[1] *Sense and Sensibility*, p. 78.
[2] Tests of the heroine's virtue in, respectively, Mrs. West's *Gossip's Story*, and Mrs. Hamilton's *Memoirs of Modern Philosophers*.

In fact, granted the rigidity imposed by the form, the second half of *Sense and Sensibility* is remarkably natural, flexible, and inventive. Both the sisters are presented as plausible individuals as well as professors of two opposing creeds. Another contemporary novelist—Mrs. West, Mrs. Hamilton, or the young Maria Edgeworth—would almost certainly have had Marianne seduced and killed off, after the errors of which she has been guilty. For during the first half of the novel Marianne has stood for a doctrine of complacency and self-sufficiency which Jane Austen as a Christian deplored:

Teach us to understand the sinfulness of our own hearts, and bring to our knowledge every fault of temper and every evil habit in which we have indulged to the discomfort of our fellow-creatures, and the danger of our own souls. . . . Incline us to ask our hearts these questions oh! God, and save us from deceiving ourselves by pride or vanity. . . .
Incline us oh God! to think humbly of ourselves, to be severe only in the examination of our own conduct, to consider our fellow-creatures with kindness, and to judge of all they say and do with that charity which we would desire from them ourselves.[1]

After Allerton, Marianne failed to examine her own conduct at all. She had none of the Christian's understanding of the sinfulness of her own heart; and she showed a notable lack of Christian charity towards Colonel Brandon, Mrs. Jennings, and the Middletons. Elinor alone had exercised the self-examination prescribed for the Christian, by questioning the state of her heart in relation to Edward, and, even more, her complex and disagreeable feelings about Lucy. Elinor never had the same certainty that Edward loved her which Marianne always felt about Willoughby. 'She was far from depending on that result of his preference of her, which her mother and sister still considered as certain.'[2]

The most interesting feature of the character of Elinor, and a real technical achievement of *Sense and Sensibility*, is that this crucial process of Christian self-examination is realized in literary terms. Elinor is the first character in an Austen novel consistently to reveal her inner life. The narrative mode of

---

[1] Prayers composed by Jane Austen: *Minor Works*, ed. R. W. Chapman, Oxford, rev. ed., 1963, pp. 453–4 and 456.
[2] *Sense and Sensibility*, p. 22.

Sense and Sensibility is the first sustained example of 'free indirect speech', for the entire action is refracted through Elinor's consciousness as *Northanger Abbey* could not be through the simple-minded Catherine's. Other technical changes necessarily follow. Dialogue is far less important in *Sense and Sensibility*, since the heroine is not so much in doubt about the nature of external truth, as concerned with the knowledge of herself, her passions, and her duty. Judging by the narrative mode alone, *Sense and Sensibility* is, like *Mansfield Park* after it, an introspective novel. And yet it is clearly important to recognize that both are introspective only within closely defined limits. The inner life led by Elinor, and later by Fanny, is the dominant medium of the novel, but it is entirely distinct from the irrational and emotional states which the post-Romantic reader thinks of as 'consciousness'.

Technically, as well as intellectually, Elinor's scrupulous inner life has great importance in the novel, and Jane Austen brings it out by giving similar qualities to the two male characters who approach a moral ideal. Edward Ferrars and Colonel Brandon have the same wary scepticism about themselves. Rather to the detriment of their vitality, Jane Austen's characteristic word for both of them is 'diffident'. Diffidence helps to explain Edward's unwillingness to expatiate on matters of taste; and 'the epicurism, selfishness and conceit' of Mr. Palmer are contrasted with Edward's 'generous temper, simple tastes and diffident feelings'.[1] Robert Ferrars's complacent comparison of himself with his brother Edward enforces a similar point.[2] And diffidence, especially in relation to Marianne, is also the characteristic of Colonel Brandon as a lover.[3]

But it is Elinor alone who can be seen living through the moments of self-examination that are evidently typical of both men. The most interesting sequence in which she is shown doubting herself occurs after she has heard Willoughby's confession. Many modern critics interpret this passage as evidence that Jane Austen is qualifying her own case, in order to arrive at a compromise solution somewhere between 'Sense' and 'Sensibility'. According to Mr. Moler, for example, Elinor feels after she has heard Willoughby that her own 'Sense' has been

[1] *Sense and Sensibility*, p. 305.   [2] Ibid., pp. 250–1.   [3] Ibid., p. 338.

inadequate: 'Elinor's rationality causes her to reach a less accurate estimate of Willoughby than Marianne and Mrs. Dashwood reach with their Sensibility.'[1]

Such interpretations are interesting as evidence of the difficulty the twentieth-century reader has with the notion of an objective morality. What happens in this episode is surely that Elinor is shaken by her feelings, for she finds both that she pities Willoughby and that she has a renewed sense of his 'grace', or personal attractiveness. Her judgement is assailed by involuntary sympathy: part of her wants to excuse his injuries to Marianne and Miss Smith. Yet the fact that Willoughby was tempted—by the two young women on the one hand, and by an education in worldliness on the other—does not in fact absolve the adult man, or not, at least, if one employs the objective ethical code rather than the relativist subjective one. The progressive supposedly sees the evil in individual men as social conditioning, the operation of impersonal forces which the individual cannot help. Elinor now considers Willoughby from this point of view—which is, of course, his own—and she finds it impossible to absolve him. 'Extravagance and vanity had made him coldhearted and selfish.'[2] This is not Jane Austen qualifying Elinor's sense with a dash of Marianne's sensibility. On the contrary, she shows Elinor's judgement reasserting itself, with some difficulty, after a most effective and deeply felt appeal has been made to her sympathies:

. . . Willoughby, in spite of all his faults, excited a degree of commiseration for the sufferings produced by them, which made her think of him as now separated for ever from her family with a tenderness, a regret, rather in proportion, as she soon acknowledged within herself—to his wishes than to his merits. She felt that his influence over her mind was heightened by circumstances which ought not in reason to have weight; by that person of uncommon attraction, that open, affectionate and lively manner which it was no merit to possess; and by that still ardent love

---

[1] *Jane Austen's Art of Allusion*, p. 70. For other expositions of the view that JA is 'ambivalent' between sense and sensibility, see Mary Lascelles, *Jane Austen and her Art*, p. 120; Andrew Wright, *Jane Austen's Novels: A Study in Structure*, pp. 30–1 and 92; and Lionel Trilling, 'A Portrait of Western Man', *The Listener*, 11 June 1953, 970.

[2] *Sense and Sensibility*, p. 331.

for Marianne, which it was not even innocent to indulge. But she felt that it was so long, long before she could feel his influence less.[1]

It is easy to mistake Elinor's sense for coldness. She is intended to be quite as loving and quite as accessible to 'feeling' as Marianne. The difference between them is one of ideology—Marianne optimistic, intuitive, un-self-critical, and Elinor far more sceptical, always ready to study the evidence, to reopen a question, to doubt her own prior judgements. She can be ready to revise her opinion of Willoughby. She can admit her mistakes, as she does of her wrong estimate of Marianne's illness.[2] The point about both episodes is that Elinor was never intended to be infallible, but to typify an active, struggling Christian in a difficult world. Indeed, Jane Austen clearly argues that we do not find the right path through the cold, static correctness of a Lady Middleton, but through a struggle waged daily with our natural predisposition to err.

It is the role of Marianne Dashwood, who begins with the wrong ideology, to learn the right one. After her illness she applies her naturally strong feelings to objects outside herself, and her intelligence to thorough self-criticism in the Christian spirit. In what for her is the crisis of the book, her confession of her errors to Elinor,[3] Marianne resembles Jane Austen's other heroines Catherine, Elizabeth, and Emma, all of whom arrive at the same realization that (in the words of Jane Austen's prayer) 'pride' and 'vanity' have blinded them in relation both to themselves and to external reality.

It is quite false to assume that merely because Marianne is treated with relative gentleness, Jane Austen has no more than a qualified belief in the evils of sensibility. She spares Marianne, the individual, in order to have her recant from sensibility, the system. Even this is possible only because Marianne, with her naturally affectionate disposition and her intelligence, is never from the start a typical adherent of the doctrine of

[1] *Sense and Sensibility*, p. 333.

[2] For Mr. Moler, Elinor's complacent first opinion, that Marianne will soon recover, is further evidence that JA meant to show the limits of sense, and to strike a balance with sensibility. *Jane Austen's Art of Allusion*, pp. 62–73.

[3] *Sense and Sensibility*, pp. 345 ff.

self: youth and impetuosity for a time blinded her, so that she acted against the real grain of her nature.[1] Because Marianne is not representative, other characters are needed, especially in the second half of the novel, to show the system of self in full-blooded action. Jane Austen provides them in the group of characters who fawn upon and virtually worship that false idol compounded of materialism, status-seeking and self-interest, Mrs. Ferrars.

The leading characters who take over from Marianne the role of illustrating what worship of the self really means are Lucy Steele and Fanny Dashwood. It is clear, of course, that neither Lucy nor Fanny is a 'feeling' person at all. Both are motivated by ruthless self-interest, Lucy in grimly keeping Edward to his engagement, Fanny in consistently working for her immediate family's financial advantage. But both Lucy and Fanny, though in reality as hard-headed as they could well be, clothe their mercenariness decently in the garments of sensibility. Lucy flatters Lady Middleton by pretending to love her children. She acts the lovelorn damsel to Elinor. Her letters are filled with professions of sensibility. Similarly, in the successive shocks inflicted by Lucy's insinuation of herself into the family, 'poor Fanny had suffered agonies of sensibility'.[2] It is no accident that at the end the marriages of the two model couples, Elinor and Marianne and their two diffident, withdrawing husbands, are contrasted with the establishments, far more glorious in worldly terms, of Lucy and Fanny and their complacent, mercenary husbands.[3] Lucy and Fanny may quarrel, but it is suitable that they should end the novel together, the joint favourites of old Mrs. Ferrars, and

---

[1] Marianne's intelligence is of a kind which gives her moral stature within Jane Austen's system of belief. Although she begins the novel professing an erroneous system, it is always clear that she has the capacity for the searching self-analysis of the Christian. Simple, good characters like Mrs. Jennings are valued by Jane Austen, but she never leaves any doubt that individuals with active moral intelligence are a higher breed. See below, pp. 270–1.

[2] *Sense and Sensibility*, p. 371.

[3] Some critics have called Elinor's marriage 'romantic', Lucy's 'prudent', and the end another instance of JA's compromise between sense and sensibility. (Cf. Andrew Wright, *Jane Austen's Novels*, p. 92.) But this shows a continued misunderstanding of JA's interpretation of her two terms: her 'sense' approximates to the traditional Christian personal and social ethic, her 'sensibility' to a modern individualist ethic in two different manifestations, Marianne's and Lucy's.

forever in one another's orbit. However it begins, the novel ends by comparing the moral ideal represented by Sense with a new interpretation of 'individualism'. The intellectual position, originally held in good faith by Marianne, is abandoned; what takes its place is selfishness with merely a fashionable cover of idealism—and, particularly, the pursuit of self-interest in the economic sense. Willoughby's crime proves after all not to have been rank villainy, but expensive self-indulgence so habitual that he must sacrifice everything, including domestic happiness, to it. Lucy's behaviour is equally consistent, and it, too, is crowned with worldly success:

> The whole of Lucy's behaviour in the affair, and the prosperity which crowned it, therefore, may be held forth as a most encouraging instance of what an earnest, an unceasing attention to self-interest . . . will do in securing every advantage of fortune, with no other sacrifice than that of time and conscience.[1]

Jane Austen's version of 'sensibility'—that is, individualism, or the worship of self, in various familiar guises—is as harshly dealt with here as anywhere in the anti-jacobin tradition. Even without the melodramatic political subplot of many anti-jacobin novels, Mrs. Ferrars's London is recognizably a sketch of the anarchy that follows the loss of all values but self-indulgence. In the opening chapters especially, where Marianne is the target of criticism, 'sensibility' means sentimental (or revolutionary) idealism, which Elinor counters with her sceptical or pessimistic view of man's nature. Where the issue is the choice of a husband, Jane Austen's criteria prove to be much the same as Mrs. West's: both advocate dispassionate assessment of a future husband's qualities, discounting both physical attractiveness, and the *rapport* that comes from shared tastes, while stressing objective evidence.[2] Both reiterate the common conservative theme of the day, that a second attachment is likely to be more reliable than a first.[3] By all these characteristic tests, *Sense and Sensibility* is an anti-jacobin novel just as surely as is *A Gossip's Story*.

The sole element of unorthodoxy in *Sense and Sensibility*

---

[1] *Sense and Sensibility*, p. 376.   [2] See above, pp. 97–101.

[3] Marianne, Colonel Brandon, Edward Ferrars, the late Mr. Dashwood, and even perhaps Lucy Steele are better matched in their second choice than in their first.

lies in the execution, and especially in the skilful adjustment of detail which makes its story more natural. *Sense and Sensibility* is not natural compared with Jane Austen's later novels. Any reader will notice the stiffness of some of the dialogue, particularly perhaps those speeches early in the novel where Elinor sums up the character of Edward.[1] And yet, especially in the second half of the novel, it is remarkable how the harsh outlines of the ideological scheme are softened. Often the changes are small ones, such as turning the jilted heroine's near-obligatory decline and death into a feverish cold caught, plausibly, from staying out to mope in the rain. Alternatively the difference may show in the born novelist's sense of occasion, her flair for a scene. Twice in the latter half of the novel, for example, there are theatrical entrances, consciously worked for: Edward's, when at last he calls on Elinor in London, only to find her with Lucy Steele; and Willoughby's, when he comes to Cleveland in response to the news that Marianne is dying. Developments like this do more than rub away some of the angularities of the old nature–nuture dichotomy. They begin to make so many inroads on it (particularly in relation to Marianne) that many readers have had the impression Jane Austen was trying to break it down altogether. Certainly there is plenty of evidence in the second half of the novel that Jane Austen was impatient with the rigidity of her framework; and yet all the modifications she makes are a matter of technique, not ideology. Lucy Steele resembles Isabella Thorpe and Mary Crawford, George Wickham, Henry Crawford, Frank Churchill, and William Walter Elliott in that she does not come, like some other authors' representations, vociferously advocating free love, or revolution, or the reading of German novels. She is a harbinger of anarchy for all that.

Compared with the common run of anti-jacobin novels it is a considerable achievement, and yet it has never been found quite good enough. *Sense and Sensibility* is the most obviously tendentious of Jane Austen's novels, and the least attractive. The trouble is not merely that, for all the author's artistic tact, the cumbrous framework and enforced contrasts of the inherited structure remain. It matters far more that the most

[1] *Sense and Sensibility*, p. 20.

deeply disturbing aspect of all anti-jacobin novels, their inhumanity, affects this novel more than Jane Austen's skilled
mature work. In a way *Sense and Sensibility* is worse affected
than many clumsy works by lesser writers, because it is written
naturally, and with more insight into at least some aspects of
the inner life. The reader has far too much real sympathy
with Marianne in her sufferings to refrain from valuing her
precisely on their account. There is plenty of evidence that
Jane Austen, anticipating this reaction, tried to forestall it.
As far as possible she tries to keep us out of Marianne's
consciousness: Marianne's unwonted secrecy, after Willoughby
has left Barton, and after her arrival in London, functions
quite as effectively in restricting the reader's sympathy as in
restricting Elinor's. Merely to have Marianne's sufferings described after she has received Willoughby's letter is sufficient,
however, to revive all the reader's will to identify himself with
her. The effort to point up Elinor's feelings instead will not do:
either we do not believe in them, and conclude her frigid, or
the felt presence of suffering in the one sister helps us to
supply imaginatively what we are not told about the inner life
of the other. It is difficult, in short, to accept the way consciousness is presented in this novel. Marianne, and to some
extent also Elinor, are drawn with strong feelings which the
reader is accustomed to sympathize with, and actually to
value for their own sake. But it is the argument of the novel
that such feelings, like the individuals who experience them,
are not innately good. Unfortunately, in flat opposition to the
author's obvious intention, we tend to approach Marianne
subjectively. Right or wrong, she has our sympathy: she, and
our responses to her, are outside Jane Austen's control. The
measure of Jane Austen's failure to get us to read her story
with the necessary ethical detachment comes when she imposes
her solution. What, innumerable critics have asked, if Marianne never brought herself to love Colonel Brandon? The fact
that the question still occurs shows that in this most conscientiously didactic of all the novels the moral case remains
unmade.

CHAPTER 9

PRIDE AND PREJUDICE

O F all the Austen novels, *Pride and Prejudice* seems at first glance the least likely to yield a conservative theme. Jane Austen herself playfully confessed that the impression it made was not serious:

> The work is rather too light, and bright, and sparkling; it wants shade; it wants to be stretched out here and there with a long chapter of sense, if it could be had; if not, of solemn specious nonsense, about something unconnected with the story; an essay on writing, a critique on Walter Scott, or the history of Buonaparté, or anything that would form a contrast, and bring the reader with increased delight to the playfulness and epigrammatism of the general style.[1]

Although the remedies Jane Austen suggests are intentionally absurd, the critical observation itself reads like a genuine one. At any rate, generations of Jane Austen readers have agreed in finding *Pride and Prejudice* the lightest, most consistently entertaining, and least didactic of the novels.

It would not be in keeping with the serious-mindedness of modern scholarship to rest content with the popular view of *Pride and Prejudice* as having no meaning at all. But the commonest interpretations, however they differ from each other, agree in placing it well outside the sphere of the antijacobin novel. Many modern critics have suggested that it appears deliberately to run counter to the conservative tendency which can hardly be gainsaid in *Sense and Sensibility* and *Mansfield Park*. In appearing before her readers in the guise of Elizabeth Bennet, Jane Austen—or so the argument runs—reveals herself the critic of various forms of orthodoxy.

A powerful and systematic interpreter of *Pride and Prejudice* as a progressive novel is Mr. Samuel Kliger, author of the essay 'Jane Austen's *Pride and Prejudice* in the Eighteenth

[1] Letter to Cassandra Austen, Chawton, Thursday 4 Feb. [1813]; *Jane Austen's Letters*, ed. R. W. Chapman, pp. 299–300.

Century Mode'.[1] Mr. Kliger develops the argument that *Pride and Prejudice* uses the familiar eighteenth-century antithesis between art and nature 'as the ground of the book's action and its mode of organization'.[2] He marshals a considerable number of instances in which the antithesis appears in relation to Elizabeth. Her 'natural' piano-playing is compared, for example, with Mary's artificial performance; her impulsive walk through the mud to Netherfield contrasts with the cold, formal reservations expressed first by Mary, later by Miss Bingley. A series of episodes, in short, presents Elizabeth on the side of nature, feeling, impulse, originality, spontaneity. Mr. Kliger takes care, as he begins, to introduce a caveat. 'Although Jane Austen's partiality for Elizabeth's vivid style is obvious, it would be a serious mistake to conclude that it was possible for either Jane Austen or her period to deprecate "art" altogether.'[3] Nevertheless he does not doubt that on the whole Jane Austen sympathizes with a 'natural' Elizabeth, a view which has startling implications when he transfers his attention from style to the sphere of morals, and, especially, of class relationships. He sees the movement of the book as one of compromise and mutual instruction, as Elizabeth learns to take class into account, and Darcy comes to share 'Elizabeth's genius for treating all people with respect for their natural dignity'.[4] Nevertheless, the tendency of Mr. Kliger's closing paragraphs, in which he compares Elizabeth with the seventeenth-century Levellers, is clear-cut enough. According to this reading, Elizabeth, even if not wholly victorious, is Jane Austen's revolutionary heroine.

A totally different approach to the relationship between *Pride and Prejudice* and other eighteenth-century novels has tended to produce the same kind of result. More than the rest of Jane Austen's work, *Pride and Prejudice* has attracted speculation about its purely literary borrowings. Mrs. Q. D. Leavis believes that in its early stages the novel was a burlesque of *Cecilia*, and that Elizabeth is still discernibly an

[1] *University of Toronto Quarterly*, xvi (1946–7), 357–71.
[2] Ibid., p. 362. [3] Ibid., p. 358.
[4] Ibid., p. 367. For a sophisticated variant of this reading—that Jane Austen shows herself, through Elizabeth, a 'Tory radical', with a strong anti-aristocratic bias—see D. J. Greene, 'Jane Austen and the Peerage', *PMLA* lxviii (1953), 1017–31.

anti-Cecilia.[1] Other critics have pointed out, however, that Darcy, as a 'patrician hero', has as much affinity with Fanny Burney's Lord Orville and Edgar Mandlebert as with her Mortimer Delville. Equally Elizabeth, as a poor heroine destined to marry a wealthy aristocrat, resembles Evelina and Camilla; and in behaving with spirit (or as Elizabeth herself might say, impertinence) to the dignified hero, she reflects appositely on all three Burney heroines.[2] Alternatively one might choose to trace the influence of Richardson: critics have severally argued that in *Pride and Prejudice* Jane Austen clearly had in mind the examples of the central couples in *Pamela*, *Sir Charles Grandison*, or both.[3]

Those who see special significance in Jane Austen's debt to part or whole of the Richardson–Burney tradition usually develop their case in a particular way. They claim that the principal difference between Jane Austen's version and its prototypes is that instead of the innocent, impulsive, fallible young girl and the model of established propriety whom she worships, the heroine of *Pride and Prejudice* dislikes, teases, and ends by in part debunking the hero. Where the Burney heroine was a sycophant of social and masculine prerogative, Elizabeth Bennet is fearless and independent. The critic who compares *Pride and Prejudice* with *Evelina* or *Grandison* is tempted to stress that element of scepticism and originality in Elizabeth which brings a new element into her hackneyed situations. Viewed like this, Jane Austen criticizes literary convention, or social convention, or both, by siding with Elizabeth in her teasing of Darcy.

Recent scholarship has established beyond possibility of doubt Jane Austen's debt to the conventions of eighteenth-century fiction. The case for a previous stage or a surviving

[1] 'A Critical Theory of Jane Austen's Writings', pt. 1, *Scrutiny* x (1941–2), 61–87. Cf. R. Brimley Johnson, *Jane Austen*, London, 1927, pp. 124–7, and *Jane Austen: Her Life, Her Work, Her Family and Her Critics*, London, 1930, pp. 137–9.

[2] The relationship between Darcy and the Richardson–Burney tradition of the patrician hero is developed in Kenneth L. Moler's chapter on *Pride and Prejudice*, in his *Jane Austen's Art of Allusion*, pp. 75–108.

[3] e.g., E. E. Duncan-Jones, 'Proposals of Marriage in *Pamela* and *Pride and Prejudice*', *N & Q* ccii (1957), 76, and her 'Notes on JA' *N & Q* cxcvi (1951), 14–16. Cf. also Henrietta ten Harmsel's chapter on *Pride and Prejudice* in her *Study in Fictional Conventions*, The Hague, 1964.

element of intentional literary burlesque remains much more questionable. It is a proposition which requires us to acknowledge that at some stage *Pride and Prejudice* was a very different work from the one we have. The habit of literary allusion was so strong in the period as to amount to a literary vice: Fanny Burney, Maria Edgeworth, and Scott, for example, all have a habit of quotation which can be little more than a verbal tic, so small is the contribution to the subject in hand. While Jane Austen was verbally more discriminating than any of them, she was even more willing to use conventional plot situations. Miss Mary Lascelles has pointed out that by restricting herself to the familiar topic of love and marriage in a limited domestic setting, Jane Austen confined herself more narrowly than Maria Edgeworth to situations which had already been exploited in novels.[1] Fanny Burney's favourite plot, which is also the plot of *Pamela*, of a poor girl (in Cecilia's case, a rich girl of inferior social status) who marries above her, is one of the commonest plots of the eighteenth-century novel. Given the stock situations, many scenes and some characters readily suggest themselves.[2]

There is a stronger argument against seeing in *Pride and Prejudice* a nonconformist version of Fanny Burney. In one respect *Evelina*, if not *Cecilia*, was typical of the subjective, individualistic manner of the 1770s: the heroine is a strong focus for the audience's sympathy, and in her very artlessness she acts (though not very consistently) as a critic of over-sophisticated society. Bage and Maria Edgeworth further develop the element of social criticism that the Burney framework offers; Jane Austen is the only one of the four to turn her back on the obvious thematic opportunity. Unlike her possible prototypes, Elizabeth is not employed to survey society, whether urban or provincial.

As for the comparison between the two types of heroine, meek and vigorous, it is possible to see Jane Austen making an iconoclastic point about Elizabeth only if we ignore other

---

[1] *Jane Austen and her Art*, p. 42.

[2] e.g., scenes between the hero and the heroine's embarrassing low relations, and scenes between the heroine and an arrogant woman of the hero's family. It is true that there are celebrated models for the first in *Evelina* and the second in *Cecilia*, but each is so obvious, given the plot, that even 'borrowing' seems too strong a word.

intervening versions of the Burney theme. Bage's novels regularly make the point that, of a pair of lovers, the poorer and lower-born one may be morally the more worthy, and may rightly disdain marriage with the man or woman whom the world thinks remarkably eligible.[1] In *Belinda* Maria Edgeworth gives moral value to her clever, independent-minded, disinterested heroine, through whom she certainly means to criticize feminine passivity and mindlessness.[2] It seems incredible that if Jane Austen wished to make the same individualistic point, she should have done so in a manner so much obscurer than the models known to her. Incredible, moreover, that she should have badly fudged the moral issue. The conclusion of Bage's *Hermsprong* shows signs of trimming when Hermsprong turns out not to be a man of no name after all. But if *Pride and Prejudice* ever intended to cock a snook at snobbish novels, the ending, with its clear feeling that a poor girl has made good, is far more deplorable than the mild backsliding of Bage. The fact is that *Pride and Prejudice* does not read like satire at all. Generations of readers have received its love-story as archetypally romantic, and they have been right to do so. What is true even of *Northanger Abbey*, that it is a novel rather than an anti-novel, is the very essence of *Pride and Prejudice*.

Nonetheless, intentional or unintentional, right or wrong, the tendency of the considerable scholarship which has gone into the sources of *Pride and Prejudice* has been to bring general support and comfort to critics like Mr. Kliger who associate Jane Austen intellectually with Elizabeth's individualism. If these critics are right, *Pride and Prejudice* is a very different novel from *Sense and Sensibility*, which precedes it, and *Mansfield Park*, which follows it. In both of these the heroine, with the author's obvious approval, stands for a point of view which is explicitly orthodox and Christian, and hence, according to the conventions of ideological debate in the period, politically conservative.

Far from being deterred by the strange apparent inconsistency of Jane Austen, Lionel Trilling emphasizes the contrast

---

[1] See above, p. 77. For evidence that Jane Austen possessed a copy of Bage's *Hermsprong*, see above, pp. 85–6. She alludes to *Belinda* in *Northanger Abbey*, pp. 37–8.   [2] See above, pp. 140 ff.

with *Mansfield Park*, and finds in iconoclasm the special glory of *Pride and Prejudice*:

A way of describing *Mansfield Park* is to say that it is almost the opposite of *Pride and Prejudice:* almost every virtue of freedom, vivacity and consciousness that is celebrated in *Pride and Prejudice* is condemned in *Mansfield Park*. Mary Crawford of *Mansfield Park* is in every detail of temperament the counterpart of Elizabeth Bennet, the perfection of whose qualities needs no proof, yet Mary Crawford, after having been allowed to charm us, is entirely condemned . . . *Pride and Prejudice* is militantly anti-snob. It sides with the young against the old. It is anti-religious in its implications, or at least anti-Church. . . . But [in] . . . *Mansfield Park* Jane Austen marshals every defence of the old way of life against the new.[1]

It may be important that both Mr. Trilling and Mr. Kliger see in *Pride and Prejudice* what they clearly like to see. They rate the novel high precisely on account of its supposedly radical theme. It has become very popular of recent years in the Austen canon, and many of its admirers, though not quite all, evidently find it attractive because they read into it social observation which is both penetrating and independent. 'Is not *Pride and Prejudice* in the very movement of its plot the representation of a great change that was overtaking society, the movement of a formerly depressed class into a position of power, and of a formerly powerful class into a position of compromise?'[2] Elizabeth and her family (or the maternal side of it) represent a rising middle class, with its money made in trade, and its characteristic virtues of independence and value for the individual rather than for his status in society. Darcy represents the old aristocracy, whose family must learn to respect merit, whatever its origin. Read like this, the novel moves towards a social synthesis as Elizabeth and Jane marry into higher ranks than their own: but the harmony of the conclusion is achieved largely at the expense of the pompous aristocrats and their hangers-on. Energetic, feeling, informal, a modern 'personality' rather than a pre-Romantic character, Elizabeth attracts critics of diverse liberal tendencies because

[1] 'A Portrait of Western Man', the *Listener*, 11 June 1953, 970.

[2] Mark Schorer, Introduction to the Laurel Jane Austen, New York, 1961, p. 8. Cf. E. Rubinstein, *Jane Austen's Novels: the Metaphor of Rank, Literary Monographs*, vol. ii, University of Wisconsin, 1969, pp. 101–233, *passim*.

they are predisposed to like a heroine who champions individualism against the old social order.

The more one examines the novel the more difficult it becomes to read into it authorial approval of the element in Elizabeth which is rebellious. It is true that, like all Jane Austen's fiction, *Pride and Prejudice* has an element of antithetical patterning. It is not true that the pattern is adequately summarized in the terms 'nature' versus 'art'. To begin with, Mr. Kliger's simple transition from the aesthetic sphere to the socio-political sphere is a long step, far too long one suspects for Jane Austen. He remarks of the aesthetic discussion that the taste and temper of the times 'required that excellence be found in a mean between two extremes'.[1] It may be true of art, but it is not true of politics, especially in the aftermath of the French Revolution. There the debate is about the nature and hence the rights of man, and it scarcely admits of trimming. As it happens, all novels built on the consciously antithetical pattern, from Sterne's comparison in *Tristram Shandy* of the feeling with the intellectualizing, to Maria Edgeworth's many comparisons of the rational with the unthinking, are about the human question, not the aesthetic question, and are—as one would expect—perfectly clear about which side they favour.[2]

In fact the antitheses in the novel by no means match Mr. Kliger's equation. They are far more complex and bewildering, since in many respects they cut across one another. To be sure Elizabeth, independent and informal, can be contrasted with Darcy, who is socially established and formal; Elizabeth's 'low' mother, sisters and aunt offer themselves for comparison with Darcy's haughty aunt and cousin. But, equally, Elizabeth and Darcy together, each of them complex and censorious, are balanced against the simpler Jane and Bingley, and this may prove in the long run to be the more significant comparison. The obvious social contrasts between the two extended families and their connections have encouraged, latterly, some unduly sociological interpretations, in which the characters come to stand for certain classes and class attitudes. Elizabeth and Darcy, for example, believe respectively in 'a

[1] Kliger, op. cit., p. 358.   [2] See above, e.g., p. 13.

personalist ethic' and 'a prudent and social point of departure', and the parties behind them follow suit: 'the novel is structurally balanced between the basic orientation of the two principals.'[1] Yet of all the points made by the complex action, the most decisive are surely those which affect Darcy and Elizabeth in their private capacity, as individuals. And if this is true, the notion of a structure which opposes the two is at best a half-truth, at worst misleading.

When Darcy and Elizabeth are first introduced, we are aware of great differences of personality between them: enough, one might think, to justify the idea that they are indeed presented as polar opposites. At the first assembly Darcy is 'discovered to be proud, to be above his company, and above being pleased; and not all his large estate in Derbyshire could then save him from having a most forbidding, disagreeable countenance'.[2] His hauteur seems as different as possible from Elizabeth's informality. 'She had a lively, playful disposition, which delighted in anything ridiculous.'[3] Elizabeth certainly continues in the notion that she and Darcy are so different as to be totally incompatible. Her teasing of him while they dance reveals the extent of the contrast as she sees it:

'. . . for the advantage of *some*, conversation ought to be so arranged as that they may have the trouble of saying as little as possible.'

'Are you consulting your own feelings in the present case, or do you imagine that you are gratifying mine?'

'Both', replied Elizabeth archly; 'for I have always seen a great similarity in the turn of our minds.—We are each of an unsocial, taciturn disposition, unwilling to speak, unless we expect to say something that will amaze the whole room, and be handed down to posterity with all the éclat of a proverb.'

'This is no very striking resemblance of your own character, I am sure', said he. 'How near it may be to *mine*, I cannot pretend to say.'[4]

This, then, ironically conveys Elizabeth's view that there is no similarity in the turn of their minds: a hasty conclusion

---

[1] Alistair M. Duckworth, '*Pride and Prejudice:* The Reconstitution of Society', *The Improvement of the Estate*, Johns Hopkins, 1971, p. 142.
[2] *Pride and Prejudice*, p. 10.   [3] Ibid., p. 12.   [4] Ibid., p. 91.

based on her hostile first impression of Darcy. And Darcy's view of Elizabeth is also coloured by his sense of a gulf between them; although for him it is not a difference of personality but of social status, an objective fact related to the dignity of his own family, and to the vulgarity of some of Elizabeth's connections.

Apparently many readers are persuaded by the opinions of the two protagonists that they should see in the love-story of *Pride and Prejudice* a meeting of opposites. Yet from the beginning the evidence supplied by independent witnesses and, surely, by the author herself shows that the two protagonists are mistaken. Whenever Elizabeth discusses Darcy's faults, she touches, though often unconsciously, upon her own. She notices at once, for example, that he is, like her, a critic of others. 'He has a very satirical eye, and if I do not begin by being impertinent myself, I shall soon grow afraid of him.'[1] In discussing his faults with Darcy, she gets him to admit to what he calls resentfulness, which is an unwillingness to change his mind once he has decided to censure someone. 'My good opinion once lost is lost for ever.'[2] Elizabeth calls this 'a failing indeed'; but Darcy's disapproval of Wickham is not more obstinate (and of course it turns out to be more reasonably founded) than Elizabeth's own wilful dislike of Darcy. Although for different reasons, both are equally likely to be severe on others:

'There is, I believe, in every disposition a tendency to some particular evil, a natural defect, which not even the best education can overcome.'
'And *your* defect is a propensity to hate everybody.'
'And yours', he replied with a smile, 'is wilfully to misunderstand them.'[3]

Darcy's theory of human nature implies a curiously blended attitude towards his own: in theory he admits he is fallible, but the real impression left is one of pride. For Elizabeth, too, the quality that goes with severity about others is complacency towards the self. As Jane Austen's prayers show, this

---

[1] Ibid., p. 24.   [2] Ibid., p. 58.

[3] Ibid. In this case, as in many others, Elizabeth's phrasing is far more exaggerated, and in fact untrue, in relation to Darcy, than his perfectly accurate observation about her. For the use of dialogues between them to expose Elizabeth's more pronounced intellectual errors, see below, p. 209.

disposition to think well of the self and ill of others is the opposite of what she conceives to be the Christian's duty:

Incline us oh God! to think humbly of ourselves, to be severe only in the examination of our own conduct, to consider our fellow-creatures with kindness, and to judge of all they say and do with that charity which we would desire from them ourselves.[1]

In *Pride and Prejudice* Jane Austen presents Miss Bingley and her sister Mrs. Hurst, who are 'proud and conceited', and, because fashionable, conceive themselves 'entitled to think well of themselves, and meanly of others'.[2] These have also been Darcy's faults, as eventually he humbly confesses:

'I have been a selfish being all my life, in practice, though not in principle. As a child . . . I was given good principles, but left to follow them in pride and conceit. . . . I was spoilt by my parents, who . . . allowed, encouraged, almost taught me to be selfish and overbearing, to care for none beyond my own family circle, to think meanly of all the rest of the world, to *wish* at least to think meanly of their sense and worth compared with my own. . . . You taught me a lesson, hard indeed at first, but most advantageous. By you, I was properly humbled.'[3]

The subject of *Pride and Prejudice* is what the title indicates: the sin of pride, obnoxious to the Christian, which takes the form of a complacency about the self and a correspondingly lower opinion, or prejudice, about others. Darcy's pride is humbled mid-way through the novel, when he proposes to Elizabeth and to his astonishment is rejected. The lesson he has to learn is not quite that it is hard for a rich man to enter the kingdom of heaven; it is more that we have no innate worth, either of social status or abilities. We have to earn our right to consideration by respect for others, and continuous watchfulness of ourselves.

Elizabeth's corresponding sin is more subtle and her enlightenment requires the space of the whole book. To begin with she seems unconscious that she suffers from pride at all. Quick of observation, encouraged by her father's example to take delight in the follies and vanities of others, she sees everyone's mistakes but her own. The false proffers of friendship from Miss Bingley and Mrs. Hurst do not deceive her:

---

[1] See above, p.189 .   [2] *Pride and Prejudice*, p. 15.   [3] Ibid., p. 369.

she already has too low an opinion of them. She is quick to
see and enjoy the foibles of Mr. Collins, as she has always
taken pleasure from those of Sir William Lucas. But she also
quite unreasonably persists in thinking ill of Darcy, and, just
as perversely, in thinking well of Wickham, even when the
evidence that he is a fortune-hunter is placed before her.
Elizabeth's pride in her own fallible perceptions is her governing characteristic.

There has been a curious tendency to take 'Pride' and
'Prejudice' to be polar qualities, like 'Sense' and 'Sensibility',
whereas in the course of the novel we generally see them
associated within the same character.[1] The proud Lady
Catherine is certainly prejudiced, and the prejudiced Elizabeth
can validly be accused of pride. Caroline Bingley after all
declares that her manners are 'a mixture of pride and impertinence',[2] and though we need not take the jealous Miss
Bingley too literally as to Elizabeth's manners, on Elizabeth's
moral character she probably speaks more truth than she
knows. So does the sententious Mary. Her pompous definitions
follow Elizabeth's flippant reference to her own pride as well
as to Darcy's:

'... I could easily forgive *his* pride, if he had not mortified *mine*.'
'Pride', observed Mary, who piqued herself upon the solidity of
her reflections, 'is a very common failing I believe. By all that I
have ever read, I am convinced that it is very common indeed,
that human nature is particularly prone to it, and that there are
very few of us who do not cherish a feeling of self-complacency
on the score of some quality or other, real or imaginary. Vanity
and pride are different things, though the words are often used
synonimously. A person may be proud without being vain. Pride
relates more to our opinion of ourselves, vanity to what we would
have others think of us.'[3]

It is a distinction which on the whole works in the book,
for both Elizabeth and Darcy are too proud to be vain.
Elizabeth, who is so quick about the mistakes of others,

[1] But cf. Andrew Wright, *Jane Austen's Novels: A Study in Structure*, p. 106:
'Darcy's pride leads to prejudice, and Elizabeth's prejudice stems from a pride
in her own perceptions'; and E. Zimmerman, 'Pride and Prejudice in *Pride
and Prejudice*', *Nineteenth Century Fiction*, xxiii (1968).
[2] *Pride and Prejudice*, p. 35.
[3] Ibid., p. 20.

has no inkling of her own fallibility until Darcy's proposal and the explanatory letter which follows it. The confrontation between these two central characters naturally brings about mutual illumination, not because one has opposite qualities which the other must learn to adopt, but because each discovers the other to be worthy of respect: the very admission of the value of an opponent forces both Elizabeth and Darcy to be more humble about themselves. Elizabeth's first concession is relatively trivial: she sees initially that she has been mistaken about Wickham. But it is more than this. As she examines her own mental processes, she notices that she has never been objective about him. She never tried to check his account of himself against information about his early life, if she could have acquired any, or even against what would have been available, 'some instance of goodness, some distinguished trait of integrity or benevolence'.[1] On the contrary, the subjective impression had been enough for her. 'His countenance, voice and manner, had established him at once in the possession of every virtue.' She now perceives that there *was* objective evidence; that Wickham, a stranger, ought not to have spoken so freely; that, contrary to his boast, he had not stood his ground, but had avoided Darcy; yet at the time she persistently ignored every pointer. Conversely she begins to see that apart from her own antipathy she has no case against Darcy.

> She grew absolutely ashamed of herself.—Of neither Darcy nor Wickham could she think, without feeling that she had been blind, partial, prejudiced, absurd. 'How despicably have I acted!' she cried.—'I, who have prided myself on my discernment! I, who have valued myself on my abilities! who have often disdained the generous candour of my sister, and gratified my vanity, in useless or blameable distrust.—How humiliating is this discovery!—Yet, how just a humiliation!—Had I been in love, I could not have been more wretchedly blind. But vanity, not love, has been my folly.—Pleased with the preference of one, and offended by the neglect of the other, on the very beginning of our acquaintance, I have courted prepossession and ignorance, and driven reason away, where either were concerned. Till this moment, I never knew myself.'[2]

---

[1] *Pride and Prejudice*, p. 206.   [2] Ibid., p. 208.

Later, in her confession to Jane, she is equally self-abasing:

'. . . I meant to be uncommonly clever in taking so decided a dislike to him, without any reason. It is such a spur to one's genius, such an opening for wit to have a dislike of that kind. One may be continually abusive without saying anything just; but one cannot be always laughing at a man without now and then stumbling on something witty.[1]

The last statement is perhaps the most perceptive utterance of Elizabeth's self-examination over her earlier treatment of Darcy. In his excellent essay on *Pride and Prejudice*, Mr. Howard S. Babb shows how in conversation with Darcy Elizabeth has indeed preferred wit to justice, and has steadily shown herself more fallible than he is. Elizabeth prides herself on her individualism and trusts her perceptions, never recognizing that her judgements are really grounded in her feelings. While Darcy is equally assured, his generalizations tend to be those of society at large, and he is far more careful than Elizabeth to base his arguments upon reason. Among the many instances cited by Mr. Babb is the scene at Rosings where Darcy replies with scrupulous accuracy to Elizabeth's persistent and perverse teasing:

'I shall not say that you are mistaken', he replied, 'because you could not really believe me to entertain any design of alarming you; and I have had the pleasure of your acquaintance long enough to know, that you find great enjoyment in occasionally professing opinions which are not your own.'[2]

Jane Austen has to allow time for her lovers to come together, and especially for Elizabeth to change her emotional antipathy for Darcy into a predisposition to love him, and she also needs time to bring Elizabeth to a full sense of right reasoning. In the second half of the book an event occurs, Lydia's elopement, which Elizabeth must concede gives objective support to Darcy's dislike of her connections. But the event has richer significance than this, since it provides a test of Mr. Bennet's character as a father. And Mr. Bennet, with his satirical view of human folly, his irresponsible detachment

---

[1] Ibid., pp. 225–6.
[2] *Pride and Prejudice*, p. 174. Cf. H. S. Babb, *Jane Austen's Novels: The Fabric of Dialogue*, Columbus, Ohio, 1962, p. 137.

from it as it is manifested in his own family, is shown to be morally very defective indeed. Elizabeth, trying to comfort him when Lydia's affairs are at their worst, begs him not to be too severe upon himself:

'You may well warn me against such an evil. Human nature is so prone to fall into it. No, Lizzy, let me once in my life feel how much I have been to blame. I am not afraid of being overpowered by the impression. It will pass away soon enough.'[1]

And it *does* pass away. At least, Mr. Bennet soon resumes his characteristic tone, his ironic detachment, and his tendency to enjoy his own cleverness at the expense of others. 'For what do we live, but to make sport for our neighbours, and laugh at them in our turn?' His remarks about Wickham as a son-in-law are heavily ironic; yet he does enjoy him, as he enjoys Mr. Collins, precisely because he can see through them:

'Much as I abominate writing, I would not give up Mr. Collins's correspondence for any consideration. Nay, when I read a letter of his, I cannot help giving him the preference even over Wickham, much as I value the impudence and hypocrisy of my son-in-law.'[2]

The moral exposure of Mr. Bennet is a further examination of the vices that Elizabeth, to a less culpable degree, has shared: for she is quite as much the product of her father's influence as Darcy was of his. It is from her father that she derives the tendency that is in her to misanthropy, before her reformation begins: 'The more I see of the world, the more am I dissatisfied with it; and every day confirms my belief of the inconsistency of all human characters, and of the little dependence that can be placed on the appearance of either merit or sense.'[3] No wonder, then, that she is brought to a proper view of Darcy's pride and prejudice, which, although excessive, was still in its way more reasonable, more based on objective evidence, than her own. Like Darcy, she emerges from a period of introspection concluding that, partly through a wrong upbringing, she has consistently over-valued herself. 'For herself she was humbled; but she was proud of him.'[4]

The most central of the antitheses in the novel is the one which contrasts the attitudes of the two pairs of central

---

[1] *Pride and Prejudice*, p. 299. [2] Ibid., p. 364.
[3] Ibid., p. 135. [4] Ibid., p. 327.

characters to the people around them. Darcy and Elizabeth
are similar in being 'satirical': they tend consistently to adopt
a low opinion of others. In this they are continuously compared with the other couple, Bingley and Jane, who are
modest about themselves and charitable about others. 'Your
humility, Mr. Bingley, must disarm reproof',[1] says Elizabeth,
in pointed reference to the arrogance of Darcy. Bingley thinks
well of the people of Meryton, Darcy ill. The arrogant Darcy
is convinced, wrongly, that Elizabeth loves him; Bingley is too
diffident about himself to believe that Jane returns his feeling.
The same contrast is more thoroughly worked out in the conversations between Elizabeth and Jane, where it is of more
moment because Elizabeth's moral errors matter more to the
reader than Darcy's. Elizabeth has always admired Jane for
her 'candour', her generous capacity to think well of others,
and at several points in the novel she pays general tribute to
the quality while in the individual case persisting in her own
characteristically astringent view.[2] Jane is surely too kind in
thinking Charlotte's motives in marrying Mr Collins may not
be narrowly prudential; she has to admit that she was over-
charitable about Miss Bingley; she did not see through
Wickham; but she was right in two important instances, in
detecting goodness where it really was—in Bingley and in
Darcy. After Wickham has spread his slanders about Darcy at
Meryton, Jane alone resists taking a prejudiced, hasty, or ill-
natured view:

. . . everybody was pleased to think how much they had always
disliked Mr. Darcy before they had known any thing of the matter.
Miss Bennet was the only creature who could suppose there
might be any extenuating circumstances in the case, unknown to
the society of Hertfordshire; her mild and steady candour always
pleaded for allowances, and urged the possibility of mistakes—
but by everybody else Mr. Darcy was condemned as the worst of
men.[3]

Elizabeth's conversations with Jane, in which she is gently
urged to take a more candid view, counterpoint her conversations with Darcy, in which we see her ill-founded prejudices in
action.

[1] Ibid., p. 48.   [2] Ibid., pp. 14–15, 116–20, 134–7, 147–9, 224–7.
[3] Ibid., p. 138.

Now this clearly *is* the kind of antithesis in which a balance is meant to be struck. Many critics have echoed Elizabeth's remark, 'intricate characters are the *most* amusing'.[1] We would not exchange Elizabeth's intelligence for Jane's innocence, nor Darcy's consistency for Bingley's pliancy, even though the faults of the central couple lead them into worse moral error. But in fact the author does not want us to—it is clear that her view of the truly Christian character blends the best qualities of all four. Elizabeth and Darcy take a properly pessimistic view of human liability to err, and, rightly applied, their perceptiveness will be a great moral quality: for Jane Austen insists that the scrupulous self-knowledge which she prizes is the product of their kind of sceptical intelligence. The example of the other couple helps them to harness their talents to more Christian ends, by showing charity towards others and humility towards themselves. To this extent Mr. Kliger's generalization applies: in the comparison between the two central couples, faults are identified with excesses in either extreme, and excellence lies in the mean. But the different beliefs that divide Elizabeth and Jane are not fundamental, for they concern the proper application of principles which they both share. Elizabeth's satire versus Jane's candour is a very different polarization from nature versus art, and it can never suggest to us that over the novel as a whole Jane Austen compromises between two views of human nature. Her moral ideal is clear: it is most nearly approached by Darcy and Elizabeth at the point when they have acknowledged the necessity of Jane and Bingley's humility and candour. In their ultimate state of enlightenment, Jane Austen's hero and heroine illustrate a view of human nature that derives from orthodox Christian pessimism, not from progressive optimism. The theme of the moral education of Elizabeth, which is paralleled by that of Darcy, does not sanction but rebukes the contemporary doctrine of faith in the individual.

If in nothing else, a clue to the conservatism of the novel lies in the original title, 'First Impressions'. Mr. B. C. Southam has suggested that *Pride and Prejudice* may have begun as a burlesque on that popular theme.[2] Jane Austen had already

---

[1] *Pride and Prejudice*, p. 42.
[2] *Jane Austen's Literary Manuscripts*, London, 1964, pp. 59–62.

employed it satirically more than once, for both *Love and Friendship* and *Sense and Sensibility* mock the convention of love at first sight; and, in doing so, express conservative scepticism about the 'truth' of man's spontaneous feelings. It is possible that Jane Austen meant to ridicule the hackneyed theme by standing it on its head: what *she* offers is hate at first sight. In any case, as she develops her plot in the final version, it is clear that to her love at first sight and hate at first sight are essentially the same. Both are emotional responses, built on insufficient or wrong evidence, and fostered by pride and complacency towards the unreliable subjective consciousness. It may well have been that with such a title the early version was more dogmatic: it belongs, after all, to 1796–7, years of great partisan activity in the novel, and approximately the era of the early work on *Sense and Sensibility*. Yet, for all its polish and technical maturity, the finished *Pride and Prejudice* has not, evidently, modified its ideological stance. As a novel it is far better than *Sense and Sensibility*, but no less conservative.

An explanation of *Pride and Prejudice* based on the theme of Elizabeth's moral enlightenment accounts for about three-quarters of the novel; and, like most other obvious explanations, it leaves a number of problems unresolved. What, for example, of the theme so beautifully established in the first sentence—'It is a truth universally acknowledged, that a single man in possession of a good fortune, must be in want of a wife'? It is a topic which brings Darcy's relative and Elizabeth's, Lady Catherine de Burgh and Mrs. Bennet, unexpectedly together, since both are venal about marriage, and blind to its moral significance for the individuals concerned. If we make this theme important, we perceive that there is after all *some* social criticism in the novel. The progress of the two central couples towards matrimony shows what the state ideally means. But for representative people of very different classes in society, it is a transaction involving merely money and status.

However, it is one thing to see a parallel between Lady Catherine and Mrs. Bennet, another to discern quite how the subject which links them together is supposed to work in

relation to Elizabeth's own marriage. If Jane Austen meant
to enforce the moral contrast between her ideal couples and
her matchmakers, it is strange that she allowed Elizabeth's
intermittent reflections on the subject of prudent marriage to
be so disconnected and (from the general ideological point of
view) so pointlessly inconsistent. It is true that she is appalled
by Charlotte's loveless marriage for financial security. (She is
equally shocked by Lydia's reckless pursuit of passion.) But
Elizabeth's readiness to condemn Charlotte operates more as
a means of throwing light on her own wavering judgement
than as an insight into marriage-in-society: for the next time
we hear of the subject is in relation to Wickham, whose plans
for a prudent marriage to Miss King Elizabeth is so incon-
sistently ready to condone.

The marriage-and-money theme operates in an even more
baffling way when Elizabeth herself comes to marry. Walter
Scott has been teased for declaring that Elizabeth decides to
marry Darcy because when she sees Pemberley 'her prudence'
begins 'to subdue her prejudice'.[1] Of course we are not supposed to take so literally her own joke to Jane that she must
date her love for Darcy from first seeing his beautiful grounds.[2]
The fact remains that Elizabeth *does* make what from the
materialistic point of view is a glorious match, the most
glorious of any Austen heroine, and that its material splendour is pointedly put forward. Quite what, then, is the connection between the heroine's personal progress, and minor
characters' satirized attitudes to husband-getting?

Marriage at the end of a conservative novel should be, and
is, the fulfilment of a personal moral quest. An impulsive or
mistaken protagonist, frequently someone whose first choice
in love was rash, now uses sober judgement and external
evidence to select a partner in marriage. Usually it is a girl,
a Marianne or a Camilla, who wisely chooses a guardian-like
husband; occasionally, for the point is not a sexist one, an
Edward Ferrars or an Edmund Bertram arrives at *his* second
choice, to find a wise mentor in an Elinor or a Fanny. The
personal implication in every case, given the prudence of the
partner, is that by the act of choice the erring lover gives up

---

[1] 'Emma', *Quarterly Review*, xiv (1815), 194.
[2] *Pride and Prejudice*, p. 373.

his or her youthful waywardness; all at once, it seems time to grow up. The 'true' marriage which follows close and sceptical analysis of the self is also the marriage which commits a couple to a responsible leading role in society. Jane Austen's heroines have a tendency to end up married to clergy or landowners, the spiritual or material leaders of a local community.

Unquestionably the marriage of Elizabeth and Darcy in *Pride and Prejudice* suggests all these traditional aspects. For both, but in our eyes more essentially for Elizabeth, it represents the arrival at true criticism of the self via correct, humbling assessment of another. Pemberley is significant in this inward process, but not because it means money and status. Darcy's grounds teach Elizabeth that his taste is 'neither formal, nor falsely adorned', and thus refute her preconceived notion of his pomposity. The good opinion of his housekeeper and tenants is precisely the objective proof of character that she neglected to look for in the case of Wickham. And of course the existence of Pemberley hints at a future life of active social involvement for both Darcy and Elizabeth, a role of far more real dignity than the self-important and selfish patronage of a Lady Catherine de Burgh.

Knowing the other five Austen novels, and a whole genre of lesser works by novelists of similar ideals, we can guess at a properly inward reading of the dénouement.[1] It would have been obvious to her first readers, who were well schooled in the ideological significance of marriage and of the processes leading up to it. But the meaning is not precisely or not sufficiently written into the text. If we return to the issue of Elizabeth's ideas about marriage in general, or to her own marriage with Darcy in particular, we find something of a vacuum. The elements in the novel which convey its meaning are the antithetical patterning, and a series of incidents; *Pride and Prejudice* tends to externalize its action, even though that action is a history of changing attitudes. The most striking omission from the novel's stylistic techniques is continuous free indirect speech, the simulated flow of the heroine's consciousness which is the narrative vehicle of the other mature novels.

[1] Cf. the eloquent discussion by Joseph Wiesenfarth, *The Errand of Form: An Assay of JA's Art*, New York, 1967, pp. 82–4.

In having a faulty heroine, *Pride and Prejudice* is comparable with *Northanger Abbey* and *Emma*; in technical sophistication it lies between the two. With *Pride and Prejudice* Jane
Austen rejects both the ironic authorial intrusions of *Northanger Abbey*, and the use of a hero who comes near to representing a moral ideal, to rely almost wholly for both narrative
and interpretation upon amusing and dramatic dialogue. The
clues for a right reading of the characters are present in
conversation for anyone acute enough to pick them up.
Darcy, though stiff, is careful, scrupulous, truthful; Elizabeth,
intoxicated by the pleasure of attacking him, often says what
she does not mean. Precisely the same technique is to be used
with greater clarity in *Emma*: for there the heroine's unreliable
thought-processes are exactly defined by the accuracy and
objectivity of Mr. Knightley's conversations with her. The
trouble with *Pride and Prejudice* is that many readers do not
perceive just how critical the author is of Elizabeth's way of
thinking. The meaning is obscure partly because Elizabeth's
thoughts are insufficiently characterized, and partly because
no character within the novel effectively criticizes her. The
reader accepts Knightley's evidence as objective, but tends
to reject Darcy's, since he too is prejudiced; alternatively,
Jane Austen does not reveal enough about what Darcy is
supposed to be thinking. In Elizabeth's crucial conversations
with Jane, the antithetical technique, contrasting Elizabeth's
satire with Jane's candour, operates in a baffling way: sometimes Jane is in the right, sometimes Elizabeth. Jane is an
ineffective guide to the failures of Elizabeth's consciousness,
since as far as the reader knows Jane herself hardly thinks at
all. Confusion enters because *as a whole* intelligence is represented as faulty in the novel. Nothing so clearly illuminates
the difference between the rationalist Maria Edgeworth and
the Christian Jane Austen as the admiration the former
bestows on Belinda's intelligence, and the scepticism with
which the latter regards Elizabeth's.

What makes *Pride and Prejudice* especially baffling is that
the form taken by intelligence in the novel is so seductive.
The reader cannot help admiring Elizabeth's wit and sharing
her lively and satirical vision. He enjoys *Pride and Prejudice*
largely for its caustic portraits of the servile Mr. Collins, the

foolish Mrs. Bennet, the sublimely insolent Lady Catherine de Burgh—which means that he looks out on the world of the novel with the eyes of an Elizabeth, even of a Mr. Bennet. The *action* may imply that this is morally a defective outlook. But, granted that the reader cannot identify himself either with Darcy or Jane, where is his alternative? Elizabeth's reformation is not complete until near the end (and everyone notices that the second, less satirical and extrovert half of *Pride and Prejudice* is less enjoyable than the first). The Gardiners, the only characters in the greater part of the novel who combine sceptical intelligence with good nature, do not offer a persuasive alternative to Elizabeth's consciousness, because during most of the action they do not know enough about what is really happening. The result is that in *Pride and Prejudice* the reader tends to feel himself in a moral limbo. The intention never was a statement about contemporary society which was 'militantly anti-snob' or 'anti-Church'. But the mistake is understandable. The inadvertent impression left by *Pride and Prejudice* is, literally, a negative one.

In spite of this, the general public has liked *Pride and Prejudice* the best of Jane Austen's novels, and it is easy to see why. Of them all, it is the most outward-looking, the most richly inventive in terms of character. Its breadth and spirit make it marvellously pleasing. There is no reason why we should object that it has no clear message; it has been compared with Mozart, who has no message either. What we can say is that in lacking clarity it is untypical of Jane Austen. It may well be that the author was more worried by the lightness of the effect than the irony of her tone when criticizing it implies; for with Fanny of *Mansfield Park* she reverted to a model heroine resembling Elinor. In this way, though setting herself great technical problems—and, most readers have felt, presenting a far less likeable central character— she at least avoided an effect dreaded by the moral novelist of the time, that of presenting a faulty heroine whose very errors were attractive. No other Austen novel except *Pride and Prejudice* can be accused of the fault most censured by Johnson, that of exhibiting virtues and vices promiscuously mixed, and by this means confusing good and evil. 'Vice . . . should always disgust; nor should the graces of gaiety, or the dignity of courage, be so united with it, as to reconcile it to the mind.'[1] The exterior Elizabeth presents to the world has all the graces of gaiety, and we do not understand her mental misdeeds clearly enough to call them vices. In *Pride and Prejudice* Jane Austen might have appeared to err from orthodoxy, not wilfully, but through a fault in the execution, and she never made the same mistake again.

[1] See above, p. 20.

CHAPTER 10

MANSFIELD PARK

With the possible exception of *Sense and Sensibility*, *Mansfield Park* is the most visibly ideological of Jane Austen's novels, and as such has a central position in any examination of Jane Austen's philosophy as expressed in her art. It is all the more revealing because here she has progressed far beyond the technical immaturity of the period when *Sense and Sensibility* was conceived, to a position where she can exploit to the full the artistic possibilities of the conservative case; and, at the same time, come face to face with the difficulties it presents. By far the most imaginative and accomplished of received anti-jacobin novels, *Mansfield Park* reveals all the inherent problems of the genre.

The superb draughtsmanship of the opening chapters of *Mansfield Park* makes it easy to forget that they present a set of themes which are entirely commonplace in the period. Its beginning must have encouraged contemporaries to believe that here was yet another novel by a female about female education.[1] Mrs. West's novels, from *The Advantages of Education* (1793) on, had hammered the theme. Mrs. Inchbald had dealt with it more elegantly and idiosyncratically in *A Simple Story*, and Fanny Burney had made it a very substantial subsidiary interest in *Camilla*. Since the turn of the century it had retained its place as perhaps the most popular of all themes of women novelists, notable examples being Mrs. Opie's *Adeline Mowbray* (1804) and Hannah More's *Coelebs* (1808). Maria Edgeworth, whose literary career was dedicated to the proposition that early education makes the man, had recently given it more extended treatment than ever before in *Patronage* (1814). The last-named novel has indeed innumerable incidental resemblances to *Mansfield Park*, which appeared later in the same year,[2] for not only is its

---

[1] See above, pp. 54–5.

[2] *Patronage* was published in December 1813, although 1814 appears on the

virtuous and well-brought-up heroine, Caroline Percy, compared with her foils, the fashionable Arabella and Georgiana Falconer, who strongly resemble the Bertram girls; but one of the most important sequences concerns the performance of a play, in which Georgiana Falconer displays herself, and Caroline Percy virtuously refuses to take part.

The reader of 1814 thus knew broadly where he, or perhaps more typically she, stood. The novel of female education criticized superficial qualities, particularly accomplishments, which were too narrowly aimed at giving a girl a higher price in the marriage-market: accomplishments and mercenary marriages tended to be coupled together. The debate was linked to, indeed was the female aspect of, that common eighteenth-century topic of educationalists, the inferiority of 'wit' or 'cleverness' to judgement. Hence the relevance of showing that the Bertram girls' education had been spent not only on their appearance and accomplishments, but also on superficial information designed to make them appear clever and well-informed in company—'. . . the Roman emperors as low as Severus; besides a great deal of the Heathen Mythology, and all the Metals, Semi-Metals, Planets, and distinguished philosophers'.[1]

The structure of *Mansfield Park* is as severely built round the contrast between the girls' education and its consequences as the see-saw structure of *A Simple Story* or *Patronage*, though Jane Austen's artistry does much to soften the outlines of the antithesis. (Technically she is now a world away from *Sense and Sensibility*, where the parallels were so much laboured.) The first part of *Mansfield Park*, until Sir Thomas's return facilitates Maria's marriage, is about the entry into life of the two Bertram sisters: their education, their values, and, especially, their inability to resist the worldly baits proffered by the Crawfords. In the second, slightly longer part, Fanny, the exemplary heroine, encounters in her turn the

---

title-page; *Mansfield Park* about five months later (it was advertised in the *Morning Chronicle* on 23 and 27 May). *Mansfield Park* was finished in the summer of 1813, and was not influenced by *Patronage*.

[1] *Mansfield Park*, ed. R. W. Chapman, Oxford, 1923, pp. 18–19. Cf. Maria Edgeworth's *Good French Governess*, quoted above, p. 133.

temptation of Henry's love, and Mary's friendship,[1] and prevails. Her endurance sets right the wrongs done at Mansfield by the older girls, just as in the second part of *A Simple Story* Miss Milner's daughter restores the family which was shattered by her mother's lapse from virtue.[2]

Maria Bertram especially is a girl according to the female moralist's common formula. Having demonstrated her vanity and superficiality in adolescence, she grows up with the typical ambition of marrying for money. 'Being now in her twenty-first year, Maria Bertram was beginning to think matrimony a duty; and as marriage with Mr. Rushworth would give her the enjoyment of a larger income than her father's, as well as ensure her the house in town, which was now a prime object, it became, by the same rule of moral obligation, her duty to marry Mr. Rushworth if she could.'[3] This 'duty' is one of the few Maria acknowledges, for as their father's daughter neither she nor her sister Julia feels any obligation. They are not fond of Sir Thomas Bertram, whose role as parent has hitherto been a negative one, and accordingly they feel nothing but a sense of release when he departs for Antigua. 'They were relieved by it from all restraint; and without aiming at one gratification that would probably have been forbidden by Sir Thomas, they felt themselves immediately at their own disposal, and to have every indulgence within their reach.'[4]

But, though the Bertram girls resemble other novelists' shallow females, the ideal figure set up in opposition to them is slightly more distinctive. In characterizing her heroine, Fanny, Jane Austen illustrates her ideological disagreement with Maria Edgeworth. Caroline Percy of *Patronage*, like Belinda, Leonora, and other Edgeworth model characters, is essentially a rationalist. Fanny Price is a Christian. The clue lies in those characteristics in which the Bertram girls are deficient—'It is not very wonderful that with all their promising talents and early information, they should be entirely deficient in the less common acquirements of self-knowledge, generosity, and humility.'[5] Immediately afterwards, Fanny,

[1] For the frequent reappearance of the lover and the sentimental friend as tempters, see Mrs. West's novels (above, pp. 96–104), and Jane Austen's *Catharine* and *Northanger Abbey* (above, pp. 170 ff).

[2] See above, p. 54. [3] *Mansfield Park*, pp. 38–9.
[4] Ibid., p. 32. [5] Ibid., p. 19.

in conversation with Edmund, is shown to have the qualities her cousins lack. Humility is obviously an appropriate virtue for the Christian heroine; but equally important in Jane Austen's canon is, as always, the impulse towards self-knowledge. Fanny's sense as a Christian of her own frailty, her liability to error, and her need of guidance outside herself, is the opposite of the Bertram girls' complacent self-sufficiency. For Jane Austen 'vanity', the characteristic of the fashionables, is a quality with a distinctly theological colouring. It means both an unduly high opinion of oneself, and a pursuit of worldly goals, 'vanities'. Such an error arises from an inability to place oneself in a larger moral universe, a context in which the self, and the self's short-term gratifications, become insignificant. As an ideal this is wholly different from the Edgeworthian belief in individual self-realization, leading to greater—not less—personal independence.

The entrance of the Crawfords soon extends and enriches the didactic case. The Crawfords are sophisticated, fully aware disciples of a worldly creed to which the Bertram girls merely veer unconsciously, on account of the vacuum left in their education. Mary Crawford has actually been instructed, by her social circle in general, the marriage of her uncle and aunt in particular, in a wholly sceptical modern philosophy. Her doctrine includes the notion that there are no values but material ones, and that the gratification of the self is the only conceivable goal. Mary's comments about marriage, uttered to her sister Mrs. Grant in the first scenes in which we meet her, are obviously meant to be compared with Maria Bertram's reflections about Mr. Rushworth. Where Maria is confused as to her values, and barely half aware of the moral implications of what she is doing, Mary sounds, and is, knowingly cynical. 'Everybody should marry as soon as they can do it to advantage. . . . Everybody is taken in at one period or other. . . . It is of all transactions the one in which people expect most from others, and are least honest themselves.'[1] Even more clearly, Henry Crawford's amoral determination to make the Bertram girls fall in love with him compares with their vague, complacent, and far less formulated readiness to be fallen in love with. The Crawfords, who know

[1] *Mansfield Park*, pp. 43–6.

precisely what they are doing, are infinitely more dangerous than the Bertrams. More than that, the Bertrams are peculiarly vulnerable to be made the Crawfords' dupes, since their attitudes to life already half incline them to throw off restraint and pursue the self-gratification which the Crawfords' creed allows. It is dangerous to be exposed to worldliness without the worldly-wisdom which goes with it.

The triple contrast, of three kinds of education, three kinds of moral attitude, is maintained in every early scene. The cynical Crawfords, planning their pleasures with cold selfishness; the Bertram girls, equally selfish but more naïve; Fanny, who alone after a few days retains enough insight and objectivity to see that Henry Crawford is still plain. Whatever the topic of dialogue, the moral landscape of the various characters is what really receives attention. Mary, for instance, brings up the question of whether Fanny is 'out' or 'not out', so that Jane Austen can contrast two widely diverging ideals of young womanhood. Edmund considers whether, out or not out, young women act with any real modesty; Mary, whether they act in accordance with convention.[1] Similarly, when Mary borrows Fanny's horse, the thoughts and actions of three principals, Edmund, Fanny, and Mary, can be examined in turn. Edmund, who has always been considerate of Fanny, is now seduced by his physical delight in Mary into forgetting her. Fanny, after detecting her own jealousy, and struggling with motives of which she is suspicious,[2] can at least display some genuinely objective concern for the horse. Mary correctly ascribes her own behaviour to selfishness, so gaily that she proves the vice has little meaning for her.

Mansfield Park is the first Austen novel to be conceived as well as executed after the appearance of Maria Edgeworth's social comedies.[3] Jane Austen had deployed lesser characters in a stylized pattern around her heroine before, but she had not exploited in any sustained way the typical Edgeworth intellectual comedy. The brilliant dialogue in *Pride and*

[1] Ibid., p. 50.

[2] As usual in Jane Austen, an awareness that one is influenced by ulterior motives is a sign of grace, not weakness. See the discussion of Elinor above, pp. 190-2.

[3] But cf. Mrs. Q. D. Leavis, 'A Critical Theory of Jane Austen's Writings', *Scrutiny*, x (1942) and xii (1944).

Prejudice is the natural culmination of a technique Jane
Austen had used since *Catharine*: it gives the reader and heroine simultaneously an objective insight into character. In the
first part of *Mansfield Park* a new element is added: the
subject-matter of a conversation becomes as important as the
insight it offers into character, because conversation becomes
the occasion for the clash of distinct systems of value. Three
key topics recur, all of them often found in anti-jacobin novels
of the 1790s. The first is Nature, and is illustrated by contrasting the attitudes of different characters towards living
in the country. All late-eighteenth-century moralists of whatever colouring prefer the country to the town,[1] but Jane
Austen's Fanny does so as a typical conservative: because she
associates it with a community, in which individuals have
well-defined duties towards the group, and because physically
it reminds her of the wider ordered universe to which the
lesser community belongs. Urban life, on the other hand, has
given Mary selfish values: she betrays her egotism when she
laughs at the farmers who will not let her have a wagon to
move her harp, and her materialism when she comments that
in London money buys anything. The second issue that will
recur in conversation in the novel, though sometimes allusively in association with Nature, is religion; the third is
marriage. All three come to the fore in the sequence that
provides an ideological key to the book, the visit to Sotherton.

The Crawfords' indifferent and even destructive attitude
to the country emerges when the visit to Sotherton is first
projected, for they go there as improvers. Essentially their
feelings are negative about the external scene they propose
to deal with. Utility is not a criterion which concerns them.[2]
Nor do they respond to the sentimental connotations of a
feature of landscape, the link with the past provided by
Sotherton's heavy, ancient avenue of trees. It is actually Mary
who first voices the idea that change must temporarily at least
mean disequilibrium: she remembers the time when her uncle
improved his cottage at Twickenham as a period of anarchy.

[1] See above, pp. 97–8 and 110. The Rousseauist of course preferred the
country for very different reasons, because it enabled him to be morally
independent and left him free to cultivate the self.
[2] Cf. Henry's later cavalier dismissal of the farmyard at Thornton Lacey.
Mansfield Park, p. 242.

But she is restless for novelty, and improvements are fashionable; in the arbitrary name of fashion she urges Mr. Rushworth to employ a landscape artist such as Repton. It does not occur to her, as it does to Fanny, to regret the destruction of the trees, since she is scarcely aware of inanimate nature, or the wider physical universe beyond herself and the few people she cares for. Sotherton itself is, or ought to be, a Burkean symbol of human lives led among natural surroundings, man contiguous with nature and continuous with his own past. Fanny finds it both these things, when she sees the grounds and begins to walk around the house. But Mary is bored and even hostile.[1]

In interpreting the meaning of the house within its grounds, and the chapel within the house, the two minds are joined by a third, Mrs. Rushworth's. She has learnt her speech parrot-fashion from the housekeeper, and her interest is far more in the grandeur of the outward appurtenances than in the quality of the life lived. Her casual remarks about the chapel—that the seat-covers were once less tasteful than they are now, and that it was her husband who discontinued the religious services—show clearly enough how superficial her values are. ' "Every generation has its improvements",' remarks Mary: and between Rushworth senior, who gutted the house in the interests of modernity, and Rushworth junior, who with Henry Crawford's help proposes to do the same for the grounds, there is morally little to choose.

The scene in the chapel, where Mary is offensive about clergymen, brings out for the first time in full the gulf between the Crawfords and religious orthodoxy. In discussing the suspension of chapel services, Mary thinks only of the immediate convenience to individuals who might have had to attend; while Fanny and Edmund have two concerns—the well-being of the individual, *sub specie aeternitatis*, and the social validity of established forms of worship:

'It is a pity', cried Fanny, 'that the custom should have been discontinued. It was a valuable part of former times. There is something in a chapel and chaplain so much in character with a great house, with one's ideas of what such a household should be! A whole family assembling regularly for the purpose of prayer, is fine!'

[1] Ibid., p. 85.

Mary in her individualism cannot even begin to apprehend the social value Fanny sees in religion:

'At any rate, it is safer to leave people to their own devices on such subjects. Every body likes to go their own way—to choose their own manner and time of devotion. The obligation of attendance, the formality, the restraint, the length of time—altogether it is a formidable thing, and what nobody likes. . . .'

Such an argument demands to be answered in terms of the individual, and Edmund does answer it:

'. . . We must all feel *at times* the difficulty of fixing our thoughts as we could wish; but if you are supposing it a frequent thing, that is to say, a weakness grown into a habit from neglect, what could be expected from the *private* devotions of such persons? Do you think the minds which are suffered, which are indulged in wanderings in a chapel, would be more collected in a closet?'[1]

The double function which Fanny and Edmund see religion as serving is important in the novel, and is developed more fully in subsequent conversations between Fanny, Edmund, and Mary. In the wilderness Edmund speaks of the social role of the country clergyman, his influence by example and precept on the minds of his parishioners.[2] Later, when Fanny discusses Dr. Grant with Mary, it is she who raises the more private, spiritual aspect:

'I cannot but suppose that whatever there may be to wish otherwise in Dr. Grant, would have been in greater danger of becoming worse in a more active and worldly profession, where he would have had less time and obligation—where he might have escaped that knowledge of himself, the *frequency*, at least, of that knowledge which it is impossible he should escape as he is now.'[3]

Mary is clearly equally indifferent both to the social aspect of religion ('duty' and 'morals'), and to its spiritual demand of self-knowledge, since she accepts no reality outside her own sensations. But to Fanny and Edmund the two meanings of religion are interdependent, and 'knowledge of the self' and knowledge of a reality outside the self cannot be disassociated from one another.[4]

---

[1] *Mansfield Park*, pp. 86–7.   [2] Ibid., pp. 92–3.   [3] Ibid., pp. 111–12.
[4] The question of Fanny's religion is generally dealt with indirectly, for reasons of taste. The nearest suggestion to a religious *experience* is the occa-

The theme of marriage is first glanced at in the chapel when Julia spitefully refers to Maria's coming marriage to Mr. Rushworth. In the hollow sham of a chapel the full emptiness of the proposed ceremony is felt. Afterwards, in the strangely diagrammatic sequence in the wilderness, we see sketched out the shadowy future, or at least tendency, of the various sexual relationships which are developing in the novel. Edmund and Mary walk up and down, supposedly for a finite time, and within the wilderness; but Edmund, not for the first or last time, forgets his promise to Fanny and strays further than he meant. Henry and Maria arrive with Mr. Rushworth at the gate, and while he (their future dupe) is away fetching the key, they escape through the palisade into the liberty of the park. Julia, who acts with the same impatience of restraint as they, and to the same end, is less guilty because she is not escaping from an acknowledged fiancé in the company of a desired lover. And so on. In any other novel such a miming of future events would seem an intolerable contrivance; but, extreme though it is, in *Mansfield Park* it does not seem illegitimate. The action of the novel is so entirely bound up with the value-systems of the various characters that they are always to a greater or lesser extent illustrating, acting out, their beliefs.

The sequence in the grounds, with Fanny still and alone on the seat, the others walking about, is especially expressive in terms of their relative roles. The worldly characters are the real subject of the first half, and Jane Austen is ingenious in letting them occupy the centre of the stage while Fanny as yet remains in the wings. Her consciousness is deliberately left slightly childish and unformed. Instinctively she tries to tell right from wrong, but as yet she lacks the ability; by contrast the Bertram sisters have the decision that comes with greater assurance and maturity, but they have no moral discrimination. Fanny's turn to act is to come, but her role of wondering observer of her cousins' doings is in itself expressive, suggesting as it does the virtuous person's struggle towards judgement and knowledge that is being neglected by

---

sion when she contemplates the stars and reflects that there would be less evil and sorrow in the world if 'people were carried more out of themselves by contemplating such a scene'. (*M.P.*, p. 113.)

the active characters. She has the role which often carries so much prestige in eighteenth-century literature, that of the thoughtful bystander. Like Gibbon's 'philosopher', she strives to interpret, to make some sense out of the superficial chaos of events. However unformed her opinion and inarticulate her expression of it, her anxious vigil on the bench in the park is enough in itself to remind the reader of a long tradition of men who have been wise in retirement, whose ascendancy lay in detachment from the actors and the common scene.

The conclusions Jane Austen tries to direct her reader's attention to are encouraged by Fanny's demeanour, yet not dictated by her at all. Jane Austen is not interested in impressions conveyed by subjective identification with a heroine. While Sterne or Mackenzie induce the reader to act the part of the man of feeling,[1] she casts the reader as a moral arbiter. If there must be identification, it is with Fanny's role, not with her individual responses, which (at least as they affect Edmund) are depicted with ironic detachment. Meanwhile the reader's judgements are guided by other, more objective means. References to familiar issues are no doubt among the most important. But equally interesting, and in actual practice more original, is the extremely detailed presentation of what, after all, Jane Austen wants us to value. For the first time she gives her external world a solidity and scale which eventually belittles individual characters.

Although the scene at Sotherton is stylized, it is also very natural—in its setting, as far as concerns the house and grounds, and in the sense it conveys of the day as a rather unsuccessful outing, an occasion felt in mixed and on the whole uncomfortable ways by the many people involved. The result of this curious blend of stylization and naturalism is to give flesh to the conservative case as no one else had done except Burke. As in the *Reflexions on the French Revolution*, with its reiterated references to hearths, homes, and families, so in the scene at Sotherton society takes on visible shapes.[2]

[1] See above, p. 19.

[2] For a more detailed discussion of Jane Austen's handling of her two great houses in *Mansfield Park*, and the implicit parallel with Burke, cf. Alistair M. Duckworth, *The Improvement of the Estate*, John Hopkins, Baltimore, 1971, pp. 46 ff.; and A Fleishman, *A Reading of Mansfield Park*, Minneapolis, 1967, p. 23.

The house and grounds are old, impressive, handsome, but under the rule of the Rushworths hollow, without the core of belief (symbolized by the chapel) which could give meaning to so much pompous grandeur. The cynical Crawfords have appeared, like Satan in the Garden of Eden, hostile to the old ethos of the place and bent on destruction. Every detail of what they say and do suggests their self-willed lawlessness: Mary, irrationally challenging the dimensions of the wilderness because she happens to feel tired; Henry, defying the restraint imposed by the limits of the ground and the locked gate. Yet the Crawfords' encroachment at Sotherton, dangerous though it seems, remains in the end curiously ineffective —for, like Burke, Jane Austen not only locates the enemy but diminishes him. In the Bertram sisters and in Henry there is an odd, wilful capacity for self-destruction. They are more likely to reject a momentary restraint than to attack restraints systematically. In escaping into the park, Henry, Maria, and Julia go off in a different direction from their supposed objective, the avenue of oaks; which accordingly survives the threat they originally offered it. Sotherton, although an empty shell, remains intact. By the end of the story it is only individuals, Maria and to a lesser extent Henry, who have destroyed themselves. A little through direct description, more through our sense of the weariness of the characters, we retain an impression of the heaviness, the largeness, but also the age and endurance of Sotherton, which is an important part of the moral framework for what follows.

Although some of its meaning has become obscured by purely historical difficulties of interpretation, the play-sequence remains the most masterly part of *Mansfield Park*. Unlike the account of Sotherton, where the naturalism and the scheme sometimes jar, it is equally fine on its many levels. Best of all is the presentation of that distinctive technique of the first volume of *Mansfield Park*, the serial treatment of several consciousnesses. At the beginning of volume i, chapter xii, for example, we enter successively the minds of Mary Crawford, the Bertram sisters, Henry Crawford, and Fanny. The next chapter, the thirteenth, takes us into and out of the consciousness of Mr. Yates; through the views of all the characters involved, first directly in dialogue and then in reported speech; to the silencing of Edmund when Mary joins in, and the happy concurrence of Mrs. Norris. There is no other comparable sequence of a Jane Austen novel so independent of the heroine. It is as though the movement of the sentimental period, towards distinguishing the central character by special insight into his inner life, has been put into reverse. The characters in this part of *Mansfield Park* each have their speeches, their scenes, like characters in a drama.

This, since it is a play they are rehearsing, is wholly appropriate. But what amuses Jane Austen—and even amuses Fanny—is that each actor continues to be selfishly absorbed by personal feelings, in spite of the corporate activity they are engaged in. Fanny is 'not unamused to observe the selfishness which, more or less disguised, seemed to govern them all.'[1] Many of the actors—Mr. Yates, Tom, and Mr. Rushworth, for example—clearly think in terms of the effect they will make in acting their own parts. Maria and Henry, though not motivated by the vanity of the actor, are bent on self-gratification of an even more culpable kind. Mary, and even Edmund, focus intently upon the significance to them of their own scenes. Apparently comic dialogues, in which plays and parts are argued over—and the selfishness of the actors revealed—have simultaneously a serious level of meaning. Not one of the actors, not even Edmund, has a proper sense of what it is as a whole that they are doing. When issues of propriety arise, even the more intelligent of them persist in looking at their own speeches: Mary admits that some of hers should be cut, Edmund is embarrassed by his. Only Fanny, the detached bystander, reads the play through and reacts to it as a whole.

Fanny's most important function here is that she alone perceives something pitiful and wrong in solipsism. 'Fanny saw and pitied much of this in Julia; but there was no outward fellowship between them. Julia made no communication, and Fanny took no liberties. They were two solitary sufferers, or connected only by Fanny's consciousness.'[2] As at Sotherton, she never directs the reader's opinions in detail: her watchfulness gives the necessary clue. When it comes to discussion of the general issue, to act or not to act, she can seem madden-

---

[1] *Mansfield Park*, p. 131.   [2] Ibid., p. 163.

ingly inarticulate. Her general opinion about the play is the
bald conclusion, 'everything of consequence was against it'.
Pressed to take part herself, she is merely depicted showing
the outward signs of confusion and distress.[1] Later, when she
is alone in the East room, the reader has his first real insight
into her attempts to sift right from wrong. But these do not
in fact throw much light on the general issue. What is important about Fanny's cogitations is that they involve scrupulous
self-examination, the critical mental process that everyone
else in the novel neglects.

For a general judgement of the play-acting, therefore, the
reader must not rely on Fanny's articulation but on an independent understanding of the issue, informed as at Sotherton
by a subtle network of allusion. The reader's efforts to understand are expected to parallel Fanny's, but to be more mature,
more experienced about the world and its pitfalls. There
seems to be no doubt, for example, that Jane Austen takes as
read our familiarity with the common contemporary arguments against amateur acting, even though no one in the
novel alludes to them plainly. By 1814 the increasingly strong
Evangelical movement had sufficiently publicized the link
between upper-class immorality and its rage for private
theatricals.[2] A common and important leading objection is that
play-acting tempts girls especially into an unseemly kind of
personal display. In his *Enquiry into the Duties of the Female
Sex*, 1797, which Jane Austen read with approval in 1805,
Thomas Gisborne declares that acting is 'almost certain to
prove injurious to the female sex'.[3] Even granted that the

[1] *Mansfield Park*, p. 146.
[2] David Spring, 'Aristocracy, Social Structure and Religion in the Early
Victorian Period', *Victorian Studies*, vi (1962–3), 263–80. Some critics see
special significance in the fact that by acting the Bertrams are aping the
aristocratic friends of the Hon. Mr. Yates—himself a typically profligate
representative of his class. (See below, p. 285.) The case against acting as given
within the novel is an example of Jane Austen's Tory preference for the
soberer *mores* of the gentry against those of the Whig aristocracy. See D. J.
Greene, 'Jane Austen and the Peerage', *PMLA* lxiii (1953), 1017–31, and
A. Fleishman, *A Reading of Mansfield Park*, Minneapolis, 1967, p. 29.
[3] Quoted by Frank W. Bradbrook, *Jane Austen and her Predecessors*, Cambridge, 1966, p. 36. Cf. *Jane Austen's Letters*, ed. R. W. Chapman, p. 169.
In two of the best-known novels of the same year as *Mansfield Park*, Fanny
Burney's *The Wanderer* and Maria Edgeworth's *Patronage*, the heroine also
has scruples about acting for reasons similar to those given by Gisborne.

chosen play 'will be in its language and conduct always irre-
prehensible' (a condition certainly not met by *Lovers' Vows*),
Gisborne believes that acting will harm a young woman
through encouraging vanity and destroying diffidence 'by the
unrestrained familiarity with the other sex, which inevitably
results from being joined with them in the drama'.[1] Fanny's
principal doubts seem to relate to the women's parts of
Amelia and Agatha.[2] Unquestionably Jane Austen expects us
to see the play as a step in Maria Bertram's road to ruin.

For the four principals, Maria and Henry, Mary and
Edmund, the play represents an elaborate exercise in 'encouraging vanity' and 'destroying diffidence'. Unlike Mr.
Rushworth or Mr. Yates, not one is vain in the trivial sense of
seeking self-display; but all are after the kind of worldly
'vanity' that concerns Jane Austen in *Mansfield Park*, since
all equate the pretended stage love-making with real love-
making. *Lovers' Vows* gives them a licence for what would
normally be entirely improper. Their scenes together permit
physical contact between the sexes (as when Henry holds
Maria's hand) and a bold freedom of speech altogether outside
the constraint imposed by social norms. Lionel Trilling has
ingeniously but anachronistically suggested that Jane Austen
objects to the insincerity involved in acting a role.[3] This is
surely near the opposite of the truth. In touching one another
or making love to one another on the stage these four are not
adopting a pose, but are, on the contrary, expressing their
real feelings. The impropriety lies in the fact that they are *not*
acting, but are finding an indirect means to gratify desires
which are illicit, and should have been contained. The unbridled passions revealed by the play-acting are part of the
uninhibited selfishness which it has been the purpose of the
sequence to bring out. The point is underlined by the casting,
for the actors play exaggerated versions of themselves. Mr.
Rushworth plays Count Cassel, a foolish and rejected suitor.
Mary plays the forward and free-thinking Amelia. Edmund
plays a lovelorn clergyman. Maria plays a fallen woman. The
stage roles of all these imply not insincerity, but liberation.

[1] Quoted by Frank W. Bradbrook, p. 39.   [2] *Mansfield Park*, p. 137.
[3] Lionel Trilling, 'Mansfield Park', *The Opposing Self*, New York, 1955,
pp. 218–19.

The imagined free world which comes into being on the
stage is a comprehensible entity, the clearest image in all Jane
Austen's novels of what she is opposed to. And meanwhile the
'real' world of Mansfield, which is suddenly neglected and at
risk, also begins to take on solidity. As at Sotherton, the most
eager disciples of the dangerous activity—there it was im-
proving, here play-acting—are those who should be the
guardians of the place. Tom is the play's producer, while Mrs.
Norris happily (and economically) presides over the physical
damage caused to Sir Thomas's property. Yet at Mansfield
Park, as at Sotherton, the really dangerous figures are the
Crawfords: a fact which we see fully only if, like Fanny, we
look at the play as a whole.

Ideologically, the choice of play is crucial. Kotzebue's
Lovers' Vows counterpoints what the rehearsals have revealed
of the actors' selfishness and reckless quest for self-gratification, since its message is the goodness of man, the legitimacy
of his claims to equality, and the sanctity of his instincts as
a guide to conduct. It is, in fact, the dangerous foreign reading-
matter which so often appears in anti-jacobin novels, though
wonderfully naturalized. Nor could any literate reader of the
period be unaware of the connotation of the play. Quite apart
from its successful runs at Covent Garden, Bath, the Hay-
market, and Drury Lane between 1798 and 1802, the name
of Kotzebue, by far the most popular, or notorious, of German
playwrights in England at this period, was quite enough to
indicate what *Lovers' Vows* was likely to be about.[1] He was
the most sanguine of optimists about the beauty and innocence of human nature left to follow its own instincts. One
of his heroines[2] marries her brother and has children by him,
until her happiness is unnecessarily destroyed by the revelations of a meddlesome priest. Another innately virtuous
victim of prejudice is the pregnant nun sentenced to death
by an alliance of king and priestly hierarchy (in *The Virgin of
the Sun*); she is made touchingly innocent, and her persecutors
either cowardly or bigoted. This play was not well known in

[1] For an allusion to the plot of *Lovers' Vows* which assumes that the public
still knows it well in 1812, see above, p. 93. Information about performances
if the play is given in Walter Sellier's unpublished German thesis, 'Kotzebue
in England', Leipzig, 1901, pp. 19–20.

[2] In *Adelaide von Wulfingen*, trans. B. Thompson, London, 1801.

England, but Sheridan scored a tremendous success with the less controversial sequel, *Pizarro*, in 1799. A third Kotzebue play as often seen as *Lovers' Vows*, and even more notorious, was *The Stranger*, in which the heroine is a guilty runaway wife, who is (rightly, the play makes clear) forgiven and reinstated by her husband. There could thus be no doubt in the minds of Jane Austen and most of her readers that the name of Kotzebue was synonymous with everything most sinister in German literature of the period. A sanguine believer in the fundamental goodness and innocence of human nature, the apostle of intuition over convention, indeed of sexual liberty over every type of restraint, he is a one-sided propagandist for every position which the anti-jacobin novelist abhors.[1] Unless the modern reader feels, like Fanny, the anarchic connotation of the whole play—rather than, like Edmund and Mary, the daring of individual speeches—he is in no position to understand its significance in relation to Mansfield Park and its owner, Sir Thomas.

Like other plays in the Kotzebue canon, *Lovers' Vows* attacks the conventions by which marriage upholds existing rank, and exalts instead the liaison based on feeling. In the main action Baron Wildenhaim, who has endured years of loneliness and remorse since refusing to marry the peasant girl whom he seduced, is persuaded to think more rightly by their illegitimate son, Frederick. In the subplot the Baron's daughter, Amelia, persuades the clergyman, Anhalt, to overlook the fact that she is a woman—by convention passive—and a noble—by convention debarred from marrying a bourgeois; her argument is that in defiance of convention they should obey their impulse.[2] Thus Frederick and Amelia are the

---

[1] For discussion of the relationship of Jane Austen's novel with Kotzebue's play, cf. E. M. Butler, 'Mansfield Park and *Lovers' Vows*', *MLR* (July 1933), and the reply by H. Winifred Husbands, *MLR* (April 1934); and William Reitzel, 'Mansfield Park and *Lovers' Vows*', *RES* (October 1933). On the whole critics have concentrated on whether the reader of *M.P.* is expected by JA to know the roles of individual characters in *Lovers' Vows*. I believe, and have tried to show, that some passages in the novel are enriched by our perceiving a connection between play characters and novel characters, yet it seems to me that JA does not *rely* on our knowing so much. What she does expect (more reasonably) is that we will have a general impression of the ideology of the play.

[2] For a summary of the play's attack on rank, see Crane Brinton, *The Political Ideas of the English Romanticists*, London, 1926, p. 39: 'Society—

two characters in the play who expound Kotzebue's message of freedom in sexual matters, and defiance of traditional restraints. They are played by the Crawfords, who thus again in their play-acting adopt not an assumed role but a real one. During the rehearsals they have often seemed almost diffident. It is only in relation to their parts in the play that they are revealed once more as the advocates of social and moral anarchy.

The affront felt by Sir Thomas has puzzled some observers more than it should. He returns home to find some material damage to his house, and his study in confusion. After discovering this, he steps out on to the stage for an irresistibly comic moment, his startled confrontation with the ranting Mr. Yates. Because our insight into the scene is through Tom's eyes, we interpret it as Tom does—in the spirit of pure comedy—and are liable to miss the underlying point of the meeting. The head of the house, upholder in the novel of family, of rank, and of the existing order, is confronted at the heart of his own terrain by a mouthing puppet who represents a grotesque inversion of himself: the dignified baronet meets the 'Baron' whose play-function is to abandon his dignity and to legitimize his mistress. Sir Thomas and Baron Wildenhaim are the heads of their respective worlds, and the sudden meeting emphasizes their significant relationship. In the future, the fact that Sir Thomas both resembles and differs from the Baron appears even more ironically, for he is called upon to deal with Maria's real-life lapse from virtue. At the time it is sufficient that a character who is central to the play's ethos makes a direct challenge to the house and its owner. Even the Crawfords, who have abstained from general discussion of the propriety of acting, know immediately that this father will not permit the play to go on. They retreat, as at Sotherton. And, though, as at Sotherton, they appear at first to have done little harm, this time they have made more significant inroads than ever before into the fabric of the Bertram family. The individuals who have sampled what the play means, who have thrown off restraint, are the more likely to do the same again. Much later, after Maria's flight

cultivated society—is always wrong. The individual who has courage to act against it is always right.'

with Henry, Tom describes the 'dangerous intimacy of his unjustifiable theatre' as an ancillary cause of his sister's fall.[1]

But this is not the story of the whole book. After the climax created by Sir Thomas's return early in the second volume, a major change occurs. The cast narrows dramatically: Maria and Mr. Rushworth, Julia, Mr. Yates, and Tom depart, leaving a much quieter world, and a smaller scene. From being a bystander, Fanny becomes the active heroine. Henry turns his attention from the Bertram sisters to her, and the rest of the book requires her to make a positive stand: to discern the true nature of evil, to choose the future course of her life, and, through a period of total loneliness, like a true Christian, to endure.

That the tempting of Fanny *is* now the central issue becomes clear when it is compared with a subject which seems to challenge it in interest, Edmund Bertram's love for Mary.[2] Edmund's affair remains essentially static. He is always duped by Mary, and always on the point of proposing, although in fact he never does. Edmund's courtship becomes interesting as it affects Fanny. It is the means of revealing her mental and moral stature: she is now clearer-sighted than Edmund, who educated her. Equally it is the means of at last bringing the reader close to her, through his sympathy for the painful predicament she faces when Edmund makes her the confidante of his love for Mary. While Edmund confides his feelings to Fanny we are more interested in her pain than in his.

Volume ii centres, then, on Henry Crawford's growing love for Fanny, his proposal, and her refusal. It includes a series of trials for Fanny: Mary's deceitful effort to involve her with Henry by giving her the necklace; Henry's attempt in turn

---

[1] *Mansfield Park*, p. 462.

[2] Edmund's role in the structure has often been exaggerated, because JA was thought to have said *Mansfield Park* was about ordination. The mistake arises from the punctuation of JA's letter to Cassandra Austen of 29 Jan. [1813]: *Letters*, p. 298: '. . . it [*P. & P.*] must be rather shorter than *S. & S.* altogether. Now I will try to write of something else, and it shall be a complete change of subject—ordination—I am glad to find your enquiries have ended so well. If you could discover whether Northamptonshire is a country of hedgerows I should be glad again.' The punctuation which accords with JA's meaning would surely be a full stop between 'subject' and 'ordination'. Cf. the letter of Mr. Hugh Brogan, *TLS*, 19 Dec. 1968, p. 1440.

to buy her by getting promotion for William; and the proposal itself, followed by the scene in which Sir Thomas acts as Henry's advocate. A further development of the same theme, the testing of Fanny, is the subject of volume iii. Sir Thomas believes that by sending Fanny to Portsmouth he will be putting pressure on her to marry Henry, for there she will see where her material advantage lies. Portsmouth is Fanny's exile in the wilderness, her grand temptation by the devil Mammon. As it happens, the same interval of time encompasses other characters' temptation too: Edmund hovers on the brink of proposing to Mary, Mary is coarsened and corrupted again by London, Henry and Maria resume their affair, and Julia and Mr. Yates are infected by their example. But all this is told indirectly in letters, or retrospectively in the explanatory narrative which follows Maria's elopement and Fanny's return. Until the default of the others ends her ordeal, Fanny is peculiarly alone, cut off from Mansfield Park for much of the time even by letter. Her sole contacts are in Portsmouth and in the very heart of the corruption, London, whence the devil's party, in this case the Crawfords, offer themselves as false friends. Mary by letter holds out promises of what a wealthy life in London is like; Henry comes down to tempt Fanny in person.

The testing of Fanny is thus the single pivot of the second and longer part of the novel, and the change of theme calls for a wholly new linguistic strategy. Henceforward Fanny's free indirect speech becomes the vehicle of the narrative, and the special quality of her mind colours, or dominates, the story. There is far less dialogue, and such conversations as there are tend to seem not merely unnecessary but disturbing, an intrusion upon Fanny's natural medium of quiet. To illustrate the subtle matching of word to idea, faulty or disagreeable characters in the second half of the book tend to be associated with terms like 'bustle' and 'noise'. The very idea of Mrs. Norris is inseparable from the notion of bustling. On the evening when Sir Thomas comes home she 'was trying to be in a bustle without having anything to bustle about, and labouring to be important where nothing was wanted but tranquillity and silence'.[1] The same word is applied to her activity

[1] *Mansfield Park*, p. 180.

over the play,[1] and to her manner of leaving the dinner-party at the Parsonage.[2]

Mrs. Norris's protégée, Maria, is drawn towards a way of living to which the same word can be applied. When her heart is wounded by Henry Crawford, and her liberty restrained by her father's return, she determines to 'find consolation in fortune and consequence, bustle and the world'.[3] Bustle in a similar sense is agreeable to the Crawfords: for this reason they approve both of the play and of the ball.[4] Afterwards Mary Crawford, lightly describing her own departure, diagnoses herself as correctly as when earlier she spoke of her selfishness. 'When your cousin comes back, he will find Mansfield very quiet;—all the noisy ones gone, your brother and mine and myself.'[5]

This long-laid train of association leads up naturally to a climax at Portsmouth. Mrs. Price, who combines some of the worst features of Lady Bertram and Mrs. Norris, spends her days 'in a kind of slow bustle'.[6] The word, as used in the novel, signifies a local turbulence, distracting the company from deep, lasting concerns and forcing them to focus on the material, the trivial, the everyday. When Fanny, at Portsmouth, thinks back to Mansfield Park, she concludes that

as to the little irritations, sometimes introduced by aunt Norris, they were short, they were trifling, they were as a drop of water to the ocean, compared with the ceaseless tumult of her present abode. Here, every body was noisy, every voice was loud, (excepting, perhaps, her mother's, which resembled the soft monotony of Lady Bertram's, only worn into fretfulness.)—Whatever was wanted, was halloo'd for, and the servants halloo'd out their excuses from the kitchen. The doors were in constant banging, the stairs were never at rest, nothing was done without a clatter, nobody sat still, and nobody could command attention when they spoke.[7]

The converse of noise is quiet, and of bustle tranquillity. Both words, together with the related notion of 'comfort', are continually associated with Fanny. At the ball Edmund, wearied by his doubts and disappointments in Mary, says, 'But with you, Fanny, there must be peace', and they go

---

[1] *Mansfield Park*, p. 129.
[2] Ibid., p. 251.   [3] Ibid., p. 202.   [4] Ibid., p. 225.
[5] Ibid., pp. 288–9.   [6] Ibid., p. 389.   [7] Ibid., p. 392.

down the dance together in 'sober tranquillity'.[1] Fanny's
happiness when calm is restored after the ball is contrasted
with Mary's dissatisfaction: 'what was tranquillity and comfort to Fanny was tediousness and vexation to Mary'.[2]
Again, when Edmund and Henry return to Lady Bertram and
Fanny one evening after dinner, Edmund is struck by their
'apparently deep tranquillity'.[3] Fanny's pleasures throughout
run deep and quiet. When she feels delight at going home to
Portsmouth, she is silent.[4]

Tranquillity is the natural state of Mansfield Park under
Sir Thomas. At first, after the bustle of the play, Edmund
wonders at the gravity that seems to have returned with his
father, but Fanny corrects him:

'I think he values the very quietness you speak of, and that the
repose of his own family-circle is all he wants. And it does not
appear to me that we are more serious than we used to be; I mean
before my uncle went abroad. As well as I can recollect, it was
always much the same. There was never much laughing in his
presence; or, if there is any difference, it is not more I think than
such an absence has a tendency to produce at first. There must
be a sort of shyness. But I cannot recollect that our evenings formerly were ever merry, except when my uncle was in town. No
young people's are, I suppose, when those they look up to are at
home.'[5]

And Edmund, after a moment's thought, concedes that
'the novelty was in their being lively'. In the hiatus left by the
absence of the head of the house, an anarchic disturbance set
in, during which Tom and his sisters, abetted by Mrs. Norris,[6]
helped the Crawfords to come very near destroying the peace-
ful regime normally maintained by Sir Thomas and Edmund.
Edmund's part in the customary quiet happiness of Mansfield
Park is to supply grave equivalents of gaiety—'comfort' and
'cheerfulness'. He contributes to the social, communicative

---

[1] Ibid., p. 279.   [2] Ibid., p. 285.   [3] Ibid., p. 336.
[4] Ibid., p. 369.   [5] Ibid., pp. 196–7.

[6] In his excellent article, 'Moral Integrity and Moral Anarchy in *Mansfield
Park*', Joseph M. Duffy describes Mrs. Norris as the internal agent to whom
the subversion of the household may be traced. He speaks of the 'wicked
enchantment' of her mismanagement, likening it to a fairy-tale situation.
ELH xxiii (1956), 75.

side of family life, the pleasures for example of mealtimes and family meetings. Fanny's presence can signify comfort to Lady Bertram, as at the moment when she returns from Portsmouth, but as a rule her services are stiller and only half-recognized. Her silences are more important than the talk of others. They speak, and she listens. It is not her *métier* to give positive advice, any more than she articulates for the reader what he ought to think. She cannot tell Tom what is wrong with acting the play, or Sir Thomas what is wrong with Henry Crawford, and she will not tell Edmund what is wrong with Mary. Her silences are the appropriate social demeanour of the Christian heroine, who is humble and unassertive. But in her half of the book, the second half, they also imply the strength of someone who neither needs to seek advice nor to vindicate herself, because she has a source of strength both within and without. Fanny's silence when she might ask advice is an important key to her character. She breaks it once, in order to find out how she can avoid taking the Crawfords' necklace: but this is an issue of manners rather than morals. Elsewhere she is consistent and resolute. She knows that in perpetually seeking her advice over Mary, Edmund betrays his own weakness. She rebukes Henry when he shows signs of relying on her in the same way:

'When you give me your opinion, I always know what is right. Your judgment is my rule of right.'
'Oh, no!—do not say so. We have all a better guide in ourselves, if we would attend to it, than any other person can be.'[1]

Her silence can be taken by Sir Thomas for the opposite of what it is. He thinks Fanny 'self-willed, obstinate, selfish and ungrateful', when she refuses to accept her friends' advice on Henry Crawford's proposal. Yet even at the time Sir Thomas is uneasy; when Mrs. Norris calls Fanny 'independent', he knows that she has never seemed so. The least assertive of characters, she is wholly schooled in submitting her personal will to something outside herself. But she is far less ready than Edmund to bow to general or worldly opinion, as she shows in the crises that end the first volume (the play) and the second (Henry's proposal). When challenged on these

1 *Mansfield Park*, p. 412.

occasions she resists, with the aid of a strength shown to be as different as possible from self-will.

It is in the light of this developing theme of stillness as opposed to bustle that we can see the relationship of the Portsmouth episode to the rest of the book. The ugly turbulence there is expected by Sir Thomas, in his worldliness, to drive Fanny towards London and Mr. Crawford:

He . . . wished her to be heartily sick of home before her visit ended; and that a little abstinence from the elegancies and luxuries of Mansfield Park, would bring her mind into a sober state, and incline her to a juster estimate of the value of that home of greater permanence, and equal comfort, of which she had the offer.[1]

Equally she might have been driven to the same decision by considering her own consequence (and Sir Thomas also considered this a valid argument for her marrying Henry).[2] In Portsmouth she was supernumerary, ignored. At Everingham and in London, as Mrs. Henry Crawford, she would have enjoyed personal consequence, even, in a fashionable sense, triumph. These were certainly considerations which would have weighed heavily with the two 'anti-heroines' who faced similar temptations in the first half of the book—Maria and Julia. Fanny's choice of Mansfield is very far from being, as is commonly said, a choice of wealth in preference to the poverty of Portsmouth.[3] The implicit alternative home is Everingham, and in opting for Mansfield Fanny volunteers to continue in her personal obscurity, her life of somewhat undefined usefulness in a subordinate role. Its central personal significance for her is that only at Mansfield can she satisfy the religious side of her nature. That this is the crucial element in Fanny's choice of Mansfield can be felt in the nuances of that much-quoted sentence—'The elegance, propriety, regularity, harmony—and, perhaps, above all, the

[1] Ibid., p. 369.

[2] 'She had tasted of consequence in its most flattering form; and he did hope that the loss of it, the sinking again into nothing, would awaken very wholesome regrets in her mind.' *Mansfield Park*, p. 366.

[3] See for example Marvin Mudrick, *Jane Austen: Irony as Defense and Discovery*, Princeton, 1952, p. 174; Andrew Wright, *Jane Austen's Novels: A Study in Structure*, pp. 128–9; and Moler, op. cit., p. 152. But for a minority view closer to my own, cf. Howard C. Babb, *Jane Austen's Novels: the Fabric of Dialogue*, Ohio, 1962, p. 146.

peace and tranquillity of Mansfield, were brought to her remembrance every hour of the day, by the prevalence of everything opposite to them here.'[1] Living in incessant noise was, we are told, the greatest evil; and that surely because it was destructive of the inner life. Religion in the novel partly means private meditation, a consciousness of our own failures and a will to do better (or, as Edmund puts it to Mary, 'knowledge of ourselves and of our duty'). Now it is true that the Christianity of *Mansfield Park* also requires the individual to adopt a role of social utility within an ordered social framework, for to perceive the orderliness of this world is a first step to perceiving a grander order. Most critics have supposed that Fanny's choice of Mansfield signifies no more than this. But as the novel is written, Fanny's rejection of Portsmouth also means something personal to herself. It is the climax of a trial imposed upon her, during which worldlier spirits propose that she should equate personal ease and dignity with marriage to Henry Crawford. What is significant at this moment is that she breaks away not from Portsmouth (which was not set up seriously as a temptation) but from Henry's much more seductive prospect of a life of bustle; and that she chooses peace.

Fanny's story undoubtedly takes on colouring of a special kind from the period in which it was written. There can be no doubt that many of the central themes of the book have been modified by the spirit of Evangelicalism. That movement received its impetus when the tide of prosperity brought sections of the middle class, historically puritanical and Calvinistic, into social contact with their former superiors. The plot of *Mansfield Park* has suggestive echoes of the clash of life-styles that followed. The humble Fanny's immediate hostility to the fashionable, amoral Crawfords, her censure of the absence of religion at old-established Sotherton, her clear-sighted view of the 'vanity' involved in the aristocratic pursuit of play-acting, all suggest the current campaign being waged against high-life *mores*. Fanny's romantic view of the chapel,

[1] *Mansfield Park*, p. 391. Those critics who wish to emphasize the role of Mansfield Park as a moral and social ideal sometimes leave out the phrase about peace and tranquillity, which fits their interpretation less well than the rest of the sentence.

and her effusions when looking at the stars, remind one of the emotional content which Evangelicalism derived from its uneasy contact with Methodism. But more important, the Evangelical concept of the Good Life—visibly Christian, humble, contemplative, serviceable—is realized in Fanny, while it is markedly absent from the restrained, undemonstrative demeanour of Elinor; for Elinor openly to display piety would have been felt in the world of *Sense and Sensibility* as a breach of social decorum. One reading of Fanny's pilgrimage is that after acting as a negative, passive bystander in the first half of the book, she takes up a more active burden of service to Mansfield at the end. Again—and this must have been among the most fashionable of all popular-novel themes in 1814[1]—Fanny's most important choice does not directly concern Portsmouth, for it is between the life of service at Mansfield and the glittering life of worldly vanities proffered by the Crawfords: the temptation she resists, like the humble third child in a fairy-tale, after the favoured elder cousins have succumbed. As always with the Evangelicals, there is a stress not simply on religious feeling of a private kind for its own sake, but on good works, active utility within the social world. Fanny, the steady critic of worldly vanities, is rightly to become a leader of the reformed community.

The Christianity of *Mansfield Park* thus has both an inner and an outer dimension: it is ardent and pietistical as well as practical. Yet to see the Evangelical strain in the book as socially radical—the triumph of a representative of a humbler class over the corrupt aristocracy—is to get the emphasis entirely wrong: for Evangelicalism was an essentially conservative movement, more middle-class in style but not at all dissimilar in political sympathy from the anti-jacobin reaction a decade and a half earlier.[2] Even to overrate the extent to which Evangelicalism is really felt in *Mansfield Park* is to obscure what is older and broader in the book. Many themes are brought together during Fanny's temptation in the Portsmouth wilderness, and the most important is the fundamental

[1] It is a principal theme of *Patronage* and *Discipline* in the same year (see above, p. 54), and of Alicia Catherine Mant's *Caroline Lismore* (1815). Cf. Gillian Avery, *Nineteenth Century Children, 1780–1900*, London, 1965, pp. 36–7.

[2] See below, pp. 284 ff.

conflict between Fanny's own Christian values and what she now perceives as a many-sided, anarchic, irreligious modernity. Ideologically the coherence of the novel depends on the reader's being able to make the connection Fanny makes, the subtle association between Portsmouth and London. In both towns, people's lives are dominated by one form or other of materialism. Petty details of life obscure the eternal verities. Worst of all, perhaps, there can be no love, no 'natural' family feeling: for in a materialist world, every individual is loud, self-assertive, at war with the interests of others. Mary's letters, which Fanny receives at Portsmouth, reflect a high-life equivalent of Mrs. Price's concerns. Mary writes about the size and splendour of her friends' houses; Mrs. Price worries about the servant problem. Mary's friends judge Edmund, favourably, by his appearance and manner; Mrs. Price's friends judge Fanny, unfavourably, by hers. One is a sardonic parody of the other. But within the novel Fanny alone feels a connection, for to worldly eyes like the Craw-fords' and Sir Thomas's the two places are poles apart. The people in both lead characteristic modern lives directed at materialistic ends. The subtle alignment of the two in Fanny's consciousness, which is implied in the whole handling of the Portsmouth episode, illustrates Jane Austen's great technical sophistication. For the low-life sequence is yet another cliché of the anti-jacobin novel, its usual function being to depict anarchy actually operating, and thus to suggest what a world run by revolutionaries would be like. It is also an occasion to draw 'real' human nature: the apostles of modernity are the first to prove low, selfish, and self-interested. In *Mansfield Park* no one talks of revolution. There is no sordid con-spiracy, no drunken philosopher or cobbler preaching the overthrow of the gentry and the sharing of wealth. Instead there is Mr. Price, who proves to be enough for partisan pur-poses. As Fanny's real father he ought to value and protect her. Instead he illustrates non-ideal human nature as it commonly is, by an ugly way of life led without interest in others, without any sense of order because he does not even perceive the existence of such an ideal. The connection with the values of the Crawfords is not less strong for not being spelt out. Since the point attempted is ideological, it is better suggested through associating the same intellectual concepts with both places (selfishness, bustle, anarchy) than through a plot concocted of threadbare conspiracies and deliberate villainy. Fanny rejects London and Portsmouth together, finding them similar although she was expected to find them opposed. Her third alternative, Mansfield, promises her a social life of affectionate service, together with an inner life of meditation.

As a contribution to partisan literature, *Mansfield Park* thus remains to the end extraordinarily subtle and technically ingenious. After the brilliant early sequence, in which a society was sketched in objectively, and shown, through the medium of social comedy, threatened from within and without, an entirely new strategy is employed in the second half. When Maria's testing is succeeded by Fanny's, the battle moves on to a more inward plane. Champions of the two sides, evil and good, worldliness and spirituality, modern subjectivity and traditional orthodoxy, take the field and fight their conflict out to the finish—with, from the conservative viewpoint, an appropriate result. As a book which says what Jane Austen meant it to say, it is a very impressive achievement. And yet as a novel it has regularly disappointed the modern (if not the contemporary) reader. Especially after the brilliant first volume, where ideology and execution match so well—to the point that even the modern reader finds his responses correctly marshalled—the second and third volume arouse our resistance. Why?

The problems in *Mansfield Park* are associated with the presentation of Fanny. When her consciousness succeeds the Bertrams' as the *locus* of the important action, there is a movement from the plane of what could happen to the plane of what should happen, from the actual observable world to the ideal. Frequently readers have objected to the brutal seventeenth chapter of the third volume, in which life-sentences are handed down on Maria and Mrs. Norris, and the remaining characters are summarily rewarded or punished. The discomfort which some readers experience at this point is for others, and logically, an appropriate response to the entire second section. The appearance of manipulation is there from the moment that Fanny becomes the central character rather than a bystander: for once the champion of Christianity is attacked directly by the forces of materialism, she cannot be permitted to lose. Sure enough, she is never even really tempted by Henry. The action in the second half becomes exemplary, not dramatic and open-ended.

Scene by scene the second part of the novel is consistently more didactic than the first. What in the first volume is dramatized in a complex scene tends to be stated in the second half in the form of an acknowledged debate. The discussion about modernizing Edmund's parsonage at Thornton Lacey covers the same ground as the scene at Sotherton, but more thinly and, on Edmund's side, more pompously. The business of Crawford's necklace versus Edmund's chain as the right partner for William's cross is not only crude in its symbolism: it has little more than symbolism to recommend it. There is no complex interaction of character, as in the play scene, to give the episode natural life independent of its overt meaning. Although the focus of the last two volumes is intentionally more inward, the reader feels with regret the lack of external, circumstantial life.

Jane Austen is very aware of what she is doing, and she makes every effort to supply through language and treatment of character the richness that necessarily departs with so many of the lesser figures. Fanny's speech to Edmund about Sir Thomas's influence on the tone of Mansfield[1] illustrates how far her character has been made to mature from the watchful but inarticulate presence of the first part of the book. She is the mistress now of quiet, firm rhythms, a language unlike that of any other Austen character, though perhaps her distinctive note is heard more typically in inward reflection than in speech. The only earlier heroine whose mind Jane Austen had presented sympathetically, Elinor, was an apprentice job compared with Fanny, and the second part of *Mansfield Park* is really her first attempt at a sustained subjective piece of writing. And yet, the more Fanny is scrutinized, the more impossible seems the task of making her inner life the medium through which the reader receives the novel. Given the ideological theme, Fanny's experience

[1] Quoted above, p. 239.

on a subjective level cannot be the matter at issue. The theme of *Mansfield Park* is the contrast of man-centred or selfish habits of mind, with a temper that is sceptical of self and that refers beyond self to objective values. Since Fanny is the representative of this orthodoxy, the individuality of her consciousness must to a large extent be denied. Jane Austen's necessary emphasis on her stillness places her outside the range of the other characters, who verbalize freely. There is a striking difference between Fanny and those who confide in her during the last two volumes. Both Edmund and Mary use her as their reluctant confidante, both do almost all the talking in their scenes with her, and in talking both reveal the pressure of conflicting desires that they feel. Mary at times talks nervously, almost compulsively, and says far too much for our good opinion of her, both in letters and speech; as, for example, when she speculates nervously that Edmund may have fallen in love with one of the Miss Owens.[1] Edmund's short, half-contradictory sentences suggest his bewilderment. He puzzles aloud to Fanny about Mary's character, and ends no nearer a conclusion than he began.[2] The manner of speech of these two characters in near-soliloquy, like their entirely private trains of thought, is what we expect of figures in a novel for whom we have an inward understanding. But Fanny is not torn by conflicts. She is not even undecided: for though she may puzzle at times what to do, she is never in doubt what to think. The result is that by comparison with other characters her speeches and thoughts lack movement, drama, and even any strong sense of human individuality.

To some extent Fanny's is a negation of what is commonly meant by character. Jane Austen seems aware of the difficulty, for she makes clear efforts to give her a double set of traits. Her childish experiences, as innocent victim of a callous household, are in the sentimental tradition. Later Jane Austen refers to the Fanny who must watch Edmund falling in love with Mary as experiencing both 'the heroism of principle' and

[1] *Mansfield Park*, pp. 288–9.
[2] Cf. especially the letter Edmund sends to Fanny at Portsmouth, in which he discusses whether he should propose to Mary. Although supposedly written, the letter has many of the characteristics of a dramatic soliloquy. *Mansfield Park*, pp. 420–4.

'the feelings of youth and nature',[1] and many of the scenes that follow focus rather upon the feelings than the heroism. The situation that obliges Fanny to be Edmund's confidante certainly invokes sympathy; and our instinct to identify is further encouraged by seeing her the passive victim of the insensitive circle round her. But on the whole attempts to make Fanny likeable are not very successful.

Ironically, Fanny's feebleness, which modern readers tend particularly to dislike, is probably a device to make her less perfect, more 'human', and therefore more appealing. It is quite incidental, since the real significance of her character for Jane Austen is not its weakness but its strength. What we would normally think of as the heroine's 'consciousness', her fragmented, partly irrational experience, is not central to the meaning of the novel either, and operates, if at all, as a distraction. Jane Austen values a hidden, inexpressive side of Fanny, one which we have largely to read into her character through our intellectual understanding of the author's intention. Her shyness, her headaches, the childish quality of her feeling for William and even Edmund, are amiable instances of personal weakness which are supposed to give additional lustre to her powers of endurance and her eventual victory.

That Fanny is a failure is widely agreed. *Mansfield Park* is at its best when her part is smallest, in the first volume. When she merely functions to modify our view of other characters, and when she is given meaning by a richly realized setting, she is effective in invoking our powers of criticism. But at the centre Fanny is impossible. The fault lies in the incongruity of subjective, heroine-centred writing to the theme in hand; or perhaps it is more proper to say that it lies in the incongruity of the old absolutes to the novel, a form which historically is individualistic and morally relative. In the antijacobin novel 'consciousness' must be treated critically, lest it inadvertently lets in the enemy, subjectivism. Jane Austen has put much ingenuity into having her cake and eating it, but she has not succeeded.

Is there a single technical error in *Mansfield Park*? The exemplary heroine, who speaks to the intellect, and the suffering heroine, who appeals to the emotions, are certainly

---

[1] *Mansfield Park*, p. 265.

not easy characters to blend together. Fanny's real task is to excite emulation rather than sympathy—and for this reason the modern reader is justified in rejecting her as the fallible individual she looks like at first sight. The 'real' people in the book, the 'mixed' characters who belong in the naturalistic social setting, occur in the first volume. Here Jane Austen submits to the logic of her values: she depicts each individual consciousness as fragmentary, partial, spiritually cut off, and succeeds brilliantly in at once realizing the modern world, and criticizing it. Some of the best recent commentators on *Mansfield Park* have hinted that it fails for us because its conservative thinking is simply unacceptable;[1] yet the first volume succeeds, and *Emma* succeeds, and both are conservative. The failure lies not so much in the ideas, as in the attempt to use the inward life of a heroine as a vehicle for them.

The problem presented by Fanny has partly obscured the technical triumph of the first volume, a skilful dramatization of the conservative case and one of the most intelligent pieces of writing in all English fiction. If the change of strategy in the middle leads, ultimately, to artistic failure, it is valuable as a bold effort at sympathetic, 'inward' presentation of the central character. Even as it is, the novel takes Jane Austen considerably further than she had ever previously been towards mastering the technique of dramatizing consciousness on her own terms. The lessons of the first part, in which she successfully presents consciousness in error, and of the second part, where she fails with a presentation of consciousness vindicated, must have been formative for *Emma*.

[1] Cf. Lionel Trilling, *The Opposing Self*, pp. 210 ff., and Joseph M. Duffy, 'Moral Integrity and Moral Anarchy in *Mansfield Park*', *ELH* xxiii (1956), 71–91.

CHAPTER 11

EMMA

ELIZABETH's charm tends to obscure her intellectual errors; the conception of Fanny is an obvious corrective. Now Emma comes into being, again apparently in reaction to her predecessor, since she is healthy where Fanny is languishing, misguided where Fanny is essentially right. But with Emma there is no danger, as there is with Elizabeth, that the reader will fail to see the heroine's mistakes for what they are. Emma's train of thought is given in full; it is the medium of the narrative, as Elizabeth's is not; and the whole essence of the presentation is that it is unreliable. *Emma* is the greatest novel of the period because it puts to fullest use the period's interest in articulate, sophisticated characters, whose every movement of thought finds its verbal equivalent in a nuance of speech. The language of *Emma* is functional and related to the form, to a degree not found elsewhere even in Jane Austen.

The plot to which the language harmoniously relates is the classic plot of the conservative novel. Essentially, a young protagonist is poised at the outset of life, with two missions to perform: to survey society, distinguishing the true values from the false; and, in the light of this new knowledge of 'reality', to school what is selfish, immature, or fallible in herself. Where a heroine is concerned rather than a hero, the social range is inevitably narrower, though often the personal moral lessons appear compensatingly more acute. Nevertheless the heroine's classic task, of choosing a husband, takes her out of any unduly narrow or solipsistic concern with her own happiness. What she is about includes a criticism of what values her class is to live by, the men as well as the women.

The novel with a fallible heroine by its nature places more emphasis on the action than the novel with an exemplary heroine. But *Emma* is an exceptionally active novel. The point is established first of all in the character of the heroine:

Emma is healthy, vigorous, almost aggressive. She is the real ruler of the household at Hartfield—in her domestic ascendancy she is unique among Jane Austen's heroines. She is also the only one who is the natural feminine leader of her whole community. Every other Austen leading lady is socially neglected or discounted: even the confident and energetic Elizabeth is denied a positive, managerial role in events. It is a misreading of Emma's character to say that she grasps at power, for she neglects rather than exploits her opportunities at Highbury. Jane Austen's purpose in giving her an exceptionally unfettered social position is rather to leave her free to act out her wilful errors, for which she must take entire moral responsibility. The masterstroke is to make the apparent spring of the action not Emma's quest for a husband, but Harriet's. Social taboos would have prevented any young woman from taking so commanding a role in pursuing a man for herself. But Emma is unhampered by propriety when she takes the initiative in choosing a husband for Harriet.

So energetic a programme of action demands steady judgement in an inexperienced girl if it is not to lead to disaster. As a sober critic of events Emma is off to a bad start, largely because of her attitude to her mentors. Though so much luckier than the first Catharine, Emma begins the novel in the same ominous condition of self-sufficiency. Her governess Miss Taylor is being translated into Mrs. Weston; and Miss Taylor, it seems, has always supplied the soft kind of friendship that is founded on sympathy, rather than the more strenuous and critical guidance that fosters the judgement:

It had been a friend and companion such as few possessed, intelligent, well-informed, useful, gentle . . . and peculiarly interested in herself, in every pleasure, every scheme of her's [*sic*];—one to whom she could speak every thought as it arose, and who had such an affection for her as could never find fault.[1]

The replacement of Miss Taylor's companionship by Harriet Smith's is a step further in the wrong direction 'she is a flatterer in all her ways'.[2] Small wonder then that Emma, although happy to plan marriage for another, does not yet

[1] *Emma*, ed. R. W. Chapman, Oxford, 1952, p. 4. [2] Ibid., p. 38.

contemplate it for herself. At the personal level marriage would mean submitting to continued moral assessment by a mature man, who would fortify the stronger, more rational, objective, and stringent side of Emma's mind. She is much more attracted to her self-indulgent spinsterhood, which renders her unchallengeable because her supposed mentor, her father, submits to her as readily as Hariet does:

'I have none of the usual inducements of women to marry. . . . Fortune I do not want; employment I do not want; consequence I do not want: I believe few married women are half as much mistress of their husband's house, as I am of Hartfield; and never, never could I expect to be so truly beloved and important; so always first and always right in any man's eyes as I am in my father's.'[1]

Emma's presumption in thinking to direct Mr. Elton and Harriet into matrimony is an ingeniously comic revamping of the anti-jacobin plot in which some Julia or Marianne, ignoring the counsels of prudence, mistakes the nature of her man, transgresses, and does considerable damage to herself and to society. It is also a rehearsal for the more serious main action to come.

In the second and longer part of the novel, Emma casts herself with her usual confidence in the role of judge; and Jane Austen underwrites that part, in the sense that she takes very seriously the correctness, or otherwise, of Emma's observations. It is her duty to assess the two strangers, or virtual strangers, who have just entered the Highbury circle, Frank Churchill and Jane Fairfax. Clear knowledge of proffered friends, and clear knowledge of the self, are, as always in Jane Austen's world, interdependent.

Emma's judicial role is carefully established by flanking her with two other characters who aspire to the judgement-seat. The deliberations of Mrs. Weston and Mr. Knightley are of special interest to the reader, since it is Emma herself whom they watch. Although they both love her and have known her since childhood, the tone of their observations about her is very different. Mr. Knightley is balanced, analytical. 'She will never submit to anything requiring industry and patience,

[1] *Emma*, p. 84.

and a subjection of the fancy to the understanding.'[1] Mrs. Weston lets affection cancel out her memories of Emma's failings.

When, at the end of the first volume, Emma's serious test as a judge of events is about to begin, it is Mrs. Weston's indulgent example which influences her. The two of them are together reading the letter in which Frank Churchill announces his arrival, and apologizes for not coming sooner. Emma sees that his excuses are flimsy, while Mrs. Weston takes up the position of a moral relativist. 'One ought to use the same caution, perhaps, in judging of the conduct of any one individual of any one family; but Enscombe, I believe, certainly must not be judged by general rules.'[2] Later, Emma, perversely taking up Mrs. Weston's arguments, puts the very same point to Mr. Knightley. 'Nobody, who has not been in the interior of a family, can say what the difficulties of any individual of that family may be. We ought to be acquainted with Enscombe, and with Mrs. Churchill's temper, before we can pretend to decide upon what her nephew can do.'[3]

In the first part of *Mansfield Park*, Jane Austen had already tried out a heroine in the role of philosophic bystander. This time she uses the device very differently, for the 'philosopher's' pretensions are satirized, her very pose of detachment shown as a form of individualistic conceit. Emma adopts a position of compromise between the two other assessors, and, as so often with Jane Austen, the median position between the two poles of right and wrong is by no means the most morally admirable of the three. Emma's mind is potentially cool and tough, like Mr. Knightley's. For her to adopt the 'soft' position of the gentle Mrs. Weston is a sign of wilful error.

Just as the reader has been watching Emma from the first, along with Mr. Knightley and Mrs. Weston, so he shares Emma's vigil in the second and third volumes over Frank and to a lesser extent Jane. Like Frank, Jane heralds her arrival with a letter, which Emma is invited to comment on; it is a sign of her unjudicial bias against Jane that she contrives to avoid reading it. Once the two characters have

[1] Ibid., p. 37.   [2] Ibid., p. 123.   [3] Ibid., p. 146.

appeared Emma studies them, though her attitude to Jane remains careless and prejudiced. Because the reader shares Emma's consciousness, he too is placed in the position of observer, and his insights into the mysterious couple are fleeting and tenuous. The narrative method of the second, longer part of *Emma* cleverly emphasizes the heroine's distance from real understanding, for time and again she misreads a puzzling detail in Frank's behaviour, or overhears a fragment of conversation, or intercepts a glance that has no real meaning for her. It is the motif of the second and third volumes that the two opaque new characters are submitted for inspection to the three 'wise' ones. But of the latter, both Mrs. Weston and Emma are far too much influenced by their preconceptions for steady judgement. Mrs. Weston hopes that Frank will marry Emma, Emma believes that it is she who attracts him, and so both conceive that Frank is walking to Hartfield when he is really engineering a call on Jane. They are so blinded that they can watch Frank talking to Jane, and discuss Mrs. Weston's speculation that there may be a match between Jane and Mr. Knightley. Only Mr. Knightley himself perceives that there is some prior understanding between the two strangers. In the scene in which he watches Frank tease Jane by making up the word 'Dixon', his careful, literal registering of each piece of evidence compares with the many scenes in which Emma has suppressed such facts, because they do not fit her favourite schemes.[1]

From the beginning there is perversity and injustice in the manner in which Emma meets the challenge of Frank and Jane. Because Emma fears critical, rational friendship, she tries to avoid evidence that will be in Jane's favour, and substitutes instead her own more hostile fantasies, notably the idea that Jane is in love with Mr. Dixon. It is true that Jane gives real cause for affront by her seemingly excessive reserve when Emma questions her about Frank Churchill, but Emma is far too eager to make that one instance a reason for mutual antipathy—'Emma could not forgive her.'[2] Her over-reaction

[1] This is the only moment of the novel in which the reader enters the consciousness of a character other than Emma. Jane Austen's purpose is clearly to offer Mr. Knightley's very different habits of assessment for comparison.

[2] *Emma*, p. 169.

compares with Mr. Knightley's opinion of Jane. He agrees that she is reserved, but makes a distinction between reserve founded on diffidence, and reserve occasioned by discretion; and he retains his faith throughout in Jane's fundamental integrity. He proves justified at least in the sense that Jane's part in the deception practised on Highbury is less active than Frank's. She avoids telling the full truth, but she does not tell lies, nor go out of her way to mislead others.

Frank Churchill, much the more energetic sinner of the two newcomers, is treated from the beginning by Emma with wilful indulgence. Although her previous, correct understanding was that Frank should have come to Highbury when his father remarried, she is so interested in the idea of him that she readily shares the more justified partisanship of his stepmother. Before long, during his first visit, she is more than half in love with him. Her partiality persuades her to forgive his visit to London in order (as she thinks) to have his hair cut:

'I do not know whether it ought to be so, but certainly silly things do cease to be silly if they are done by sensible people in an impudent way. Wickedness is always wickedness, but folly is not always folly.—It depends upon the character of those who handle it. Mr. Knightley, he is *not* a trifling, silly young man.'[1]

Emma notices that Frank is so determined to have the dance that he brushes aside the evidence of his tape-measure. It is the equivalent of her own kind of egotism, or self-will, or perverse subjectivity, and she easily forgives it. Her observations tell her that he is morally light, and her reason supports her observation. But the attention he pays her is flattering, and of course Emma all along has liked what is agreeable better than what is challenging. As time goes on, and she is more and more certain that she will refuse Frank, her flirtation with him takes on a worse moral colouring. Providing she is not in love with him, she sees that she preserves her autonomy, and perhaps the whip-hand over him as well. So, very gradually, she is led to the moral trap she falls into on Box Hill.

---

[1] Ibid., p. 212. Cf. Catharine's interior monologue about Edward Stanley, quoted above, pp. 171–2.

Here, as elsewhere in *Emma*, there is a discrepancy between words on the one hand, truth on the other, which affects not merely speech but also trains of thought. Emma's rudeness to Miss Bates follows a conversation in which she and Frank have flirted with outstanding insincerity:

. . . Frank Churchill grew talkative and gay, making her his first object. Every distinguishing attention that could be paid, was paid to her. To amuse her, and be agreeable in her eyes, seemed all that he cared for—and Emma, glad to be enlivened, not sorry to be flattered, was gay and easy too, and gave him all the friendly encouragement, the admission to be gallant, which she had ever given in the first and most animating period of their acquaintance; but which now, in her own estimation, meant nothing, though in the judgment of most people looking on it must have had such an appearance as no English word but flirtation could very well describe. . . . Not that Emma was gay and thoughtless from any real felicity; it was rather because she felt less happy than she had expected. She laughed because she was disappointed; and though she liked him for his attentions, and thought them all, whether in friendship, admiration, or playfulness, extremely judicious, they were not winning back her heart. She still intended him for her friend.[1]

It is clear to the reader—even the reader not yet in the secret of Frank's engagement to Jane—that he does not mean many of the compliments he pays to Emma. But her part in the flirtation is also a sham. She does not care for him, and is merely gratifying her vanity at a superficial level, using Frank to make herself the centre of attention and to stimulate her vivacity and wit. Now, therefore, Emma is also lying. She has gradually laid by any claim to be a judicious bystander. But she cannot prevent others from playing the part. It is her turn again, as she becomes aware, to be the subject of critical assessment. (' "It is rather too much to be talking nonsense for the entertainment of seven silent people." ' ' "Is Miss Woodhouse sure she would like to hear what we are all thinking of?" ') Her attempt at careless laughter shows that one part of her concedes that she is being false and self-indulgent. Nervous, uneasy, and yet intoxicated with vanity, she rides the inspiration of the

[1] *Emma*, pp. 367–8.

moment and is clever at the expense of Miss Bates. 'Emma could not resist.'[1]

Box Hill has also been Frank's moral nadir. At a first reading, when we do not know the full circumstances, we may find Frank guilty only of the same mild transgression as Emma—that of following his own gratification, amusing himself by pretending a depth of feeling for Emma which is not there. It emerges however that by flirting with Emma he has been inflicting intolerable pain upon Jane Fairfax, whom he really loves. On further examination Emma's fault also takes on another dimension. She is less guilty than Frank in relation to Jane, because, though she sees afterwards that she must have 'stabbed Jane Fairfax's peace in a thousand instances',[2] at the time she is not aware of it. Yet Emma *does* believe Harriet to be in love with the man she is flirting with, and Harriet, no less than Jane, is one of the affronted bystanders. The hurt to Miss Bates is not therefore a single instance, for there is a pattern in the novel of vulnerable single women, whom it is the social duty of the strong and rich to protect. There is accordingly a continuous link between Emma's errors and Frank's, because both arise out of related attitudes to the self and to others. Afterwards Emma discerns that Frank complicated the machinery of his plot unnecessarily, and gave Jane additional pain, because he enjoyed his own cleverness while he was deceiving people. His plot became an elaborate, indulged fantasy. He denies Emma's shrewd account, but because she knows herself better now, she knows him too.[3] His actions have been uglier than hers, and yet there has been a significant symmetry between them. To a degree that became hurtful to their friends, both have been imaginists.

The aftermath of the crisis at Box Hill, Emma's discovery that Frank and Jane are engaged, and that she loves Mr. Knightley, brings her back to the directness and truth she is capable of when her judgement is clear. Once more, as when Frank first arrived, a key conversation occurs between the two would-be moral arbiters Emma and Mrs. Weston, with Frank as their subject. Mrs. Weston wants to postpone judgement until the arrival of Frank's letter. 'It may bring

[1] Ibid., p. 370.   [2] Ibid., p. 421.   [3] Ibid., p. 478.

many extenuations. It may make many things intelligible and excusable which now are not to be understood.'[1] But Emma's immediate response, as so often with her, is forceful and true:

'It has sunk him, I cannot say how it has sunk him in my opinion. So unlike what a man should be!—None of that upright integrity, that strict adherence to truth and principle, that disdain of trick and littleness, which a man should display in every transaction of his life.'[2]

Above all she puts her finger on the social nature of the crime, the way it necessarily distorted Frank's relations with everyone at Highbury—'What has it been but a system of hypocrisy and deceit—espionage, and treachery?'[3] All forms of inwardness and secrecy tend to be anti-social. There is a moral obligation to live outside the self, in honest communication with others.

The corollary of such clear judgements about others, one forced upon her above all by the discovery of how mistaken she has been over Harriet, is a new humility about herself. At last she accepts the need for self-criticism. 'To understand, thoroughly understand her own heart, was the first endeavour.'[4] Such a recognition implies (for the first time in Emma's consciousness) total scepticism about herself, admission that her processes have been irrational, obscure, delusory. It implies the rejection, in fact, of subjective mental processes in favour of objective; rejection of individual 'lights' in favour of the more reliable guides of external evidence and impartial reasoning.

None of these discoveries means that Emma is necessarily more 'right' in any single instance at the end of the book than she was at the beginning. Even after she is humbled, she continues to make mistakes. She believes, for example, that she loves her father too much to marry Mr. Knightley, even if he should ask her. While Knightley is actually proposing, she continues to think him in love with Harriet. Afterwards, in talking over Frank with Knightley, she shows signs of straying into her earlier relativism—the second time that Emma and Knightley have sat in judgement over a letter of

---

[1] *Emma*, p. 398.   [2] Ibid., p. 397.
[3] Ibid., p. 399.   [4] Ibid., p. 412.

Frank's, and the second time that Emma slides back from an earlier, clearer moral perception. She even insists comically that Knightley must be mistaken when he tells her that Harriet is already engaged to Robert Martin: ' "You were both talking of other things; of business, shows of cattle, or new drills—and might not you, in the confusion of so many subjects, mistake him?—It was not Harriet's hand that he was certain of—it was the dimensions of some famous ox." '[1]

If it is not necessary for Emma to be right in every instance after she has seen the error of her ways, nor, in Jane Austen's moral universe, is it necessary for Mr. Knightley. He admits, for example, that because he was jealous of Frank, he was prejudiced against him—'I was not quite impartial in my judgment, Emma.'[2] Some critics have concluded that because he is occasionally prejudiced or mistaken, or because he sees the truth simply, Jane Austen means to qualify what has hitherto seemed to be a clear moral tendency of the book.[3] This line of criticism seems to be based on a misconception about Jane Austen's view of character, which is no more static than it is ideal. Even Elinor Dashwood, who comes as near as any Austen heroine to real goodness, has to struggle with her own weakness and fallibility, in an effort to arrive at right judgement which, by its nature, is never-ending.[4] In one of the finest pieces of Victorian criticism of Jane Austen, Richard Simpson describes how for her characters the moral life is a continuous process:

She contemplates virtues, not as fixed quantities, or as definable qualities, but as continual struggles and conquests, as progressive states of mind, advancing by repulsing their contraries, or losing ground by being overcome . . . A character therefore unfolded itself to her . . . as a dramatic sketch, a living history, a composite force, which could only exhibit what it was by exhibiting what it did.[5]

[1] Ibid., p. 473.   [2] Ibid., p. 445.

[3] e.g. F. W. Bradbrook, *Jane Austen: Emma* (E. Arnold's Studies in English Literature, no. 3), London, 1961, p. 50. Cf. Moler, op. cit., pp. 155–85. The identity of Mr. Knightley's views with JA's is challenged radically in J. F. Burrows, *Jane Austen's Emma*, Sydney Studies in Literature, Sydney, 1968, pp. 9 ff.

[4] See above, pp. 190–2.

[5] Anonymous article, 'Jane Austen', *North British Review*, April 1870; ed. B. C. Southam, *Jane Austen: the Critical Heritage*, London, 1968, pp. 249–50.

By the end of the action, and throughout when she is with Mr. Knightley, Emma has that capacity for penetration to the truth which is the real hallmark of Jane Austen's admired characters. Instead of investing one character throughout with right opinions, as the lesser anti-jacobins do, Jane Austen depicts even the best minds as continually fallible, inder the pressure of new evidence, and potentially undermined from within by selfishness. Her only constants are abstract qualities—directness, honesty, sincerity, humility— the characteristics striven for by people who care about truth. She sees perfectibility as a condition of human life, but not perfection. The continuous effort necessary in her moral world is one of the few points at which she seems almost Godwinian.

The theme, then, is the struggle towards a fixed and permanent truth external to the individual; and chastening, necessarily, to individual presumption and self-consequence. It is more vigorously enacted than in any other Austen novel. Yet to say this is an apparent paradox, for at one level of reading 'action', exceptionally little happens in *Emma*. The scene never moves from Highbury: while, in spite of Jane Austen's declared preference for '3 or 4 families in a village', none of her other novels is restricted to one setting. The reason that *Emma* nevertheless gives so powerful an impression of sustained and vigorous movement is that its conflicts are translated more fully than in any of the other novels into the medium of language.

From the beginning Jane Austen has of course been using her two most familiar techniques, a narrative prose capable of suggesting the heroine's thought-process, and dialogue which conveys character with the objective detachment of the dramatist. In the past she has made most effective use of dialogue where the evidence it affords is required to correct the heroine's failures in judgement: the best dialogue to date is in *Pride and Prejudice* and in the first part of *Mansfield Park*, where Fanny is still young. The second part of *Mansfield Park*, on the other hand, has little call for dialogue, since Fanny hardly needs more evidence about the Crawfords, while it contains Jane Austen's most sophisticated experiments yet with free indirect speech. A full, consistent, and dramatic interaction between the two narrative modes has to wait for *Emma*.

The decisive difference between Emma's thought-processes and Fanny's is that the former's are essentially unreliable. In tracking her interior monologue, therefore, Jane Austen has to convey Emma's impetuosity, her quick habit of reaching a decision against the evidence; while at the same time the reader is discreetly made aware of these deviations from truth. Most of the staple of the narrative purports to be Emma's thought-process, or a summary of the action as it might be seen through Emma's eyes; though in either case small objective touches, a discriminating word, perhaps, or a hint at Emma's impatience, marks the reservation of the watchful author:

The longer she considered it, the greater was her sense of its expediency. Mr. Elton's situation was most suitable, quite the gentleman himself, and without low connections; at the same time not of any family that could fairly object to the doubtful birth of Harriet. He had a comfortable home for her, and Emma imagined a very sufficient income; for though the vicarage of Highbury was not large, he was known to have some independent property; and she thought very highly of him as a goodhumoured, well-meaning, respectable young man, without any deficiency of useful understanding or knowledge of the world.[1]

Overtly it is simply what Emma thinks; but the alert reader notes the detail which simultaneously characterizes Emma's thought as censurable. The terms Emma applies to Mr. Elton and the prospective marriage are not quite worthy: 'expediency', 'suitable', 'well-meaning', 'without low connections', and 'without any deficiency of useful understanding'. Moreover, Emma's mind is unobtrusively changing. 'The longer she considered it . . .' She is talking herself into her own idea at every step.

The subtlety and flexibility of Jane Austen's mature prose has been the subject of critical effort in recent years.[2] We have

[1] *Emma*, p. 35.
[2] See for example Howard S. Babb, *Jane Austen's Novels: The Fabric of Dialogue*, Ohio, 1962; K. C. Phillips, *Jane Austen's English*, London, 1970; K. Kroeber, *Styles in Fictional Structure: the Art of Jane Austen, Charlotte Bronte, George Eliot*, Princeton, 1971; N. Page, *The Language of Jane Austen*, Oxford, 1972.

learnt to notice her skill in modulating between the heroine's
unreliable cast of thought, and her own ironically detached
judgement of it; and the syntactic invention and freedom
with which she modifies her normally even style in order to
convey the rhythms of agitated emotion:

> The hair was curled, and the maid sent away, and Emma sat down
> to think and be miserable.—It was a wretched business, indeed!—
> Such an overthrow of everything she had been wishing for!—Such
> a development of everything most unwelcome!—Such a blow for
> Harriet!—That was the worst of all. Every part of it brought pain
> and humiliation, of some sort or other; but, compared with the evil
> to Harriet, all was light; and she would gladly have submitted to
> feel yet more mistaken—more in error—more disgraced by mis-
> judgment, than she actually was, could the effects of her blunders
> have been confined to herself.[1]

The paragraph beautifully conveys its subject: feeling
necessarily pent up in the first sentence, while the maid is
present, breaking out in the short exclamatory rhythms that
follow, and soberly expending itself in the long, dismal close.
Prose such as this is essentially dramatic, wide-ranging in its
effects, and also economical. It can incorporate for example
much reported dialogue, of a kind which neatly identifies
and characterizes the speaker, and at the same time saves
the proliferation of unduly prosaic conversation:

> Emma was in the humour to value simplicity and modesty to the
> utmost; and all that was amiable, all that ought to be attaching,
> seemed on Harriet's side, not her own. Harriet did not consider
> herself as having anything to complain of. The affection of such a
> man as Mr. Elton would have been too great a distinction.—She
> never could have deserved him—and nobody but so partial and
> kind a friend as Miss Woodhouse would have thought it possible.[2]

Most analysts of Jane Austen's language have tended to
track her development as though it were even and consistent, and, moreover, independent of the techniques of her
contemporaries, a feature of her novels alone. However, just
as Maria Edgeworth is capable of using dialogue in a similar
way, so she tends to employ a normal narrative prose that
cleaves to a character's thought-processes, with a similar

---

[1] *Emma*, p. 134.   [2] Ibid., pp. 141–2.

freedom to move into overt authorial comment on the one hand, or on the other to hint allusively at dialogue:

'The duchess of Torcaster's carriage stops the way!'—a joyful sound to colonel Heathcock and to her grace, and not less agreeable, at this instant, to lady Langdale, who, the moment she was disembarrassed of the duchess, pressed through the crowd to lady Clonbrony, and addressing her with smiles and complacency, was charmed to have a little moment to speak to her—could *not* sooner get through the crowd—would certainly do herself the honour to be at her ladyship's gala. While lady Langdale spoke, she never seemed to see or think of any body but lady Clonbrony, though, all the time, she was intent upon every motion of lord Colambre; and whilst she was obliged to listen with a face of sympathy to a long complaint of lady Clonbrony's, about Mr. Soho's want of taste in ottomans, she was vexed to perceive that his lordship showed no desire to be introduced to her or to her daughters; but, on the contrary, was standing talking to miss Nugent.[1]

There is, however, a crucial distinction between Maria Edgeworth's usage and Jane Austen's, which in its origins is not so much linguistic as ideological. We have seen that Maria Edgeworth's heroes and heroines tend to be critics of their world, and that commonly their criticism, being analytical, is approved by the rationalistic author. On relatively rare occasions Maria Edgeworth employs a fallible central figure, whose intellectual errors become the leading subject of the narrative. Such a central figure is the devious Mrs. Beaumont, heroine of *Manœuvring*, whose subtle inward processes and summarized speeches are presented in a manner not altogether remote from Emma's (though morally the character is a good deal blacker):

Mrs. Beaumont was, in her turn, in unfeigned astonishment; for Mr. Palmer took the matter more seriously, and seemed more hurt by this discovery of a trifling deviation from truth, than she had foreseen, or than she could have conceived to be possible, in a case where neither his interest nor any one of his passions was concerned. It was in vain that she palliated and explained, and talked of delicacy, and generosity, and pride, and maternal feelings, and the feelings of a friend, and all manner of fine and double-refined sentiments; still Mr. Palmer's sturdy plain sense could not be

---

[1] *The Absentee*, 1st ed., London, 1812, ch. i; *Works*, ix. 5–6.

made to comprehend that a falsehood is not a falsehood, or that deceiving a friend is using him well. Her son suffered for her, as his countenance and painful and abashed silence plainly showed.[1]

Needless to say, here the moral commentary is intruded upon the character's thought in a cruder fashion than the delicate style of *Emma*. But over Maria Edgeworth's work as a whole the difference is not, or not only, a matter of skill. Essentially—though the fact appears nowhere so clearly as in *Emma*—Jane Austen has a wholly distinct attitude to the inward thought-process, and to dialogue, and therefore to the proper relation between the two. Private imaginings tend, as she conceives them, to be irrational and fallible; direct speech may be right or wrong, true or false, but crucially it has become externalized, evidential, a part of the given world of fact. For Maria Edgeworth, there can be no such distinction between exterior speech and interior. There is rationality and irrationality; the mind—if it *is* a mind—is potentially the source of truth. It is because Jane Austen does not believe in the truth of the unaided subjective process that in her great work, *Emma*, her linguistic range is so much wider than Maria Edgeworth's, and wider indeed than in those of her own novels where the heroine's opinions coincide with her own. Although her characteristic theme is always the distinction between subjective and objective modes of perception, it is only in *Emma* that she consistently contrasts two styles, making language itself enact the disharmony between the false and the true.

The fact that the story is to be worked out on a peculiarly verbal level is established in the comic prologue to the action, the Elton episode, where Emma allows herself to be deceived against her own better judgement by an assumed style. Mr. Elton's sycophantic manner always grates on her. She knows that he must be flattering her when he praises her drawing; and whoever it is meant for, the poem which ascribes 'soft eye' and 'ready wit' to the same person is something less than meaningful. But she deliberately suppresses the ideas of

[1] *Manœuvring*, ch. xii; *Works*, vii. 159.

truth and accuracy which are natural to her. Mr. Elton's
docility leads her by a natural association to think of him in
conjunction with the humble Harriet. ' "It will be an Exactly
so, as he says himself" ',[1] she thinks, falling into his habit
of inaccuracy as she apes his phrase. In fact Mr. Elton's soft
manner is one of the falsehoods he assumes for the purpose
of courting Emma. Mr. Knightley, who knows him in other
contexts, sees through the speeches to the hard motive
beneath. ' "Elton may talk sentimentally, but he will act
rationally." '[2]

Emma lives with the flattery she receives from her preferred
companions and from her own easy conscience. She and the
reader hear a very different tone, one which jars indeed
in its abrupt, unequivocal rhythms, when at intervals she
encounters Mr. Knightley for one of the brief conversations
that sound a counterpoint throughout the novel. Sometimes
with his habitual brevity he offers her fundamental, unpalatable truths. ' "You have been no friend to Harriet
Smith." '[3] Emma catches his tone when she talks to him,
and their dialogues together are quick, direct, amused, concerned, decisive, the rhythms of two mature people who
accept the otherness of other people and know how to communicate with them. An example is their brief exchange on the
snowy night at the Westons, which contrasts pleasingly with
Mr. Elton's blandness and Mr. John Knightley's brutality:

'Your father will not be easy; why do not you go?'
'I am ready, if the others are.'
'Shall I ring the bell?'
'Yes, do.'[4]

Direct authorial interventions in the narrative are relatively rare in *Emma*. Yet the language is morally unambigu-
ous: one style is very much to be preferred to all the others.
Emma's dialogues with Mr. Knightley stand in the same
relation to her own interior monologues as Robert Martin's
prose does to Mr. Elton's poetry. One is manly and direct,
the other over-elaborate, devious, and unreliable. Once we
have heard Mr. Knightley, and heard Emma in conversation

---

[1] *Emma*, p. 49. [2] Ibid., p. 66.
[3] Ibid., p. 63. [4] Ibid., p. 128.

with him, we know how to assess the indirections, equivoca-
tions, and back-trackings of her train of thought. Her first,
truthful responses include the admission that Robert Martin's
letter is good, and that Harriet shows bad taste when she
prefers Mr. Elton's poetry. In every case Emma's self-will suppresses the conclusion her reason has just reached on the
basis of the evidence. And the reader always knows when she
is wrong, because the novel's other style has given him the
unmistakable note of simplicity and sincerity.

In order to understand Emma's role in the novel, we have
to recognize her natural affinity with the truth. It is only a
temporary perversity that leads her astray, a fact suggested
by her firm, strong tone when she talks to her natural equal,
Mr. Knightley. Not for her—or, at least, not then—the moral
failings of the other female characters with whom she is
compared: the soft palliations of Mrs. Weston, the constraint
of Jane Fairfax, the mindless, characterless indecision of
Harriet. Although Jane Austen called Emma 'a heroine whom
no one but myself will much like',[1] many readers have found
her attractive: as attractive, indeed, as any heroine in fiction.
In discussing Emma's charm, Lionel Trilling quotes Cardinal
Newman's observation, 'she makes me want to be kind to her',
and adds on his own account that we exist in a peculiarly
intimate relationship with her, as with the fallible side of ourselves.[2] It is an extension of this position, and lately a popular
one, that Emma's mistakes themselves are what make her
lovable; that they represent an inspired, intuitive grasping
after a higher truth than Knightley's; that Jane Austen, recognizing this, thereby qualifies the rigidities of her own ethical
position.[3] This, surely, is a misconception. Emma makes mistakes in the first instance because, like all other human beings,
she is fallible. She also makes more than she need, because for
much of the novel she underrates the need for objective self-
criticism, and positively shuns the best method of achieving
it, which is the submission of oneself and one's actions to the
honest, searching criticism of a friend. The fact remains that

[1] J. E. Austen-Leigh, *Memoir of Jane Austen*, ed. R. W. Chapman, Oxford,
1926, p. 157.
[2] Lionel Trilling, 'Emma', *Encounter*, xlix (June 1957), 54-5.
[3] Cf. common assumptions about Catherine Morland, cited above, pp. 178-9.

within the conservative ethic to which Jane Austen adheres, Emma's is a character of real moral superiority, and precisely because of its underlying truth.

As in other Jane Austen novels, alternative 'heroines' exist for the sake of comparison: Harriet and Jane. Both must be approached through their verbal mannerisms, partly because their speech is our only evidence about them (we have no access to their minds), and partly because it is through speech, in this intensely verbal novel, that we apprehend their all-important moral relationship with the truth. Harriet is a primitivist's heroine, seen with a satirical eye. She is innocent, and in all her instincts 'good'; but the shortcomings of such goodness are apparent in her speeches, ill-judging, indecisive, beneath rationality. More than once Emma exclaims that she wishes she were good in the same natural way as Harriet (or Isabella, or her father); but, as Jane Austen observes drily, 'it was rather too late in the day to set about being simple-minded and ignorant'.[1] This, indeed, is largely what Harriet's goodness amounts to, and Emma eventually submits to Knightley's opinion, that she will need the guidance of a Robert Martin if she is to be even respectable. The comparison between Emma and Harriet resembles the kind of anti-Rousseauistic point made by Maria Edgeworth in *Belinda*, when she compares her intelligent heroine with the simple Virginia. Faced with untutored ignorance, both authors are firmly on the side of 'art' against 'nature'.

At first sight Jane Austen qualifies her position by the introduction of Jane Fairfax. Jane appears to represent the other pole of art, entirely opposed to Harriet, but relatively opposed to Emma as well, since she is reserved where Emma is spontaneous, cool where Emma is warm, accomplished in the arts, where Emma's performances are unfinished. But ethically Jane's fault is not that she is too polished: it is that for once 'her affection must have overpowered her judgement'.[2] Nor, after all, does the reserve which Emma initially dislikes prove to be merely manner, an aspect of her elegant composure—as everyone discovers when the truth about the engagement emerges. Early in the novel Knightley speaks of

[1] *Emma*, p. 142.
[2] Ibid., p. 419.

the probable grounds for her reserve, diffidence and discretion; Jane's secretiveness proves to have been motivated by a culpable desire to hide a truth which should have been known. Knightley, who in general is her advocate, confesses at last that there is a censurable lack of openness about her: that all along her overt verbal style has given correct evidence about her character. There is a *real* desire in Jane to live within the self; whereas Emma, although she has been indulging her inner fantasies, is fundamentally outgoing and truthful in her dealings with others. The direct comparison between the two after the revelation of Jane's secret leaves no doubt as to which is the finer character. Emma is generous in forgiveness—'The world is not hers, nor the world's law'[1] —compensating, in this instance of moral relativism, for the injustice of her earlier judgements. She has accepted Jane's snubs as no more than she deserves, and can be wholly admiring about her attractions now that circumstances permit Jane to be more forthcoming. 'There was consciousness, animation and warmth; there was everything which her countenance or manner could ever have wanted.'[2] Not quite, however. For when Emma puts a question to Jane, the latter replies with the old reserve which is fatal to the kind of communication Knightley praises when he speaks of 'the beauty of truth and sincerity in all our dealings with each other':[3]

'And the next news, I suppose, will be, that we are to lose you—just as I begin to know you.'

'Oh! as to all that, of course nothing can be thought of yet. I am here till claimed by Colonel and Mrs. Campbell.'

'Nothing can be actually settled yet, perhaps,' replied Emma, smiling—'but, excuse me, it must be thought of.'

The smile was returned as Jane answered, 'You are very right; it has been thought of. And I will own to you (I am sure it will be safe), that so far as our living with Mr. Churchill at Enscombe, it is settled . . .'

'Thank you, thank you.—This is just what I wanted to be assured of.—Oh! ,if you knew how I love everything that is decided and open!'[4]

[1] *Emma*, p. 400.   [2] Ibid., p. 453.
[3] Ibid., p. 446.   [4] Ibid., p. 460.

Emma's gentle correction, and her forbearance in neither complaining of Jane, nor appearing to note the greater generosity in herself, are all clues to her true moral potential. In spite of everything, Emma is more truthful and more self-less. The complex inwardness of Jane's character, its capacity for withdrawal, for suffering in loneliness and secrecy, is suggested in the novel—merely, some would say critically, not to be developed. What might have made Charlotte Brontë's theme, and certainly in this action would have provided her heroine, is marginal in the comic universe of Jane Austen. But not truly marginal, after all. For if we accept Emma as the rightful heroine, her open style as the right style, and her moral progress towards truth as the central theme, we must accept that Jane Fairfax, although handled with sympathy, is almost as much an anti-heroine as Mary Crawford.

The crucial part played by Emma's openness and rationality is clinched by a consideration of the minor characters. Super-ficially the three principal comic characters in *Emma*—Miss Bates, Mr. Woodhouse, Mrs. Elton—belong to the stage tradition of the figure comically possessed by a dominant humour or obsession. Mr. Woodhouse thinks of nothing but his health, and that of those around him. Mrs. Elton thinks of her own social importance, which centres on a complex of ideas surrounding her sister Selina's house, Maple Grove. Miss Bates at first appears to be an exception, since she has difficulty in focusing her ideas upon anything; but in fact she rings the changes around a very limited number of topics— Jane, her mother, domestic trivia, the kindness of neigh-bours—a sequence accurately captured by Emma when she mimics her:

'To have her haunting the Abbey, and thanking him all day long for his great kindness in marrying Jane?—"So very kind and obliging!—But he always had been such a very kind neighbour!" And then fly off, through half a sentence, to her mother's old petticoat. "Not that it was such a very old petticoat either—for still it would last a great while—and, indeed, she must thankfully say that their petticoats were all very strong." '[1]

---

[1] Ibid., p. 225.

The dominant characteristic which makes each of these characters comic is also seen as a moral limitation. Mrs. Elton is the most obviously censurable, for her narrowness of vision (the opposite quality to that sophistication she thinks she is bringing to Highbury) is the very essence not just of vulgarity but of selfishness. Mr. Woodhouse appears at first to be a different matter, for the gentleness of his manners and the genuineness of his concern earn him more sympathetic treatment from the other characters, and Emma sincerely loves him. We should not be deceived. Nor should we take Mr. Knightley's representations of Miss Bates's worth as the final assessment of her character. It is one thing, and a valid thing, for Emma to be made to recognize the Christian virtues of good nature and humility, at points in the action where she has failed in those qualities. It is quite another to conclude—as she impulsively does—that either of these characters provides a model for an Emma. She is not really the opposite of Miss Bates or her father at all; her worst quality is not ill nature but precipitate judgement, which is just as much in evidence when she praises the meek characters too much as when she values them too little. The objective truth about Mr. Woodhouse and Miss Bates comes not from Emma, nor from Mr. Knightley when reproving Emma, but out of their own mouths. We hear it in the plaintive tones of Mr. Woodhouse as he returns to the same limited domestic conceptions, reiterating the same words:

'I am sure she will make a very good servant; she is a civil, pretty-spoken girl; I have a great opinion of her. Whenever I see her, she always curtseys and asks me how I do, in a very pretty manner; and when you have had her here to do needlework, I observe she always turns the lock of the door the right way and never bangs it.'[1]

'Pretty' is a word which Mr. Woodhouse will also apply to Emma, Jane, and Mrs. Elton. Nor can Miss Bates distinguish between the merits of Mrs. Elton and Emma, a fact which justly earns her the heroine's description at an unguarded moment, 'so undistinguishing and unfastidious'.[2] It is true that no ill-natured word passes Miss Bates's lips. But

[1] *Emma*, p. 9.   [2] Ibid., p. 85.

it is equally true that she does not finish her sentences—
and finishing them is always, as David Lodge says, a criterion
of worth in Jane Austen.[1] And if Miss Bates arrives at no
conclusions, nor does she enable her hearers to arrive at any.
Worst of all in Jane Austen's view, worse even than incon-
clusiveness, is the habit of talking in effect to oneself. All the
comic characters in *Emma* have it. Mr. Woodhouse is politely
allowed to finish his speeches, but barely: the other characters,
quite uninfluenced by his views, are only waiting for a chance
to overrule them. Mrs. Elton has more difficulty in holding
her audience, a fact which makes her patronage of the dependent Jane Fairfax—who is obliged to listen to her—both
more understandable and more disagreeable. Mr. Weston,
as soon as he has imparted his news about Frank, drifts away
from her. Mr. Knightley, who habitually listens, shuts his
mind to the meaning she intends to convey.

Miss Lascelles was the first to point out that Miss Bates
unconsciously gives a great deal of information in her speeches
about Frank and Jane, evidence which could give away
their private understanding at an early date.[2] No one in
Highbury absorbs the evidence supplied by Miss Bates,
because no one gives her words their full attention. Thus
none of the comic characters communicates. They surround
themselves with a web of words, but words which convey
their own selfhood, their individuality, and make little or no
impact upon the consciousness of others. The defect is an
important detail to notice, in a novel which focuses critically
upon selfishness. It is a moral virtue to be ready to receive
external evidence, which Emma does not always do. It is no
less a virtue to be able to convey our thoughts to others,
intelligibly and unequivocally. We live in a community, and
our verbal style is the measure of our recognition of this.

Emma differs morally from the minor comic characters,
whether well or ill intentioned, above all by virtue of her
intelligence. Jane Austen does not present stupid characters
as really good, since she thinks of goodness as an active,
analytical process, not at all the same thing as passive good
nature. But Emma also differs in that her impulses, unlike

[1] Introduction to *Emma*, Oxford English Novels, 1971, p. xi.
[2] *Jane Austen and her Art*, pp. 175–8.

those of the comic characters, are fundamentally social. At times of great personal emotion she thinks of others—of Jane when she perceives how she has injured her, of her father and Harriet when Knightley proposes. Her behaviour to her father is consistently selfless, and she seems quite unaware of it. But the fact that it is characteristic for her to think unselfishly and outwardly is best conveyed in the rhythms of her speech, its frankness and decisiveness, its quality of being immediately directed at the other person present. The comic characters are monologuists, whereas Emma, like Mr. Knightley, is supreme in dialogue:

'Whom are you going to dance with?' asked Mr. Knightley.
She hesitated a moment, and then replied, 'With you, if you will ask me.'[1]

On the one hand the novel has to do with prolific, fanciful thinkers and talkers, from Emma at her worst, and Frank Churchill habitually, down to the lesser figures. Some talk to be wrongly understood; some talk and are not listened to. Opposed to all these characters, who exist largely in a medium of words, is a firmly rendered notion of reality, linked in the novel to one laconic character. Highbury village and its main street; the rich surrounding farmland dominated by Donwell Abbey; in both these social worlds Mr. Knightley is ubiquitous, although he is seen in the novel much more continuously than he is heard. In the middle distance he is everywhere—conferring with Mr. Elton about parish affairs, or with Robert Martin about farming; detected sending apples to Miss Bates, or asking for her errands when he rides to Kingston. Highbury gatherings are not complete without him; unlike Emma, he is always present when the Coles or Eltons entertain. Compared with his active involvement in the community, Emma's conception of herself as first lady is a kind of figment of the mind. Although hers is an old and wealthy family, the Woodhouses' money has nothing to do with Highbury: they own very little land there.[2] Emma may be mindful—at intervals, that is—of the duties of the rich towards the poor. She is also capable of flirting indiscriminatingly with the fashionable stranger, the innovator: Frank

[1] Emma, p. 331.   [2] Ibid., p. 136.

Churchill, individual, naturally motivated, and nevertheless
the latest in the long anti-jacobin descent of charming, hypocritical seducers who enter a secluded community from a
corrupt wider world. Emma is vulnerable, and one reason
is that her stake in Highbury is not deep. Her very claim to
social precedence is so precarious, while she remains a spinster,
that she is superseded by Mrs. Elton. When she marries Mr.
Knightley her rank will be secured, and she will become
involved in the land by sharing in its ownership. The land,
too, will have a wholeness it never had before, since Hartfield
was 'but a sort of notch in the Donwell Abbey estate, to
which all the rest of Highbury belonged'.[1] At the end of the
novel Emma is about to assume a clearly defined and permanent role in the community, and what is left outside has
been touched with the insubstantiality which Burke gives to
the people and ideas that will not belong.

There is thus a second element of contrast in the novel:
not merely the difference between those who talk fallaciously,
insincerely, or without communicating, and those who in
Jane Austen's terms talk well; but between characters who
merely talk, and the near-silent Mr. Knightley. It is even more
than this, for Mr. Knightley has a wholly silent *alter ego*. The
goal of all Emma's deluded endeavours, of so much self-
deception, presumption, and specious inward argument—a
husband for Harriet—is found at last in a character who is
never heard to speak at all. Robert Martin acts, and simply is,
with the solidity that comes from well-defined involvement
with a physical world, and in the light of that reality the
world of thought in the novel is as flimsy as Frank Churchill's
pretended dream.

The final irony is that this most verbal of novels at last
pronounces words themselves to be suspect. It has been called
the first and one of the greatest of psychological novels. If so,
it resembles no other, for its attitude to the workings of
Emma's consciousness is steadily critical. Although so much
of the action takes place in the inner life, the theme of the
novel is scepticism about the qualities that make it up—
intuition, imagination, original insight. Where Caleb Williams
and Belinda mature by learning to think for themselves,

[1] Ibid., p. 136.

Emma matures by submitting her imaginings to common sense, and to the evidence. Her intelligence is certainly not seen as a fault, but her failure to question it is. The technical triumph is to employ the character-centred format, to place the action almost wholly within the heroine's consciousness, to enlist (as in the subjective tradition) the reader's sympathy; and at the same time, largely through the medium of language, to invoke the reader's active suspicion of unaided thought. Easily the most brilliant novel of the period, and one of the most brilliant of all English novels, it masters the subjective insights which help to make the nineteenth-century novel what it is, and denies them validity.

CHAPTER 12

PERSUASION AND SANDITON

I<small>N</small> Captain Frederick Wentworth *Persuasion* has a classic case-study of a modern-minded man from the conservative point of view. Wentworth is personally attractive and an idealist, but he has the fault of trusting too implicitly in his own prior conceptions. When, eight years before the novel opens, he first fell in love with Anne Elliott, he impulsively demanded that she should marry him, contrary to the wishes of her family, and (since he had no money for them to live on) contrary at that stage to common prudence. He put his faith in himself, and in his powers to realize his own destiny; and because, two years later, he did make a fortune, he has always blamed Anne for not showing the same degree of confidence in him, or the courage to defy her connections, know her own mind, and trust her own will. 'She had shewn a feebleness of character in doing so, which his own decided, confident temper could not endure.'[1] When he returns to the neighbourhood, and Anne has to listen to snatches of his conversation with Louisa on the walk to Winthrop, she hears him reiterate his faith in the self. Louisa states that she would rather be overturned by the man she loves than driven safely by anyone else, and Wentworth exclaims 'with enthusiasm', 'I honour you!'[2] Later, when Anne overhears their conversation within the hedge, she hears him praise 'resolution', 'decision', 'firmness', 'spirit', and finally, in truly Godwinian phraseology, 'powers of mind'.[3] His personal philosophy approaches revolutionary optimism and individualism and he is impatient of, or barely recognizes, those claims of a mentor which for him can be dismissed in the single word, 'persuasion'.

With Captain Wentworth thus established as its well-intentioned but ideologically mistaken hero, the novel takes

---

[1] *Persuasion*, ed. R. W. Chapman, Oxford, rev. ed., 1965, p. 61.
[2] Ibid., p. 85.   [3] Ibid., p. 88.

a course familiar to the reader of Jane Austen's other novels. At Lyme his eyes are opened. On the Cobb he perceives that what he took for firmness of character in Louisa is really an extreme self-will which disregards rational restraints. After the accident, Anne's behaviour reveals to him another kind of strength, which includes self-forgetfulness, self-control, and the ability to act. He reflects over the lessons of the incident, and afterwards is able to admit to Anne that his judgement of her was prejudiced by his bitterness at the broken engagement. He learns to accept that Anne's submission to Lady Russell was neither a symptom of weakness, nor cold-hearted prudence, but a further sign of principle and fortitude. In the image characteristic of Jane Austen's faulty heroines—that of blindness upon which light suddenly breaks—he says of his own errors, 'I shut my eyes, and would not understand you, or do you justice.'[1]

The problem about this explanation of the action of *Persuasion* is that although Captain Wentworth is the protagonist of the novel he is not the central character. What *happens* in *Persuasion*, Wentworth's choice of Anne for a wife, and the discovery of true values which is implicit in that choice, remains in line with the conservative philosophy of all of Jane Austen's other novels. But the novel's actual effect is, notwithstanding, distinct, because many of its techniques lead the attention away from the moral implications of action, and the kind of truth expressed by over-all form.

On the whole, though it is not clear how far this effect is intended, the action and most of the characters in *Persuasion* seem meaningful primarily in terms of the impression they make upon Anne. The slow, static, at times rather laborious opening is indirectly all about her: its function is to establish her setting, first in an atmosphere of bankrupt family pride and cold formality at Kellynch Hall, and afterwards among the comfortable, unexacting Musgroves at Uppercross. Morally the Musgroves are not nearly as censurable as the Elliotts. If we feel that there is a great deal wrong with them, it is largely because they are stupid and undiscriminating about Anne.

Just as the first half of the first volume is written in a way

[1] *Persuasion*, p. 247.

to bring out the sorrows of Anne's situation, so Captain Wentworth's entrance is delayed for the same purpose. When at last they meet, the scene is given through the blurred, rushed imprint it makes on Anne's senses:

Mary, very much gratified by this attention, was delighted to receive him; while a thousand feelings rushed on Anne, of which this was the most consoling, that it would soon be over. And it was soon over. In two minutes after Charles's preparation, the others appeared; they were in the drawing-room. Her eye half met Captain Wentworth's; a bow, a curtsey passed; she heard his voice —he talked to Mary, said all that was right; said something to the Miss Musgroves, enough to mark an easy footing: the room seemed full—full of persons and voices—but a few minutes ended it. Charles showed himself at the window, all was ready, their visitor bowed and was gone; the Miss Musgroves were gone too, suddenly resolving to walk to the end of the village with the sportsmen; the room was cleared, and Anne might finish her breakfast as she could.

'It is over! it is over!' she repeated to herself again, and again, in nervous gratitude. 'The worst is over!'

Mary talked, but she could not attend. She had seen him. They had met. They had been once more in the same room![1]

In *Emma* syntax is used to suggest heightened emotion, but there is nothing approaching the exclusively subjective viewpoint of *Persuasion*. In the earlier novel dialogue is important, and even Emma's free indirect speech can incorporate the tones of another character's conversation.[2] Here Anne is before us, and no one else. Her selective view of external 'reality', her overwhelming emotional sense of a climax that is also anti-climax, is suggested by the novelist's distortion of the two 'normal' outward dimensions: time is recklessly speeded up, space grotesquely contracted. The implication, as so consistently in the presentation of Anne, is that the senses have a decisive advantage over reason and fact. 'Alas! with all her reasonings, she found, that to retentive feelings eight years may be little more than nothing.'[3]

Especially after the cold, distanced beginning to the novel, with its unsympathetic handling of Elliotts and Musgroves, the intimacy with which Jane Austen approaches Anne's consciousness appears to be something extraordinary. So, too, is the effect of high-wrought nervous tension, compared with

[1] Ibid., pp. 59–60.   [2] See above, p. 262.   [3] *Persuasion*, p. 60.

the mental worlds of other characters, whose attention is dissipated among the trivia of their external relationships. Unlike the lesser figures, Wentworth is certainly capable of feeling, but immediately after his meeting with Anne we are deliberately shown that his frame of mind is calm and nearly dispassionate. Every technique of contrast is used to throw her abnormally intense experience into high relief.

There is nothing in subjective writing in any earlier English novel to compare in subtlety of insight or depth of feeling with the sequence of nervous scenes between the hero and the heroine in *Persuasion*. The rival realist Maria Edgeworth correctly singles out three episodes for special praise:

Don't you see Captain Wentworth, or rather don't you in her place feel him taking the boisterous child off her back as she kneels by the sick boy on the sofa? And is not the first meeting after their long separation admirably well done? And the overheard conversation about the nut?[1]

Overheard conversations are part of the technique of *Emma*, but there the inference is that the evidence supplied by the dialogue approaches objectivity; it is the interpretation placed upon the conversation by its observer which is liable to be biased and faulty. When Anne overhears Captain Wentworth's remarks to Louisa about the nut, the two elements, the heroine's consciousness and the hero's conversation, have precisely the reverse connotations. Captain Wentworth's praise of the beauty of the nut, his symbol for hidden richness, perfection, and strength, suggests an intelligent, attractive, witty man, of high moral aspirations; but at the same time a man who is in the grip of a strongly subjective frame of mind, a personal bias which perverts his judgement. Anne, the hidden listener, has, as we already know, and he will rediscover, all the richness and secret strength he is attributing to Louisa. Once again the inference is that Anne's inner life has an unassailable quality and truth. Nothing like this image of the nut—richest at the kernel, made private by its strong, defensive exterior—is even suggested in an earlier Austen novel.

It is of course precisely this 'inward interest' of *Persuasion*,

[1] Maria Edgeworth to Mrs. Ruxton, 21 Feb. 1818: Mrs. Edgeworth, *Memoir of Maria Edgeworth*, priv. printed, 1867, ii. 6.

its access to Anne's feelings, that has given it a relatively
high standing in the twentieth century. A very large factor
in securing the admiration of posterity must be the subjectivism of later thinking. We find the book peculiarly 'true',
that is to our current attitudes, while *Emma* is true only to
itself and to Jane Austen's so-called 'Augustan' objectivity.
The sad scenes of autumn in the novel, the desolation of
winter rain, are as they are because they are felt by Anne.
The world of her consciousness is so all-absorbing that it is
not clear whether the outer world (the farmer's outer world,
for example) has objective existence or not.

And yet, even while she seems to invite the reader's
emotional identification with Anne, Jane Austen orders other
parts of her novel in terms that imply her continued acceptance
of the old ethical certainties. Both at the beginning of the
first volume, where she contrasts the values of Kellynch and
Uppercross, and at the end, with the big set-piece scene at
Lyme, she reverts to a form of presentation which is near-
objective and presented to the reader dramatically rather
than refracted through Anne's consciousness. At Lyme we
continue to be aware of Anne's emotion. But the meaning of
the accident on the Cobb—that Anne is strong while Louisa
is only childishly wilful—is directed at the moral understanding of Captain Wentworth and of the reader. The change of
focus, or the dual focus, is awkward, and it points to the
weakness of *Persuasion*.

That weakness, a failure to integrate the novel's two planes
of reality, becomes more acute when in the second volume
the scene moves to Bath. In so far as Jane Austen is writing a
novel of subjective experience, she continues to do it beautifully. Anne's nervous impatience, her acute state of suspense,
is beautifully countered within her own consciousness by
her mature knowledge that she and Captain Wentworth must
eventually make their feelings known. But enveloping this
nineteenth-century novel of the inner life is an eighteenth-
century novel in search of a centre. The cold prudential
world of Sir Walter and Elizabeth properly belongs within
a two-dimensional tradition of social comedy, such as Fielding's. Within such terms they would convince: put in the

same novel as Anne, they seem out of focus, and for various reasons. One is that the pain they give Anne, and the spiritual isolation they impose on her, are out of scale in comedy.[1] Another is that beside Anne's consciousness their very being seems sketchy. In no other Austen novel since *Sense and Sensibility* is the social group surrounding the heroine so thin as the Elliotts' circle at Bath.

Far more glaringly wrong—and perhaps more relevant to the question of Jane Austen's mastery of her material—is Mr. William Walter Elliott, the alternative claimant for Anne's hand. His entry into the novel at Lyme, which serves no function, is unusually clumsy stage-management. In his scenes with Anne at Bath he seems curiously inexpressive and featureless. Jane Austen's unease in dealing with him is reflected in the inferior writing he inspires. He provokes from Anne herself some moralistic reflections which include a piece of prudery as disconcerting as anything uttered by Fanny Price.[2] Mrs. Smith's history of his past, that outworn cliché of the eighteenth-century novel, is a device which Jane Austen otherwise allows herself only in *Sense and Sensibility*. The manœuvre by which Mr. Elliott is disposed of, his *affaire* with Mrs. Clay, seems decidedly undermotivated and inconsistent with the worldly wisdom which has hitherto been his leading characteristic. Worse than any of these things, perhaps, is that Mr. Elliott has little or no place in Anne's consciousness. Apparently she does not respond to him as Elizabeth does to Wickham and Emma to Frank. He never represents any kind of real temptation to her. Belonging as he does to the usual Austen format, a novel of moral choices in which each choice is given external bodily reality, in this novel he inevitably loses most of his substance. Failure to define the tempter-figure is surely the most significant of the failures of *Persuasion*. For elsewhere in Jane Austen it is the villain who

---

[1] Relatives who embarrass the heroine are a familiar motif in the eighteenth-century novel. Elizabeth Bennet's sufferings on account of Mrs. Bennet are in a similar though less vulgar vein to Evelina's at the hands of her grandmother, Mme Duval. (See above, p. 200.) The difference in kind of what Anne suffers when Wentworth marks Elizabeth's insolence is very notable. (*Persuasion*, pp. 226–7.) Cf. Rachel Trickett, 'Jane Austen's Comedy and the Nineteenth Century', *Critical Essays on Jane Austen*, ed. B. C. Southam, 1968, London, 1968, pp. 162–81.

[2] See below, p. 282.

has always in some form or other embodied self-sufficiency, a whole intellectual system of individualism or self-interest that the more social and outward-turning ethic of the novel was designed to counter. Here, where Anne's inner world is implicitly vindicated, there is very little that is significant for William Walter Elliott to represent.

Persuasion's uneasy compromise between old techniques and new is best exemplified by its two alternative endings. In the original version of the last two chapters, a strong comic plot of a more or less traditional kind binds the events consequentially together. The characters around Anne act in the belief that she is about to marry Mr. Elliott. Anne herself is under the immediate influence of Mrs. Smith's revelations about him, which themselves came about because Mrs. Smith had heard rumours of an engagement. On her way home from talking to Mrs. Smith in Westgate-buildings, Anne encounters Admiral Croft. He too has heard that she is engaged to Mr. Elliott, and assumes that the family may want Kellynch Hall back so that the couple can live there. He takes her into his lodgings and asks his brother-in-law, Wentworth, to find out from Anne if her father would like Kellynch Hall vacated. Wentworth has to account for the question by referring to the supposed engagement; Anne replies by denying it; and the *éclaircissement* is made. In a sense, of course, Mr. Elliott's role is not great, even in this version, since Anne never intended to marry him. But the fact that she has just come from hearing a story which proves him unfit to marry seems to give a moral colouring, in the characteristic Austen fashion, to her acceptance of Wentworth.

The earlier version differs from the dénouement as we know it primarily because it is an essentially objective account of external events, which follow one another in a seemingly rational sequence. Unveiling the truth about Mr. Elliott appears to clarify the attitudes of hero and heroine towards each other—just as the discovery of Frank Churchill's secret brings about the explanatory conversation of Knightley and Emma. The original end of *Persuasion* was to have used the well-tried machinery of Jane Austen's other dénouements.

The new version is a marvellous technical adjustment, in the unique manner of *Persuasion*: it is infinitely better in its access to the feelings. The second volume has been a nervous sequence of half-articulate meetings between Anne and Wentworth—as they shelter from the rain, pass on opposite sides of the street, are separated by circumstances and by Mr. Elliott at the concert. Such occasions are tracked in Anne's consciousness, woven in with intensity among the cold externals of the Elliotts' social life. The first new element of the revised ending is another of these scenes, a meeting which fails to bring about any clarification because Wentworth and Anne are prevented by the crowd from communicating directly with each other.[1] The entirely new-written chapter ten brings the Musgroves to Bath to buy wedding-clothes for Henrietta and Louisa. Shelving her intention to reveal the truth about Mr. Elliott to Lady Russell, Anne goes instead to visit the party from Uppercross at the White Hart hotel. There she also meets Captain Wentworth, and attempts to set his fears at rest about Mr. Elliott, but in the hurried circumstances the task of explaining herself is still left incomplete. The new chapter eleven again reverts to the topic of Mr. Elliott—only, once more, to shelve it:

One day only had passed since Anne's conversation with Mrs. Smith; but a keener interest had succeeded, and she was now so little touched by Mr. Elliott's conduct, except by its effects in one quarter, that it became a matter of course the next morning, still to defer her explanatory visit in Rivers Street.[2]

She goes instead to spend the day pleasurably with the Musgroves at the White Hart, where she finds Mrs. Croft, Captain Harville, and Captain Wentworth. There follows Anne's beautifully conceived and moving conversation with Harville about the duration of love, which Wentworth over-hears: his turn to hear Anne, and to hear her eloquent and unconfined by the hurry and constraint of all their attempted conversations together. She is gentle with Harville; judicious in revealing her own story; rational and general on the subject at issue; but at the end, when her deepest feelings are touched, she speaks straight from her own experience. ' "All the privilege I claim for my own sex (it is not a very enviable one,

[1] The noise, triviality, and nuisance of the repeated crowd-scenes are further elements which seem to favour the individual's inner life.
[2] *Persuasion*, p. 229.

you need not covet it) is that of loving longest, when existence
or when hope is gone." [1]

All Anne's characteristics find expression in this conversation: her fortitude, gentleness, modesty, integrity. The ideal
Wentworth outlined in the conversation she overheard, when
he spoke of the hazel-nut, comes vividly to life. Wentworth
hears, and writes his letter of proposal, so that she receives it
when she is alone; for, in this novel of little dialogue, hardly
any of the protagonists' utterances are directed openly to
one another. The positive value of replacing the Gay-street
proposal scene with the two chapters at the White Hart
rests on this change from a direct confrontation between the
two (which has never yet occurred successfully throughout
the course of the novel) to an indirect one, in which first
Anne speaks her thoughts as it were in soliloquy, then Wentworth speaks his through the medium of the pen. The effect
is in keeping with the other techniques original to *Persuasion*, for it puts a premium on expression of the self, and
avoids direct communication between the self and another.

There can be no question that, of these two endings, the
second and final version is infinitely more pleasing—even
though it is achieved at the cost of Mr. Elliott's meaningful
place in the action. By the same token, Anne, though so out
of scale in her social setting, is many people's favourite among
Jane Austen's heroines. With an inner life that is rich and
feeling, an outer environment that is barren, she looks forward to Maggie Tulliver and Dorothea Brooke. Unfortunately
she also looks backward to Elinor and, more immediately,
to Fanny. Matching her to her world is not the only problem.
Jane Austen has further difficulties within the character—
in reconciling Anne's feelings, which are often indistinguish-
able from those of a victim of her environment, and her
exemplary role, which is that of the resolute Christian.

Like Fanny, she is a perceptive bystander, implicitly the
conscience and censor of her world. She rebukes the Elliotts
because she is above worldly vanity; the Musgrove elders
because she is meditative; unlike Louisa, she has the real
strength which derives from reflection, principle, and a sense

[1] Ibid., p. 235.

of duty. Anne comes near to being dangerously perfect: 'she is almost too good for me.'[1] Although it is given less explicit Christian colouring than Fanny's, her intense, withdrawn inner life would suggest the 'Saint' even without her hints to Captain Benwick on moral and religious reading, and her sober distaste for Mr. Elliott's Sunday travelling.[2]

The strong contrast between worldly vanity on the one hand and an exemplary train of thought on the other is quite as marked in *Persuasion* as in *Mansfield Park*. Anne's pain at the vanity, selfishness, and inutility of her father and sister have to be lightly touched upon, because a daughter's denunciations would hardly be in good taste; but the author's severe handling of the baronet comes as near to social criticism as anything she ever wrote. The comparison Jane Austen makes between an idle, useless 'gentleman' proud of his rank, and the eminently useful sailors, has been seen as a notable example of Jane Austen's willingness to be radical.[3] So too has her perception that Lady Russell's wrong advice stemmed from a refined kind of worldliness. On the contrary, the tone of Jane Austen's criticism of her novel's father- and mother-figure—together with its fictional source, in the conscience of a selfless and dutiful daughter—belong to a familiar kind of conservative social comment.

Examination of *Mansfield Park* has already shown that in her last years, when touched by Evangelical influence, Jane Austen was very ready to find fault with the aristocracy. The Evangelicals were dedicated critics of moral backsliding among the governing classes: their campaigns against worldliness, triviality, and irresponsibility in high life were central to their effort. Halévy observes that the two most powerful intellectual movements of the age, Evangelicalism and Utilitarianism, though antipathetic in some areas, were surprisingly close in others.[4] Both creeds are essentially of the

---

[1] JA to Fanny Knight, 23 Mar. 1817: *Letters*, p. 487.

[2] *Persuasion*, pp. 101 and 161.

[3] See especially Joseph M. Duffy, 'Structure and Idea in *Persuasion*', *Nineteenth Century Fiction*, viii (1953), 272–9 (with R. W. Chapman's reply, ibid., ix (1954), 154).

[4] *History of the English People in the Nineteenth Century*, i: *England in 1815*, London, 1961, pp. 485 ff. In this connection it is interesting that Maria Edgeworth, who became more utilitarian as JA became more evangelical, also

middle class. Both see the individual's life in society as rightly active and useful. Both therefore dislike the idleness implicit in a pastime like play-acting, or in a life like Walter Elliott's. It is true that Evangelicals also recommend that individuals should inwardly experience a change of heart, in order to arrive at a private spiritual state which is elevated and intense. But this is certainly not meant to imply doubt of the value of a life led effectively in society. On the contrary, it is meant to enable society's natural leaders to do their duty better. Jane Austen's plots express a typical conservative middle-class ethic of the day. When her principal characters experience an inward reform—as, in each of the novels, some of them do—it is so that they can see their way to a marriage promising continued self-discipline, and a higher commitment than ever before to service to the community. Those marriages which conclude the Austen novels imply a great deal more than the routine comic resolution: since in all the maturer novels there is a morally dominant partner, Darcy or Knightley, Fanny or Anne, to guarantee that the life to come is to be one of duty and service. If Fanny Price's inner life is a silent rebuke to Sir Thomas Bertram's failed leadership, or Anne's to her father's, the *form* of each novel makes it clear that Jane Austen looks to a new generation of leaders who are on the point of redeeming the mistakes of the old. The Evangelical colouring of her Christianity in the later novels blends imperceptibly with her earlier conservatism, since the goal of Evangelicalism was generally to fortify middle-class life by arming it from within; rather than, like Methodism, to appeal via the heart to the population at large. The Evangelical movement's clear sense of itself as both middle-class and innately conservative was the pre-condition of its influence:

It had to be, and was, a cardinal principle of the reformers' strategy not to allow themselves to be confused with the Calvinistic or any dissenters, with radicals or liberals, or with the Methodists. The great were strongly opposed to Calvinism, were not fond of dissenters, owned an immense part of all English property, had a strong

---

took up the theme of the socially useful life, notably in her greatest critical success, *The Absentee*, 1812.

sense of their financial well-being, and thought the Methodists were fanatical in religion and subversive in politics and economics. The frequently expressed belief that Evangelicals were liberals, still more the frequently expressed belief that Evangelicals and Methodists can be lumped together into something called 'the Evangelical Revival', wholly miss the nature and accomplishment of this reform movement.

Not political reformers, not dissenters and not Methodists but deeply conservative members of the Established Church, the Evangelicals were concerned with no reform but the reform of vice and sin and of the infidelity that to their mind was the sole cause of vice and sin. Their only object was to have a nineteenth century peopled by Evangelical Christians leading moral lives of a puritannical kind.[1]

The Jane Austen of 1816 and 1817 was very ready to criticize the performance of individual members of the middle classes; but the yardstick of her criticism remained a firmer conception than ever of middle-class duty. In her last fragment, *Sanditon*, which she worked at between January and March 1817, she embarked on themes which underline the striking intellectual consistency of her whole career. Mr. B. C. Southam has written well[2] of the new freedom of technique she shows in her last enterprise, her unusual interest in visual effects, in fleeting images half-perceived, in the impression left on the senses by water, wind, and sunlight. But, as in the case of *Persuasion*, experiment with a new kind of subjective writing does not imply a change of philosophy. The watering-place itself is described with much more particularity than other locations in Jane Austen's work. But when we come to assess its symbolic force we are on familiar ground, for the point is Sanditon's perversion from its earlier natural role as fishing village and agricultural community, a place where children are born and vegetable gardens flourish. Its new smart terraces are an artificial engraftment, created by an over-sophisticated society's obsession with its bodily health, and by the economic opportunism of characters like Mr. Parker and Lady Denham. The people who flock to Sanditon are of the type of gentry Jane Austen always censures: urban, rootless, irresponsible, self-indulgent.

[1] F. K. Brown, *Fathers of the Victorians*, Cambridge, 1961, p. 5.
[2] *JA's Literary Manuscripts*, Oxford, 1964, pp. 102 ff.

Criticism of the new watering-places was common in the period. Graphic artists like Rowlandson, essayists like Cobbett, and other novelists than Jane Austen thought it a vice typical of modern times that so many were eager to leave their local responsibilities for the sake of a season at 'dissipated' Brighton. Maria Edgeworth's *The Absentee* attacks the Irish gentry who flock from their estates to the capital; Scott's *St. Ronan's Well*, which is about a watering-place, is an even nearer parallel to *Sanditon*. Although it is impossible to make an extended comparison between Jane Austen's fragment and two full-length novels, one thing seems certain: Jane Austen is the most concerned of the three to compare her contemporary resort with a notional older way, an inherited organic community reminiscent of the imaginative construct made by Burke. There has been a polarization in Mr. Parker's experience, between his old, comfortable, true home, and his blue-print for a reformed Sanditon, which echoes the contrast made in the *Reflexions* between living communities and the diagrams for a reformed order drawn up by sophists, calculators, and advocates of paper Rights of Man.[1]

One after another, the characters who congregate at Sanditon are established as self-indulgent, blind to any claim but those of their own wilfully induced fantasies. Mr. Parker deludes himself with dreams of expansion and commercial prosperity. His sisters live in and for their imagined illnesses. Sir Edward Denham, presumably the villain of the piece, has taken over a ready-made fantasy world from literature. Mr. William Walter Elliott may appear to represent no observable type, or creed, very distinctly; Sir Edward Denham is, simply and classically, the philosophical would-be seducer, the bogeyman of the run-of-the-mill anti-jacobin novel of the 1790s. From his reading he has acquired a creed that appears to sanction the most perverse, violent, and anti-social behaviour. Sentimental novels have taught him that the pursuit of extreme self-gratification can be glamorous:

The truth was that Sir Edw: whom circumstances had confined very much to one spot had read more sentimental Novels than agreed with him. His fancy had been early caught by all the impassioned, & most exceptionable parts of Richardsons; & such

[1] See above, pp. 38-9.

Authors as have since appeared to tread in Richardson's steps, so far as Man's determined pursuit of Woman in defiance of every opposition of feeling & convenience is concerned, had since occupied the greater part of his literary hours, & formed his Character.— With a perversity of Judgement, which must be attributed to his not having by Nature a very strong head, the Graces, the Spirit, the Sagacity, & the Perserverance, of the Villain of the Story outweighed all his absurdities and all his Atrocities with Sir Edward. With him, such Conduct was Genius, Fire and Feeling.[1]

The sensitive, new-style descriptions in *Sanditon* occur in isolated passages, and the ordinary narrative prose is often so crude that it startles: it is surprising that even a first draft by the author of *Emma* would be quite like this. Sir Edward's caricatured literary dialogue is hardly any better than Cherubina's flights in Eaton Stannard Barrett's *The Heroine*; both belong to burlesque rather than to the novel. Presumably, if she had had time, Jane Austen could have turned even Sir Edward's speech into something more like the rodomontade of a Lucy Steele. As it is, and revealingly, it conveys the bare idea, which proves essentially to be the idea behind *Love and Friendship*—Jane Austen's suspicion of the sentimentalist's faith in human nature and ungoverned instinct:

'The Novels which I approve are such as display Human Nature with Grandeur—such as shew her in the Sublimities of intense Feeling—such as exhibit the progress of strong Passion from the first Germ of incipient Susceptibility to the utmost Energies of Reason half-dethroned,—where we see the strong spark of Woman's Captivations elicit such Fire in the Soul of Man as leads him— (though at the risk of some Aberration from the strict line of Primitive Obligations)—to hazard all, dare all, atcheive all, to obtain her.—Such are the Works which I peruse with delight, & I hope I may say, with amelioration. They hold forth the most splendid Portraitures of high Conceptions, Unbounded Veiws [*sic*] illimitable Ardour, indomptible Decision—and even when the Event is mainly anti-prosperous to the high-toned Machinations of the prime Character, the potent, pervading Hero of the Story, it leaves us full of Generous Emotions for him;—our Hearts are paralized——. T'were Pseudo-Philosophy to assert that we do not feel more enwraped by the brilliancy of his Career, than by the tranquil & morbid Virtues of any opposing Character. Our appro-

---

[1] *Sanditon*, ch. 8: *Minor Works*, ed. R. W. Chapman, Oxford, 1954, p. 404.

bation of the Latter is but Eleemosynary.—These are the Novels which enlarge the primitive Capabilities of the Heart, & which it cannot impugn the Sense or be any Dereliction of the character, of the most anti-puerile Man, to be conversant with.'

'If I understand you aright'—said Charlotte—'our taste in Novels is not at all the same.'[1]

This is the cant of the progressive side in the French Revolutionary era—or, rather, this is how their conservative opponents thought progressives wrote. The catch-phrases the anti-jacobins made such happy play with are all there, especially 'utmost Energies', 'high Conceptions', 'illimitable Ardour', and 'primitive Capabilities of the Heart'. Sir Edward is saying that intense feeling is in itself sublime; that villains arouse stronger emotions than 'the tranquil & morbid Virtues of any opposing character'; therefore, by his subjective test, that the villain is the true hero, the character to be admired and imitated. The conception of Sir Edward's character takes us back to the exaggerated terms of literary warfare of around 1798, when the tendency of alarmed conservatives to associate sentimentalism with conscious intrigue and villainy was at its strongest.

Sanditon is so firm in its sense of the organic community, so hostile to the modern tendency to social fragmentation, so sceptical towards the unbridled fantasies of individuals, so outspoken in its diagnosis of a contemporary menace, that it ought to make us very wary of any reading of *Persuasion* which proclaims a fundamental change of philosophy. Joseph M. Duffy says of the last novel that it shows the way of life of the aristocracy 'hardened to inflexible doctrine. In nature are found the threats to such a society with its excessively fixed standards, for nature implies freedom, flexibility and change.'[2] According to Robert Garis, *Persuasion* 'can hardly be anything but a conscious re-thinking of *Sense and Sensibility* ... Jane Austen comes out against caution, and for risk-taking.'[3] This however is just what she does not do. Her innovation goes no further than to alter her method of presenting the heroine's consciousness. Instead of concentrating on

---

[1] Ibid., pp. 403–4.   [2] 'Structure and Idea in *Persuasion*', p. 276.

[3] 'Learning, Experience and Change', *Critical Essays on Jane Austen*, ed. B. C. Southam, London, 1968, p. 80.

the processes of moral discrimination (as in every previous novel, even *Mansfield Park*), she dwells on Anne's sensations, her nervous responses, the natural ebb and flow of her intuitive inner life.

The pressures on Jane Austen to make some adjustments in her style were very strong indeed. By now her readers came to her from Scott, Byron, and Madame de Staël's *de l'Allemagne* (1812): it was above all the success of the last-named which ended the decade of England's cultural isolation from the heartland of Continental Romanticism. Middle-class taste now admitted enthusiasm, in moderate doses: an ardent inner life was as much a symptom of Christian orthodoxy in 1816 as it was suspect in 1796. If Jane Austen wanted to draw an exemplary Christian heroine, she must no longer concentrate on self-control and a sense of duty, as she had done with Elinor. The basic characteristic of the Christian was now felt to be her rich inner life, compared with the trivial, unthinking, external lives of those in society. Unfortunately Jane Austen's form, the basic plot of all six novels, continues to reflect the orthodoxy of the years of her youth. For all the world like Marianne, Captain Wentworth comes to recognize that he has been blinded by pride and self-sufficiency, and to admit that real strength lies outside the self. And it is the Wentworth motif—acting out, like all the Austen plots, humility and submission—which gives *Persuasion* its resolution and its over-all form; while the flow of Anne's consciousness sets the tone, and implicitly points to a very different valuation of the consciousness.

For Jane Austen to treat the inner life for the first time with unreserved sympathy required her to rethink her form. For whatever reason—insufficient time, or creative energy, or will, she did not do this, and the result in *Persuasion* is muddle. The narration is associated with Anne's consciousness, presented in the new style; and so there is no organic relationship between the novel's manner, style, and language, and the element which in the last resort must express a novel's meaning—which elsewhere *does* express Jane Austen's meaning—the form. There are recurring imbalances in *Persuasion* between the inner and outer planes of reality, precisely because the central formal difficulty is not thought through. Against the success with Anne's train of thought must be set the failure with the dialogue: the dialogue of the minor characters in *Persuasion* is perhaps as unamusing, as uninstructive, as peripheral to the real action and centre of interest, as in any Austen novel except *Sense and Sensibility*. Even in the heroine's much-admired inner free speech, there is a failure to discriminate linguistically between the inner life that is feeling and intuitive, and the inner life that is moral. It is part of the sense of intellectual uncertainty in the novel that Anne's is both at once, so that when she is among the Musgroves, for example, we must take in simultaneously her moral superiority, and the more engaging, experiential side of her, the grief, weariness, and sense of waste. She may make the nominally orthodox declaration, that she was right to defer to Lady Russell's judgement. Neither the rather shadowy Lady Russell, nor any of the book's symbols of external authority, weigh in the reader's private scale against Anne's eight years of suffering. And the insubstantial treatment of the outer world, of Kellynch or Bath, is a far cry from the meaningful solidity of either Mansfield Park or Highbury. Jane Austen's device of letting her sailors stand for her positive values, of sociable feeling and selfless service, is less eloquent than the sense of place she used earlier. Individuals are complex things to wield as moral counters. Admiral Croft's reckless driving has to balanced against Mrs. Croft's steady judgement, the Harvilles' generous hospitality against Benwick's undisciplined, emotional indulgence, and the result is that only a perplexing half-light is shed on the central action.

On the one hand, the surviving comic framework, Captain Wentworth's progress towards enlightenment, and the exemplary side of Anne, all continue to bear witness to the old certainties. On the other, Anne's deep emotional commitment to her first attachment pays unexpected homage to the truth and beauty of private experience. If *Persuasion* cannot rightly be described as a conservative novel, this is because it neither takes up an intelligible new position, nor explicitly recants from the old one. It is the only one of Jane Austen's novels that is not whole-heartedly partisan, and it is none the better for it.

CHAPTER 13

CONCLUSION

As a novelist Jane Austen draws at large on the literature of her century. She uses the insights and techniques of many earlier writers, not all of whom are by any means conservative. All late-eighteenth-century writers have a rich inheritance in the literature of reflection. Poets of a philosophical temper, like Gray and Cowper, historians like Hume and Gibbon, admire the wise man who stands aside from events both because he cannot influence them, and because they are not worth influencing. Jane Austen's novels contain central characters more given to reflection than fictional heroes and heroines of the first part of the century, and she makes it clear how much she values the probings of the rational moral intelligence. Even the sentimentalists, whom she criticizes both for their opinions and for their execution, presumably bequeathed to her a new awareness of the reader's special relationship with the hero, and an example of how it might be influenced. Her discriminating dialogue often resembles the work of progressive near-contemporaries like Bage and Maria Edgeworth; her concept of a strenuous drama within the conscious mind can seem like Godwin's. Her plots are a movement from ignorance to knowledge, culminating in a moment of intelligent discernment, and this in itself is bipartisan.

And yet she is also typical of her own generation, which was ideologically perhaps uniquely sensitive. It is a sign of her literary apprenticeship in the 1790s that she is extremely cautious and discriminating about how she applies her borrowing. Her bystanders are very unlike those of the age of Mackenzie. She is not committed in the same way to the inner life. She is not an observer of the *whole* consciousness. Except, partially, in *Persuasion*, she filters out most of the irrational elements typical of the subjective, associationist, anarchic inward experience perceived by the age of Hume. At her most brilliant technically she characterizes the inner life of her heroines, using irony and verbal nuance to give her a dramatist's detachment, so that the consciousness is only one actor in a total drama. In *Pride and Prejudice* and *Emma* the rational has more prestige than the irrational, the outer world of evidence more than the inner world of imaginings. Jane Austen's method of presentation is meant to explode the sentimentalists' claim that subjective experience is the individual's whole truth.

In this period of deep partisan feeling, the form of a novel is decisive. The degree of sympathy and inwardness of presentation of hero or heroine expresses an author's approach to human nature. The action through which the central character passes tends to reflect an ideal progress: either he is freed from social pressure, like Bage's heroes, and Maria Edgeworth's, or he is schooled in accepting it, like Jane West's and Jane Austen's. The plots of Jane Austen's six novels begin in the conservative camp and, very significantly, remain in it. She may experiment by placing her heroine in a different role in relation to the key process of self-discovery. The action itself remains essentially the same, a single all-revealing fable through which she reflects the individual's life in society. The unyielding scepticism about the individual conveyed by that plot suggests that she is innately more orthodox than either of her leading contemporaries, Scott and Maria Edgeworth. For all his personal conservatism, Scott deliberately presents his heroes as ordinary individuals whose interests tend to be in conflict not merely with historical necessity but, often, with the needs of society at large. In *Old Mortality* social duty requires so much of the hero that he barely escapes with his life; in *The Bride of Lammermoor* the outcome is wholly tragic for the individuals concerned. Scott avoids the partisan optimism of Jane Austen's conclusions. Whether his individuals assert their independence or submit, they are probably equally incapable of averting disaster. Even Maria Edgeworth, so much more heavily didactic in execution than the other two, is a genuine enough intellectual to toy with her own ideas as she goes along: on occasion, as in *Leonora*, to end with ideological contradictions. But Jane Austen never allows the inward life of a character, growing under her hand, seriously to challenge the doctrinaire preconceptions on which all her fiction is based. Even the ambivalent *Persuasion* does not read like a serious attempt to question her own beliefs.

If Jane Austen's historical context is correctly defined in these terms, some of the commonest critical assumptions about her need re-examination. The first, obviously, is that she does not involve herself in the events and issues of her time. The crucial action of her novels is in itself expressive of the conservative side in an active war of ideas. So, too, is the stylized opposition in her fictional world between certain kinds of virtuous characters, and certain kinds of villains. The heroine who is fallible and learns, and the heroine who is Christian and exemplary, are the standard heroine-types of reactionary novels of the 1790s. In Jane Austen's novels they confront, equally typically, the villains of the anti-jacobin period —plausible, attractive strangers, penetrating a community from abroad, or from dangerously up-to-date London, like wolves entering a sheepfold: and bent, especially, on winning the affections of the heroine. The idea of John Thorpe, Willoughby, Wickham, Churchill, Henry Crawford, William Walter Elliott, and Sir Edward Denham is the idea of Fitzosborne or Lord James Marauder. Jane Austen believes as Mrs. West or Charles Lucas believe; her feat is to have found so discreet a way of saying it. Technically the striking thing about her novels is indeed that they do not mention the French Revolution and barely allude to the Napoleonic Wars.

A second questionable belief about Jane Austen is that within her deliberately prescribed scene she is essentially a great naturalist, a definer of daily life as it really is; alternatively, that as her career proceeds she moves away from an inherited literary manner in the direction of naturalism. From the first her appeal to many readers has been that of an exquisite observer of village life, a carver upon ivory. But even here the ideal accompanies the phenomenal. She can be tellingly objective, but this too is part of a campaign against subjectivity. Both as a society and as a physical setting, her Highbury is altogether more notional than George Eliot's Middlemarch or Elizabeth Gaskell's Hollingworth. Although eminently believable, it is not actual for actuality's sake; so

that, unlike richer physical backgrounds, it does not function
to suggest an entire way of life, various in its possibilities, in
some way stretching boundlessly off beyond the framework
of the novel. As her career proceeds, she gives more detail of
setting, but the settings are not necessarily more 'natural'.
Barton Cottage is in a valley which is just a valley, even
though it affords a useful pretext for an ideologically significant discussion of the picturesque. The places in *Mansfield
Park*—Sotherton, Portsmouth, London, Mansfield itself—are
more elaborately invested with symbolic significance. Sanditon, the most carefully described of her villages, is also the
place which most clearly co-exists on the plane of ideas.

Nor will it do to call Jane Austen 'natural' in her portrayal
of psychology. Upon the individual's inner life she imposes
what amounts to censorship. Elizabeth and, especially, Emma,
the best of her heroines, have been thought of as psychologically truthful studies. Her outward scene might be limited;
here at least she is free to dig deep. In fact we have seen that,
natural though her portraits might seem in the manner of
presentation, they are also systematically exclusive. The
rational mind and the conscience are given an ascendancy
over irrational kinds of experience that no more seemed true
to life in Jane Austen's day than it does now. Here, especially,
she is a polemicist offering an ideal programme, and not a
realist. One of the best of her twentieth-century critics, Mary
Lascelles, defends her against the charge that she leaves a
great deal of life out by saying that she simply prefers to
write about something else.[1] But, since this implies that the
grounds for her selection are aesthetic, and personal to her,
it will not do. She chooses to omit the sensuous, the irrational,
the involuntary types of mental experience because, although
she cannot deny their existence, she disapproves of them.

As a critic of the indulged feelings, and of authors who
uncritically take characters at their own sanguine valuation,
she is the Fielding of her period, reacting against the Richardsonian individualism of the sentimental genre. It is strange,
therefore, that she is hailed as the natural heir to Richardson's
psychological novel. It is the ethical side of the mind that she
defends, as opposed to the intuitive; she is sceptical of claims

[1] *Jane Austen and her Art*, p. 123.

to virtue, and her Christians are likely to have to prove themselves, like Fielding's, by good deeds. *Pride and Prejudice* and *Emma*, two novels which are critical of the consciousness, and test their heroes by their actions, are her best achievements. It is true that of her last three novels, two, *Mansfield Park* and *Persuasion*, try a more difficult technique, in which the heroine's inner experience is more fully and less critically presented. But the provisos with which she hedges Fanny's interior monologue about, and the mixed, uncertain handling of Anne, show very clearly that she is ill at ease when she cannot view her heroine's consciousness with sceptical detachment. Both are deeply interesting novels, with fine things in them, but they no more represent Jane Austen's mastery of her medium than Fielding's half-sentimental *Amelia* represents his.

Many modern critics would agree, however, that Jane Austen does not merely hold a glass up to human affairs: that she is less a naturalist than a moralist. And this seems an accurate assessment, if we mean by it that for her the moral human being wages war with the natural human being. Her scepticism about fallen human nature has excellent Christian authority. She is indeed a moralist much as Samuel Johnson is a moralist. Yet this is not what those modern critics who call her novels moral generally have in mind.

For a liberal like Lionel Trilling, the morality of any novel is indissolubly linked with its sympathetic treatment of individual human beings. The historical Jane Austen is serious-minded and didactic, but we should not, perhaps, be over-hasty to call her *moral*—or not, at least, without more careful and accurate consideration of her real moral position. That viewpoint is a strong-minded and intellectually consistent one, a strenuous, critical code which preaches self-understanding, self-mastery, and, ultimately, subordination. What therefore it does *not* do is to give special value to the individual. It is Jane Austen's way of presenting the individual, or, more specifically, her scepticism about the subjective consciousness, that distinguishes her from the nineteenth-century novelist. She *is* a moral writer, but of a type that may be antipathetic to the modern layman.

Jane Austen's treatment of the personality has inter-

mittently troubled the conscience of some of her readers.
D. W. Harding[1] and Marvin Mudrick[2] have both noted a
vein in her that is less than enthusiastic about humanity,
even actively inhumane. Perhaps the most discussed instances
of her inhumanity have been those occasions when a character
is shown suffering, and yet the suffering has no value, is not
allowed to alter the reader's perception that it is a moral
error in the character which brings the trial about: Marianne
Dashwood's inward torments are one instance of this, Maria
Bertram's another. Most twentieth-century critics have tried
to account for Jane Austen's dispassionate attitude towards
human frailty in psychological terms peculiar to her, while
this book has sought to show that it is precisely here that she
is representative of her genre.

In lesser ways, it is true, the closer comparison of Jane
Austen with her contemporaries reveals a writer who is
relatively gentle and considerate towards the fictional
characters she creates. The male anti-jacobins are certainly
as a group more brutal, especially when they adopt the coarse
manners and horse-play of Smollett's picaresque. Their
female counterparts have more genteel tastes, but their
notions of poetic justice are strict and somewhat violent, so
that where Jane Austen sends Maria into exile, or Marianne
to a sick-bed, they kill off a seduced girl without mercy. The
most interesting comparison, as so often, is with Maria
Edgeworth. The two writers handle the consciousness in ways
that are entirely distinctive, Maria Edgeworth valuing it,
Jane Austen sceptical. *Pride and Prejudice* and *Belinda*
resemble one another in their derivation from the eighteenth-
century Burney tradition of social comedy. But in Maria
Edgeworth's novel the development of the action, the form
which effectively embodies her values, lies in the heroine's
growing mental and moral superiority to her world. For
Elizabeth, in Jane Austen's novel, arriving at maturity
means learning truths about the self which are more or less
exactly the reverse of Belinda's discoveries. Again, *Mansfield
Park* is a novel of education, like so many of Maria Edge-

---

[1] 'Regulated Hatred: an aspect of the work of JA', *Scrutiny*, viii (1940),
pp. 346–62.
[2] *JA: Irony as Defense and Discovery*, Princeton, 1952, *passim*.

worth's tales and novels. But the Austen exemplary heroine is meek, self-disciplined, and self-effacing, where her Edgeworth counterparts are confident and self-reliant. Yet, although Jane Austen has none of Maria Edgeworth's active, declared faith in the individual and his conscience, because she is the abler novelist she generally makes us care more about her characters' fates. Only rarely does she allow an un-Edgeworthian severity to sound in the justice she metes out— an iron intimation that she can forgive a Marianne or a Julia Bertram to the extent that they abjure what is rebellious or unduly private in their selfhood.

At some point it is necessary to come to terms with what cannot be explained away. Jane Austen is conservative in a sense no longer current. Her morality is preconceived and inflexible. She is firm in identifying error, and less interested than other great novelists in that type of perception for which the novel is so peculiarly well adapted—the perception that thoroughly to understand a character is to forgive him. But if this is true, are we right to call her a great novelist at all?

Of greater imaginative importance to us than Jane Austen's answer should be her question. In her day the very form of the novel prompted an inquiry of central importance and urgency: what was the moral nature of the individual, and what his true role in society? The novelist who evaded, or simply did not notice that he was called upon to put the question, was the true artistic cripple. The willingness of Jane Austen's admirers to concede that she escaped the ferment of ideas in the revolutionary period damages her more than the attempt to show that she was, in fact, a partisan.

The novelist's business is not to find solutions, or to make philosophies, but images; and perhaps no English novelist is so gifted in expression as Jane Austen. Her feat is to give life to a viewpoint that, in all other hands, proves deficient in art as well as in humanity. The richness of her allusions, the intricacy with which her form embodies her ideas, have to be allowed to compensate for what is thin or partial in her presentation of the individual. She uses images of place in order to reflect an idealized sense of community: it is a theme and a device that goes back to Pope, or beyond. Her conception of the rich, active, reflective consciousness, turned outward upon the external scene, is more typical of the later part of the century in which she was born. But the small scale and intimacy of her treatment, its power to send ordinary girls on epic journeys of intellectual discovery, involves a reach from the commonplace to high and permanent moral concerns which is probably available only to the novelist. Using fiction's chief tool, its fable, with complete conviction, Jane Austen brings Elizabeth and above all Emma to a moment of self-discovery that is the necessary condition for their maturity and happiness. Because the marriages which end her novels can be made to symbolize so much for the heroine as an individual, and for her role in society, Jane Austen's fable carries her partisan meaning further than it could be carried in reasoned argument, even by Burke.

Against her novels it may be objected that such stylized endings hint at fulfilment of a kind that scarcely belongs in the observable world. The naturalistic writer would probably feel that what Hazlitt called 'this everlasting, importunate sense of personal identity', once developed, can never recede; or that the objective plane of perception cannot be superimposed on the subjective so neatly as Jane Austen suggests. The discovery that she is not natural does not destroy the satisfying roundedness of her final effect, which is rare in the novel precisely becaue Jane Austen's desire to place the individual within a pre-ordained moral framework is, over all, so untypical of it. Her happy endings cannot resolve the clash of values which she sets out to describe, because it is hardly in the power of art to resolve them. Art merely mimes its resolutions, without real intent or power to deceive.

INDEX